IMAGES
of America

MONTGOMERY'S HISTORIC NEIGHBORHOODS

I0806480

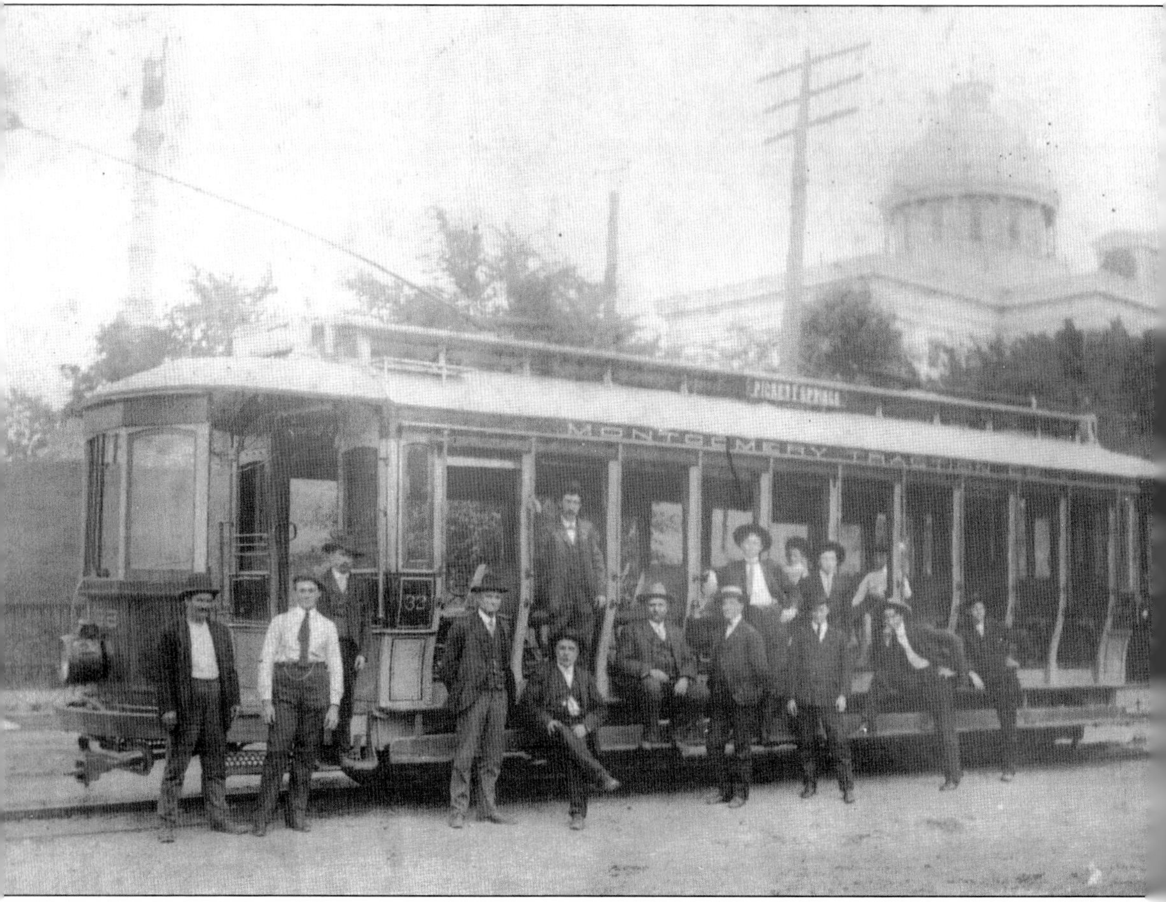

In 1887, the "Lightning Route" gave Montgomery the distinction of being the first city in the western hemisphere with an electric street railway system. The trolley provided transportation to and from downtown Montgomery, the hub of retail business and employment at the time of the neighborhoods' development, and made living beyond the city limits viable. The trolley line was discontinued in 1936, as the bus and private automobile became preferred means of transportation. (Courtesy Frazier family collection.)

On the Cover: Pictured from left to right are Fairlie Lane, Tommy Lawson, and Elizabeth Lane playing in the daffodils at Hazel Hedge in the spring of 1935. Hazel Hedge is fondly remembered as a collection of cabins and gardens owned and rented out by Jean Craik Read. Note "Miss Jean's" (as she was known) "main house" in the background. (Courtesy Fairlie Haynes.)

IMAGES
of America

MONTGOMERY'S HISTORIC NEIGHBORHOODS

Carole A. King and Karren I. Pell

ARCADIA
PUBLISHING

ISBN 978-0-7385-8620-5

Published by Arcadia Publishing
Charleston, South Carolina

Printed in the United States of America

Library of Congress Control Number: 2010922356

For all general information contact Arcadia Publishing at:
Telephone 843-853-2070
Fax 843-853-0044
E-mail sales@arcadiapublishing.com
For customer service and orders:
Toll-Free 1-888-313-2665

Visit us on the Internet at www.arcadiapublishing.com

We dedicate this book to Mary Ann Neeley: visionary, scholar, and friend. Thanks to Mary Ann's leadership in preserving Montgomery's architectural history, the majority of the neighborhoods in this book remain places where people enjoy life, friends, and family. We could not have completed this book without Mary Ann generously sharing her knowledge of Montgomery's history. We are fortunate and proud to be Mary Ann's friends and give her full credit for fostering our roles as historians and preservationists.

Contents

ACKNOWLEDGMENTS

We received images from many families and associations, and we appreciate their help. Further, we thank the following special individuals and organizations. We thank the Landmarks Foundation of Montgomery for access to their collection and for their support; we send a special thanks to Bob McLain. We are in debt to the Montgomery County Historical Society for access to their collection and technical assistance and specifically to James Fuller for sharing his knowledge and to Betty W. Pouncey for her assistance. We leaned heavily on Jeff Benton's work and thank him for his scholarship. We owe a debt of gratitude to Bob Gamble and Christy Anderson for answering our questions for months on end. We thank the Montgomery Country Club and Forrest McConnell for allowing us to print from its collection. We appreciate both Robyn Litchfield and the *Montgomery Advertiser* for the articles on our behalf. We thank Carolyn Hutcheson for interviewing us on Alabama Public Radio at Troy State. We appreciate all Mary Ann Neeley did to help us, even when her own book deadline loomed. We thank Sallie Millsap for sharing her memory book and for hot chocolate on a cold day. We thank Fairlie Haynes for digging out her family photographs from storage. We appreciate George Frazier and his family for sharing family photographs, information, and pizza. Thanks go to Ruth Ott for letting us keep her books for months and for bringing us photographs. We appreciate Phyllis Armstrong for sharing her knowledge. We appreciate Claire Bost Steindorf, Barbara Moore, Frank Broadway, and Howard Bradshaw not only for sharing family photographs but also for their patience—we kept their photographs for over a year. We appreciate Bob Thorington taking time to make us copies of the Winter Place. Our thanks go to James Bozeman for his postcard collection and to Cindy Keeping and Cindy Thornhill for transportation. We thank our families and friends for putting up with us being busy and (sometimes, admittedly) cranky. We express our gratitude to our editor, Katie Shayda, who has helped us and shown much patience and understanding.

Introduction

For over 150 years, people have been coming home to Montgomery's historic neighborhoods. Although the neighborhoods each have their own histories, and their initial developments reflect different incomes and social status, they also share important elements. The original owners, in addition to investing financially in their houses, considered their homes an investment in the comfort and safety of their families. While building houses that proudly displayed their successes, they also built homes that sheltered those close to their hearts. The neighborhoods all became comfortable and convenient communities where residents returned home from work, raised families, socialized with neighbors, attended schools, and worshipped in their churches.

Located on the Alabama River, Montgomery was a vibrant center of commerce when Alabama became a state in 1819. As the city grew, residential areas clustered around its perimeter. Since the only methods of transportation were on foot or horse, close proximity to the bustling downtown area was important in order to get to and from work and for shopping. By 1887, the electric trolley provided transportation to and from downtown Montgomery, the hub of retail business and employment, and made living beyond the city limits popular and possible. Starting from the establishment of the trolley, neighborhoods developed beyond the Montgomery city limits. Although some incorporated as separate municipalities, they are dubbed the first suburbs. Right before World War II, the last of the neighborhoods currently designated historical were built in close proximity to previous developments.

Montgomery's first neighborhoods were small antebellum enclaves built by wealthy planters and merchants who wanted town houses close to bustling downtown Montgomery. By the 1900s, these neighborhoods consisted of large spacious homes featuring architectural styles ranging from the classic Southern pillared mansions to Victorian homes with turrets and towers. Unfortunately, most of these neighborhoods can be seen only in photographs, as they have been replaced by government buildings, businesses, or the interstate. A few of the homes still stand and serve as offices or museums. Several, such as the First White House of the Confederacy (Confederate president Jefferson Davis's home while the Confederate capital was Montgomery) and the Figh-Pickett House (home of Albert Pickett, Alabama's first historian) were saved by moving them to new locations.

Cottage Hill is Montgomery's first and oldest local historic district. The residential area was planned in the 1830s by Edward Hanrick, a land speculator known as "Horsehoe Ned." Only three antebellum homes remain—both of the Winter mansions (they are connected by a second story breezeway) and the McBryde-Screws-Tyson House. The most common architectural styles are Victorian town houses and cottages that date from 1870 to 1910. Cottage Hill is a locally designated historic district and also listed in the National Register of Historic Places.

The Old Line Street neighborhood was Montgomery's southern city limit until the 1880s. Part of the neighborhood borders Cottage Hill. The main street is West Jeff Davis Avenue, named for the president of the Confederacy. Two antebellum homes still stand—the Arrington Cottage and the Opp Cottage. The area's architectural styles range from cottages to modified Victorians. The neighborhood is currently at risk.

Highland Park, dubbed Montgomery's first streetcar suburb, was platted in 1887—the same year the city's entire streetcar system converted to electricity. The shared date is not coincidental. Edwin Joseph, the president of Montgomery's electric trolley system, knew the development would increase demand for the trolley. Seeing a win-win opportunity, he became a land speculator for Highland Park. A blue-collar community, the houses are of vernacular Victorian design. The neighborhood is adjacent to historic Oak Park, Montgomery's first public park. Highland Avenue in Highland Park is a locally designated historic district.

Cloverdale was planned as early as 1887 as a separate city. Starting in 1908, the Cloverdale Homes Development Company substantially increased building. The variety of home styles included arts and crafts, neoclassical, and Spanish Mission. In addition to houses, the neighborhood included churches, schools, a business district, Montgomery Country Club, and what is now Huntingdon College. Cloverdale is a locally designated historic district, and a part of it is listed in the National Register of Historic Places.

The Garden District, a name given later to the area, was platted into lots, and homes were built as early as the 1870s and continued up to the 1930s. Two antebellum homes still stand—the Gilmer-Clitherall House and the Weiss Cottage. Styles featured an eclectic mix, including bungalows, Tudors, Italianate-influence, Colonial and Neoclassical Revivals. One of the most popular and well-known examples of the later style is the Alabama Governor's Mansion. The Garden District is a locally designated historic district and is listed in the National Register of Historic Places.

Centennial Hill became the most prosperous African American neighborhood in Montgomery between 1904 and 1908. The styles of residential architecture in Centennial Hill ranged from shotgun houses to modified Victorians. The neighborhood also featured schools, churches, and businesses. Notable among the latter is the Tulane Grocery and the Ben Moore Hotel. The most famous residence in Centennial Hill is the parsonage for the Dexter Avenue Baptist Church on 513 South Jackson Street, Dr. Martin Luther King's home while he was pastor of the church.

Capitol Heights was incorporated in 1908 as a separate city from Montgomery. Most of the homes were built from 1908 to the 1920s in craftsman, bungalows, Colonial Revival, and other style combinations. The Robert E. Lee statue that currently stands in front of Robert E. Lee High School originally served as the centerpiece of "Lee Place," a later stage of the neighborhood's development. Much of the neighborhood is a locally designated historic district.

Idlewild, also known as "Cloverdale Idlewild," was developed late considering its closeness to Cloverdale, but by 1937, homes were being built. The area's early residents, the Mastin family, built their home, Fairview, before the Civil War and remained a part of the community until the 1920s. At that time, the land was sold to Dr. Brannon Hubbard, who divided the land into lots for development. Some of the old cedar trees that lined the approach to the Mastin home still stand. Many of the homes built in the 1920s and 1930s were from plans in pattern books. Cloverdale Idlewild is a locally designated historic district.

Not all the homes and neighborhoods shown in this book still stand, but they are remembered. Not all of the homes and neighborhoods shown in this book are officially designated as historical, but they are held dear in the minds and hearts of Montgomerians. Then, as now, young families, couples, singles, and retirees agree that the historic neighborhoods' character, friendly nature, and sense of community combine with convenience, value, and ambience to create a unique and satisfying living experience. Then, and now, people love coming home to Montgomery's historic neighborhoods.

One

Downtown

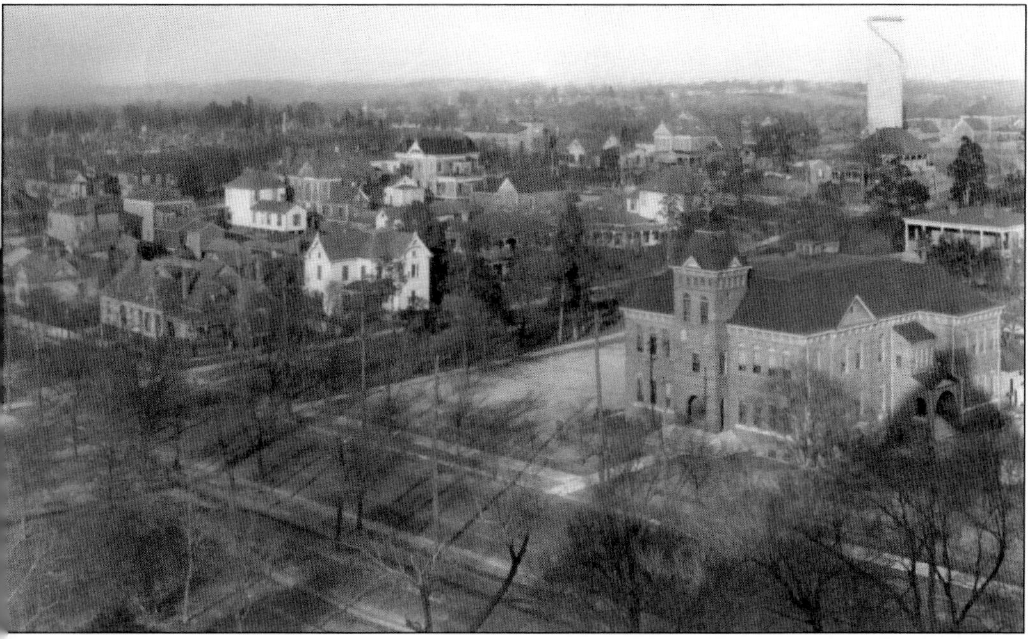

Successful merchants and businessmen built impressive homes, churches, and schools close to Montgomery's vibrant downtown. As the city grew, the need for commercial areas, combined with the trolley system that enabled suburban living, pushed the residential areas southward. Looking northeast, this 1907 aerial photograph shows a view of downtown residences behind the Capitol building along Union and Monroe Streets. Note Lafayette High School in the foreground. (Courtesy Art Work Collection.)

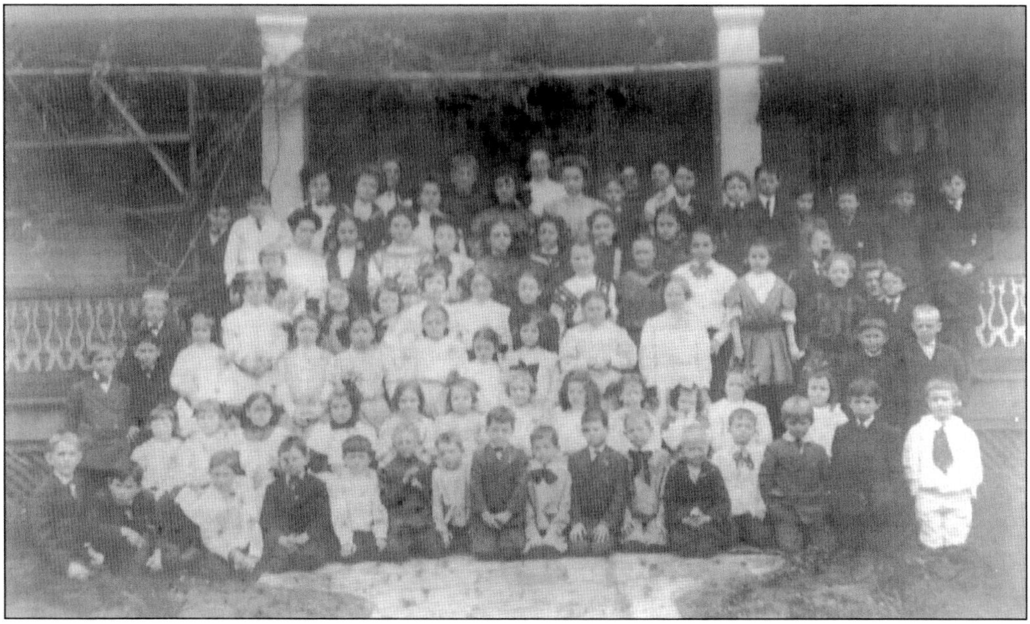

Gussie Woodruff ran a six-grade private school in a house at 201 Alabama Street from 1868 until Woodruff's death in 1927. Later the little red schoolhouse ran by the Sisters of Loretta Convent was built on that site. Currently the courthouse annex occupies the block. On graduation day, May 30, 1902, these school children gathered on the porch steps for a group photograph. (Courtesy Landmarks Foundation of Montgomery.)

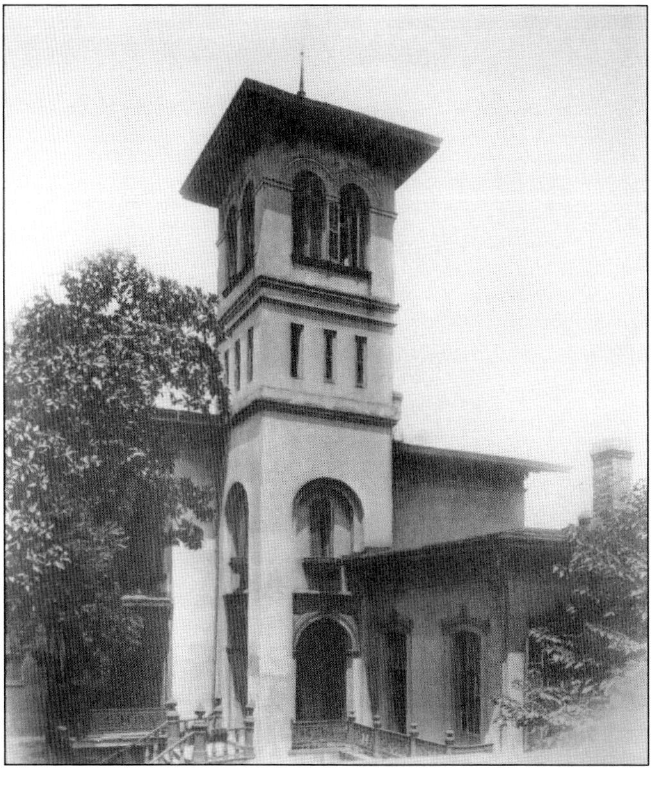

Joseph Samuel Prince Winter built this Italianate villa, designed by nationally renowned architect Samuel Sloan of Philadelphia, in 1851 at the corner of Madison Avenue and North Perry Street. In 1854, the Winter family sold the house and moved into what is now the First White House of the Confederacy. Later Colonel Winter built the Winter Place in Cottage Hill. The house at left was razed in 1919. (Courtesy Bob Thorington.)

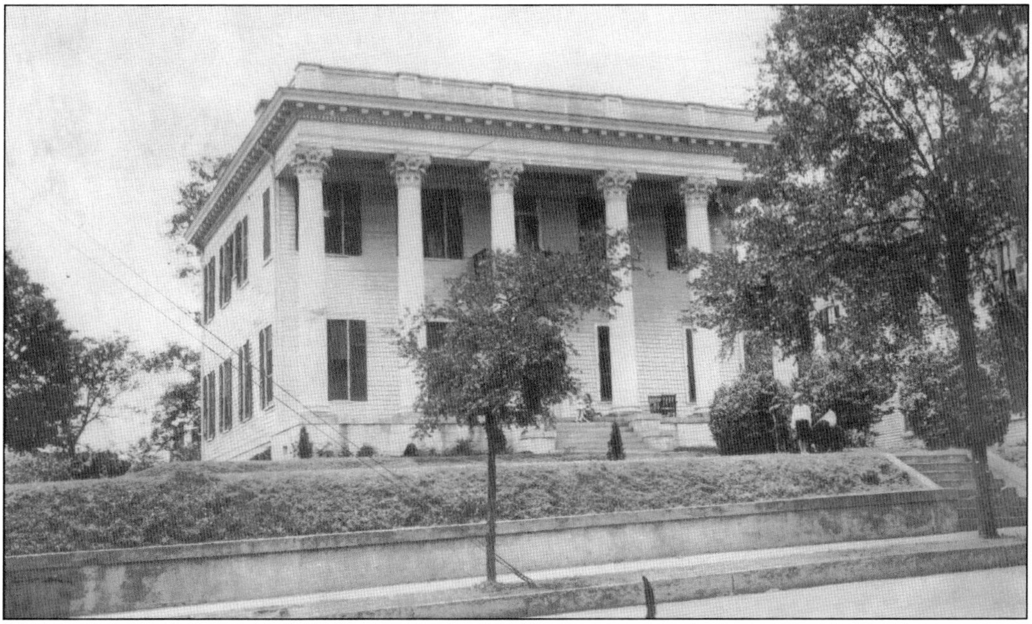

The Branch-Ray Mansion at 730 South Court Street is shown here in the 1920s, while it was still the Branch family home. On the front walk stand Edward J. Branch and William Thomas Branch. Later the house became the American Legion headquarters and part of the HABS survey in 1934. The house was lost to the interstate. (Courtesy Anne Tidmore.)

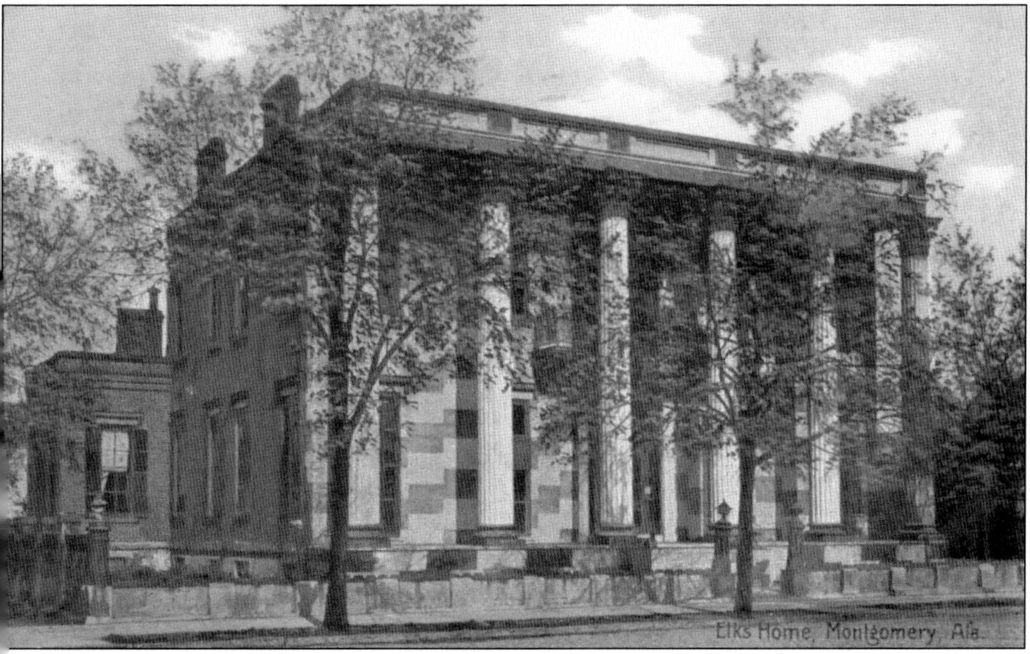

The Murphy House was built by John Murphy in 1851. The home was used as the Union army provost marshal's headquarters in April 1865. This postcard documents that the house served as the Elks Lodge from 1894 to 1970. The house currently is the office of the water works and sanitary sewer board—a connection to John Murphy, who was director of the Montgomery Water Works in 1854. (Courtesy James Bozeman.)

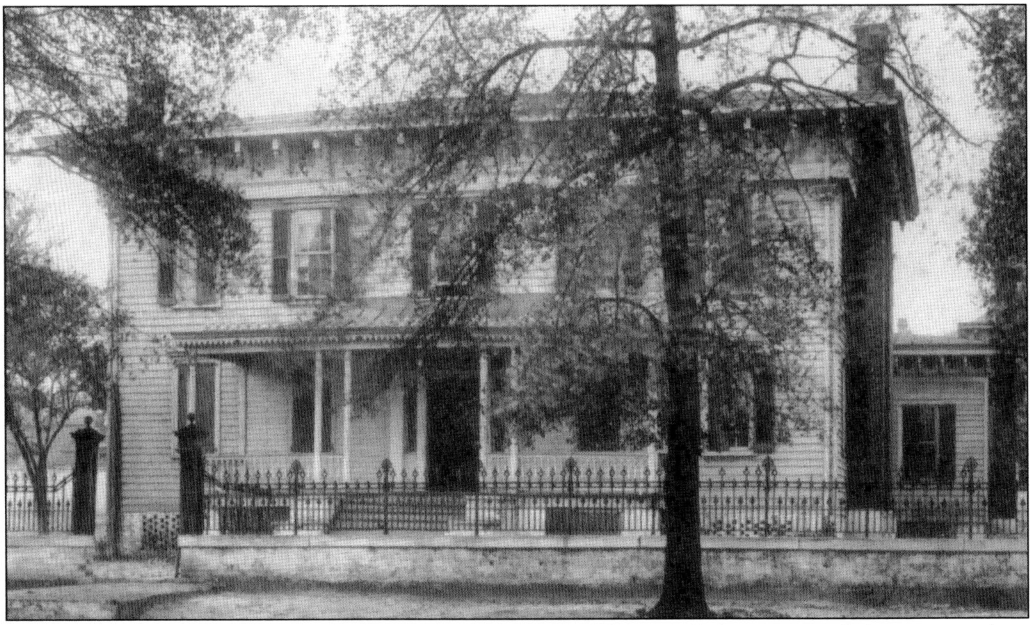

This 1894 photograph shows the First White House of the Confederacy. Confederate president Jefferson Davis and his wife, Varina, moved into the house when Montgomery became the Confederate capital. At that time, the home, built in the 1830s, stood at the corner of Bibb and Lee Streets. The house is now located next to the Alabama Department of Archives and History and is open to the public. (Courtesy Art Work Collection.)

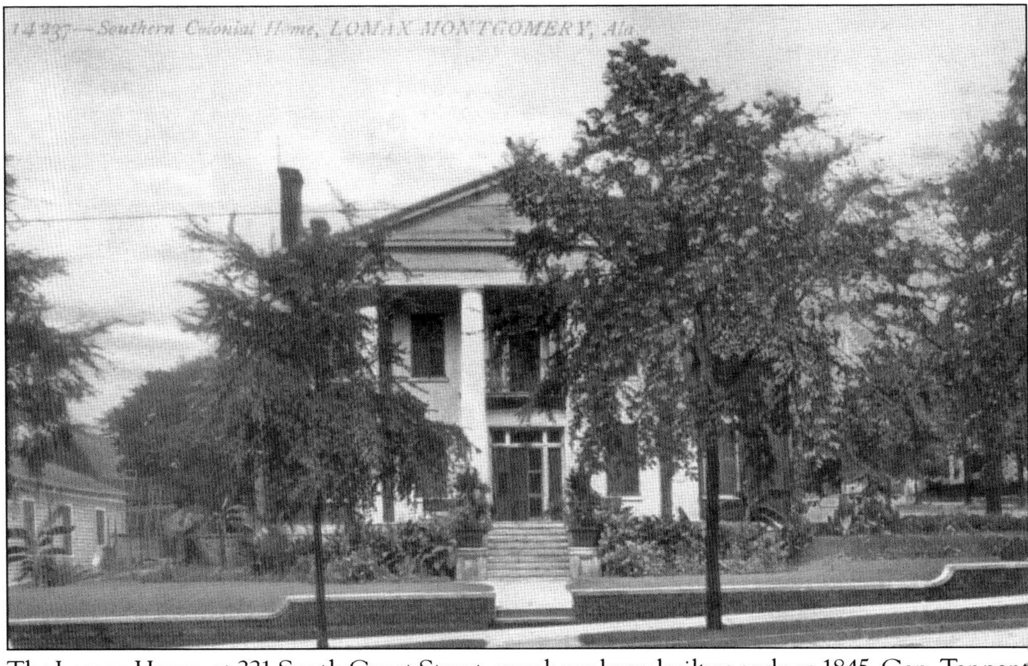

The Lomax House, at 221 South Court Street, may have been built as early as 1845. Gen. Tennent Lomax and his wife, Caroline Billingslea, moved into the house in 1857. General Lomax died in the Battle of Seven Pines, and Caroline Lomax remained in the house until her death in 1907. The home currently houses law offices. (Courtesy Art Work Collection.)

Rev. Albert Sidney Dix rests on the front porch at 423 Columbus Street during a visit to his mother and father, Rev. Alexander Franklin Dix, in 1898. Albert Dix lived with his wife and children (including Ruth in next photograph) in Georgia. (Courtesy Russell D. Whigham.)

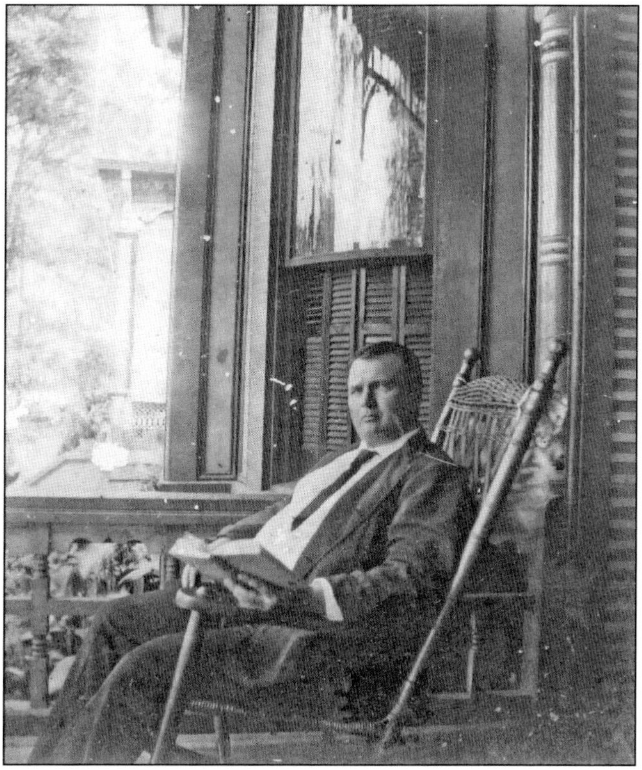

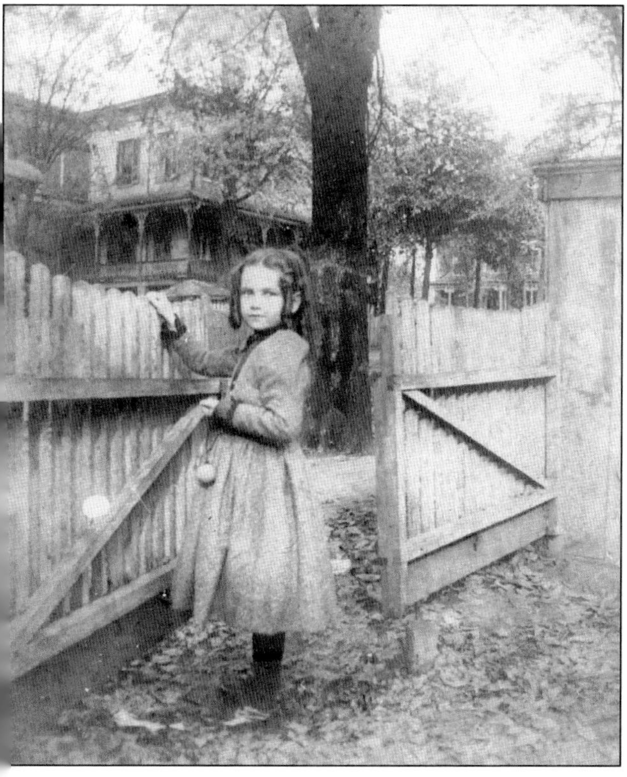

Ruth Dix visited her grandparents at their home at 515 Jefferson Street in 1899. According to family information, at the time of this photograph, Ruth was seven years and four months old. (Courtesy Russell D. Whigham.)

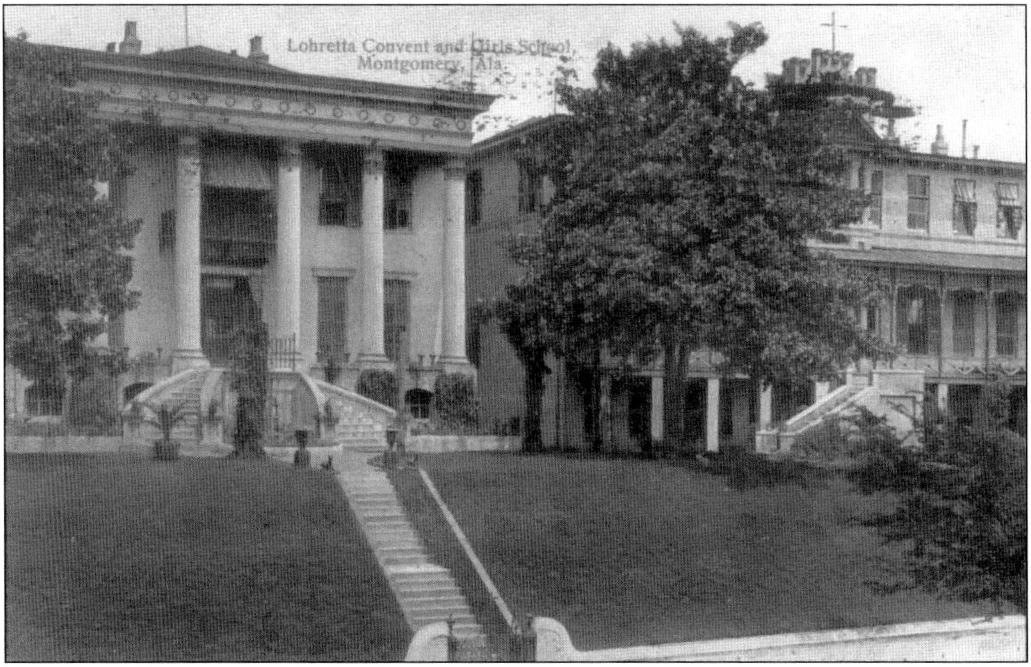

The Perley Gerald House was built around 1851 on the southeast corner of South Lawrence and Adams Streets. The Sisters of Loretta purchased and used the house as a convent from 1873 to 1962. Next to the house in 1890, the sisters built a Victorian building called the Annex for classroom space for their school, St. Mary's of Loretta Academy. The entire block is now the site of the courthouse annex. (Courtesy James Bozeman.)

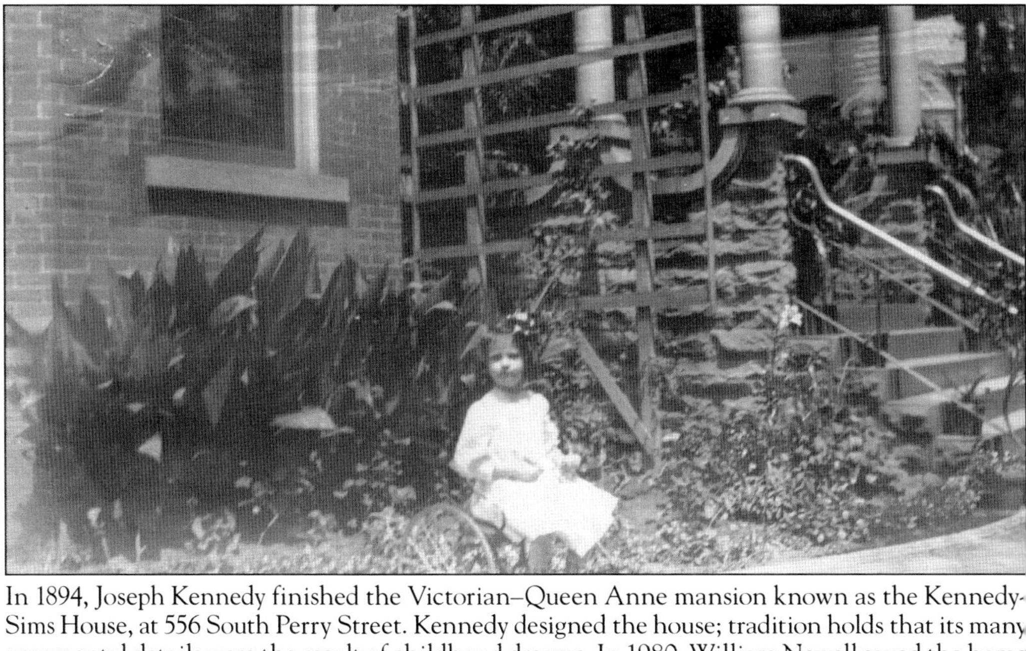

In 1894, Joseph Kennedy finished the Victorian–Queen Anne mansion known as the Kennedy-Sims House, at 556 South Perry Street. Kennedy designed the house; tradition holds that its many ornamental details were the result of childhood dreams. In 1980, William Newell saved the home and restored it. In this early 1900 photograph, an unidentified child sits in a wheelchair in the front side yard. (Courtesy Landmarks Foundation of Montgomery.)

The first governor's mansion was originally built for Moses and Hattie Sabel in 1906. It served as the governor's residence from 1911 to 1950. For a few years, the house was used as the Montgomery Academy. The home was demolished in 1963 to create U.S. Interstate 85. This postcard is postmarked 1911. (Courtesy James Bozeman and David Smith.)

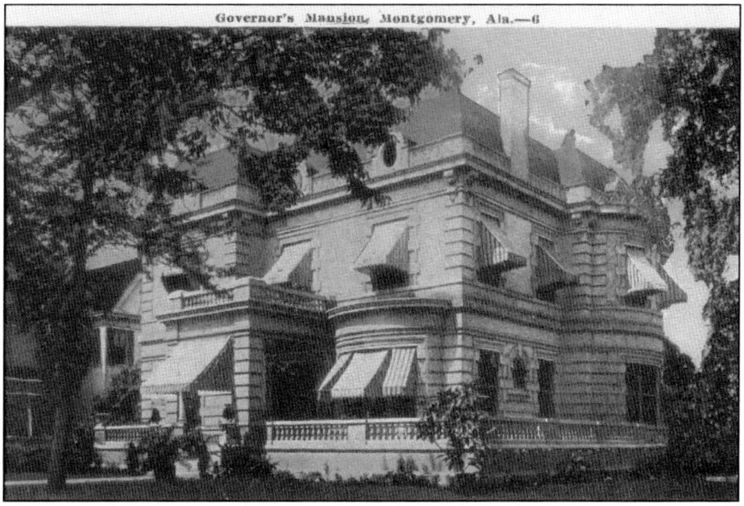

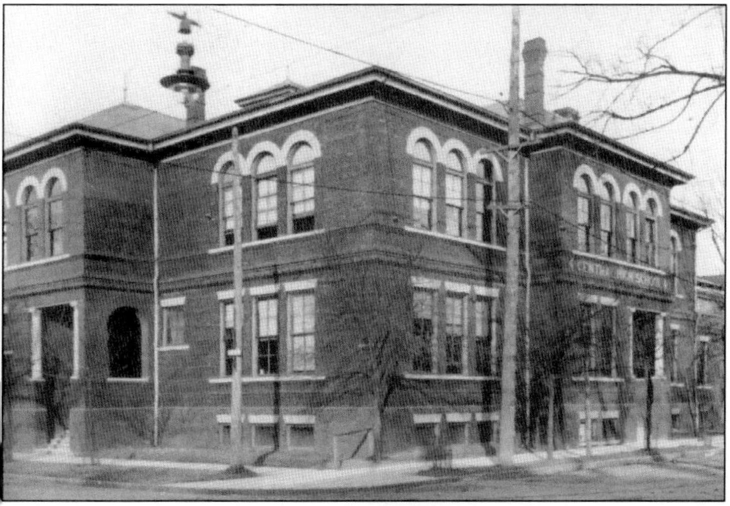

This 1907 photograph shows the Girls' High School, also known as Central High School, at the corner of Lawrence and High Streets. Young women attended high school in this building from 1894 to 1910. The building also served as an elementary school until 1924, then was used for the Montgomery Museum until it was demolished in 1959. (Courtesy Art Work Collection.)

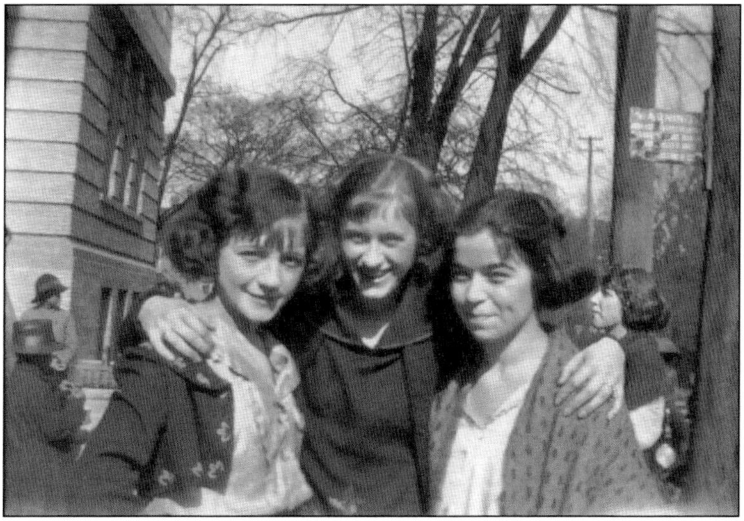

Three young women smile beside the Girls' High School; the note on the back of the picture says, "Triple Alliance." Since Sidney Lanier High School, which was coeducational, opened in 1910, this photograph was taken before 1910. (Courtesy Landmarks Foundation of Montgomery.)

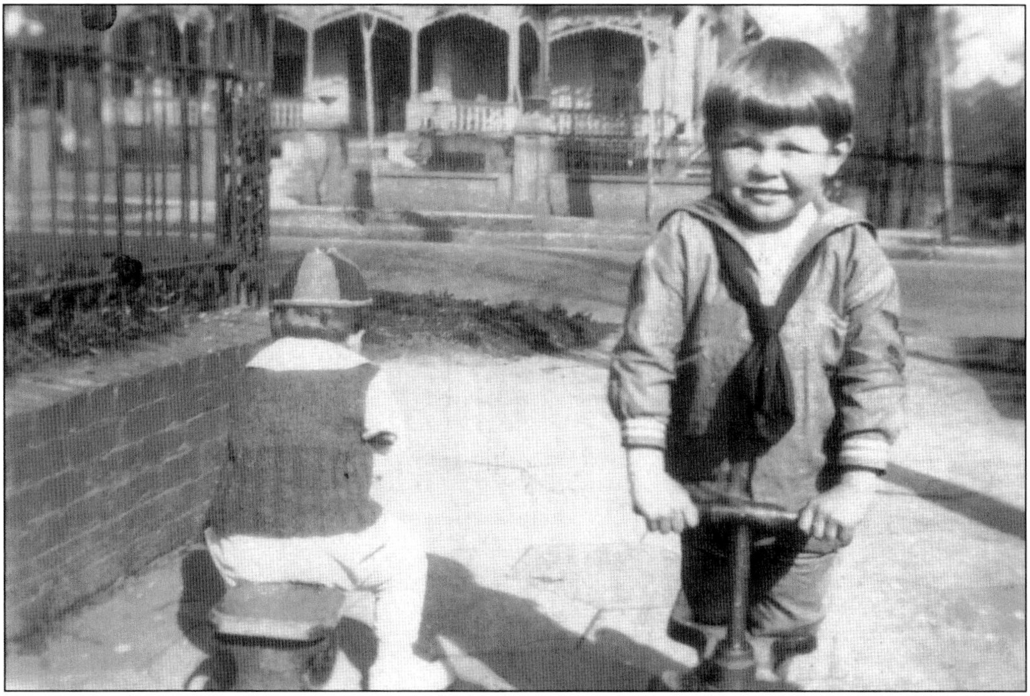

Sanford and George England cruise down an urban neighborhood street in their toy vehicles in 1919. (Courtesy Landmarks Foundation of Montgomery.)

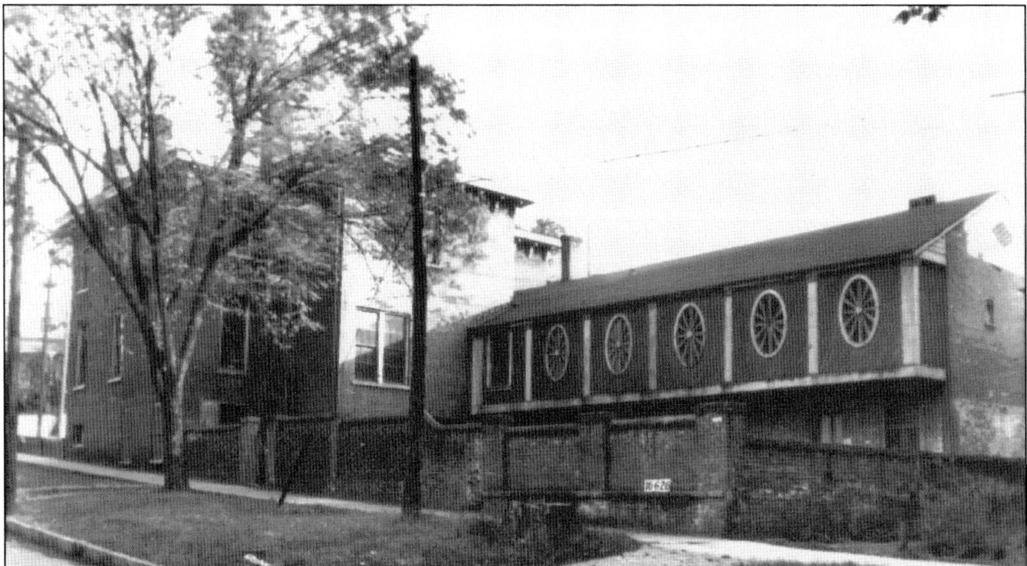

The Figh-Pickett House, the oldest surviving brick residence in Montgomery, was built about 1837 by John Figh on 14 Clayton Street. In 1858, Albert James Pickett, Alabama's first historian, bought the house. From 1907 to 1942, the house was the Barnes School for Boys. In 1996, the Montgomery County Historical Society acquired the house for its headquarters and moved the building to 512 Court Street. (Courtesy Library of Congress.)

Cowboy Peter Mastin V keeps law and order on the sidewalk on South Lawrence Street in 1943. Note the Sisters of Loretta Convent in the background. (Courtesy Mastin family collection.)

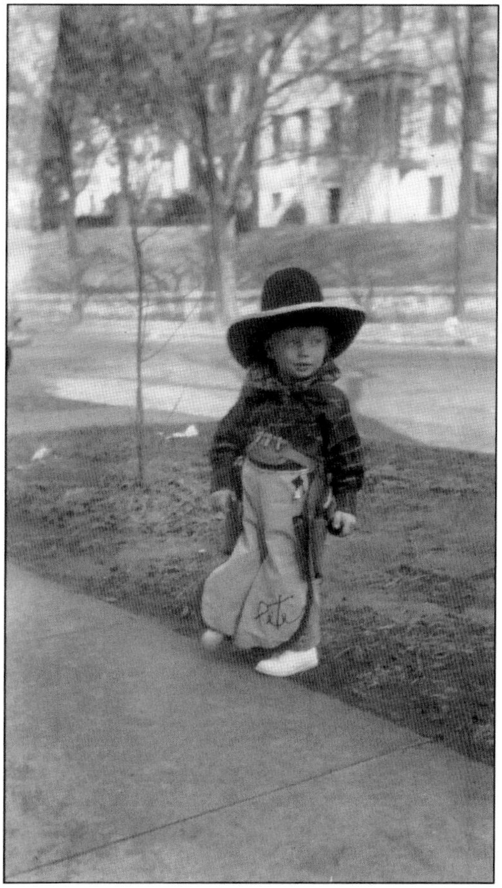

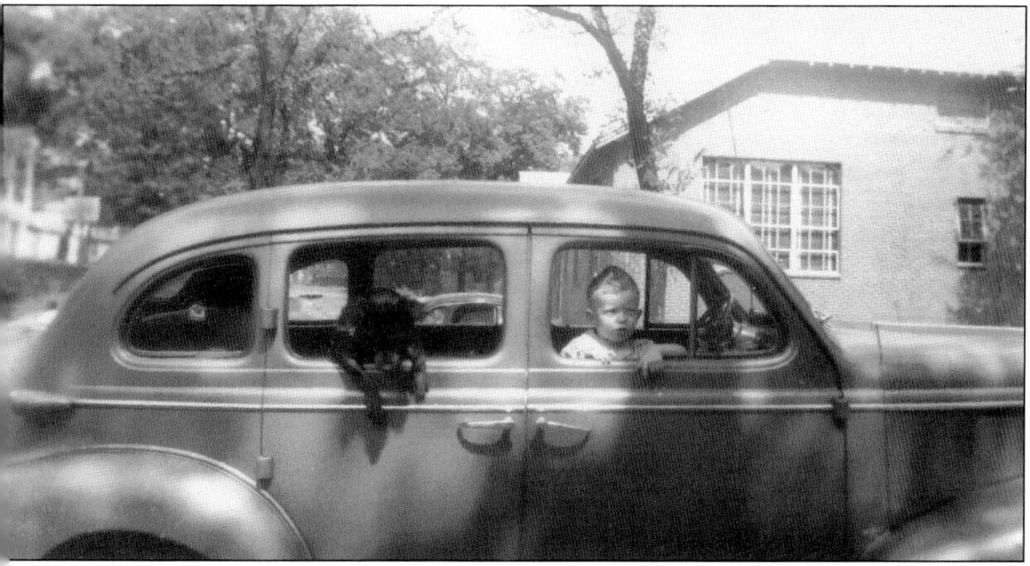

Peter Mastin V and his dog hang out of a car's windows on South Lawrence Street. Note the little red school house built by the Sisters of Loretta Convent that replaced Gussie Woodruff's school in the background. The convent and annex can also be seen. (Courtesy Mastin family collection.)

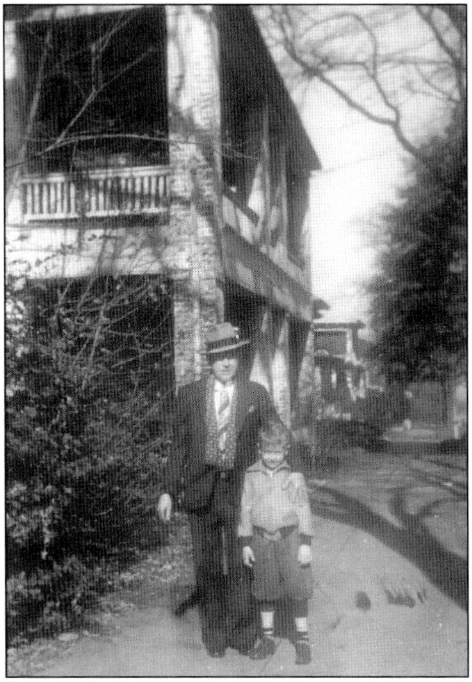

Peter Mastin V and his father, Peter Mastin IV, stand in front of the Wolff Apartments on South Lawrence Street in 1947. (Courtesy Mastin family collection.)

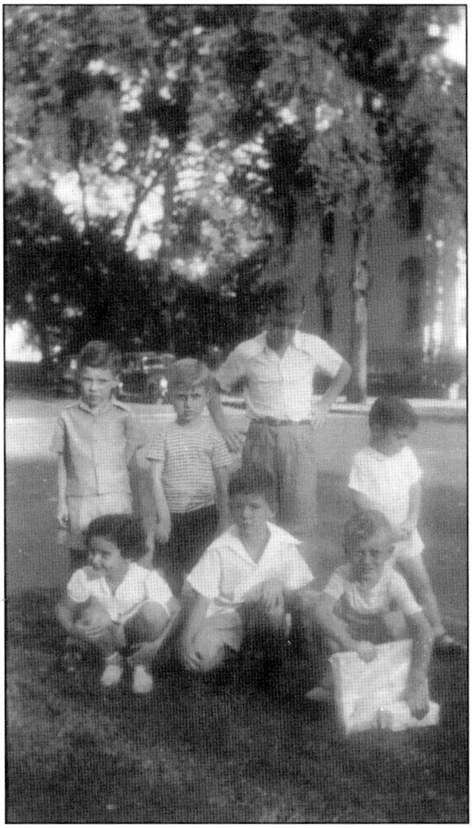

A group of unidentified children gather for a birthday party at the Wolff Apartments. Note the Governor Shorter–Griel House, built 1854–1856, which stands at 305 South Lawrence Street in the background. (Courtesy Mastin family collection.)

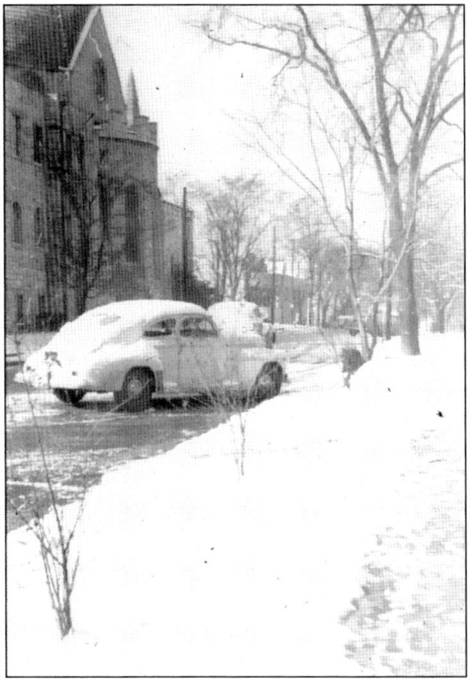

This photograph shows the side of the First Baptist Church (at 305 South Perry Street) in the 1947 snow. The church was founded in 1829 by Lee Compare, a missionary sent first to the Creek Indians in Tallassee. Construction began on this building, modeled after the cathedral in Florence, Italy, in 1905 and finished in 1923; it is the congregation's third home. (Courtesy Mastin family collection.)

This 1907 photograph shows, from left to right, Tillis Jones, Caroline (Callie) Clark Davidson, and Caroline Lee Davidson sitting on the steps of the H. C. Davidson house at 614 South Court Street. Callie Davidson is in mourning dress, as her husband, Harry Lee Davidson, had died in 1904. Callie Davidson moved to Montgomery so her daughter could know her father's family. (Courtesy Ball family collection.)

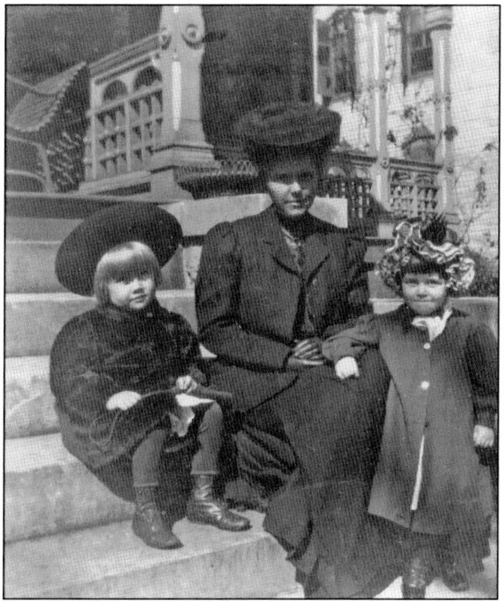

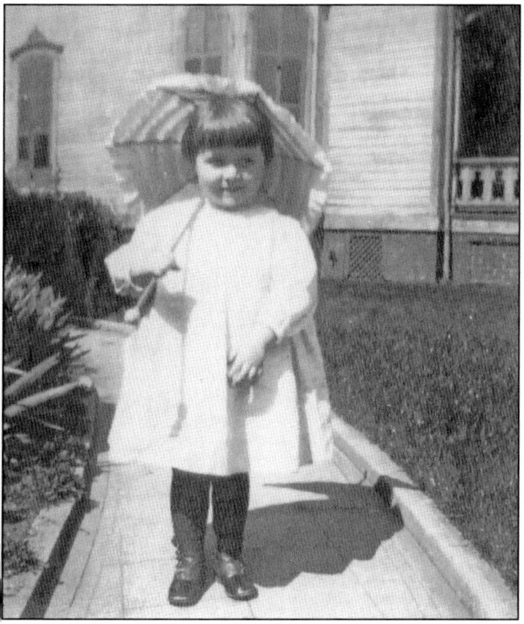

Caroline Lee Davidson strolls with a parasol along the side of 614 South Court Street around 1907. The house was built in the 1880s by her grandparents, Henry C. and Fannie Lee Davidson. (Courtesy Ball family collection.)

Henry C. Davidson and Fannie Lee Davidson built their house at 614 South Court Street in the 1880s. Henry Davidson was in the insurance and real estate business. The house was lost to the interstate. (Courtesy Ball family collection.)

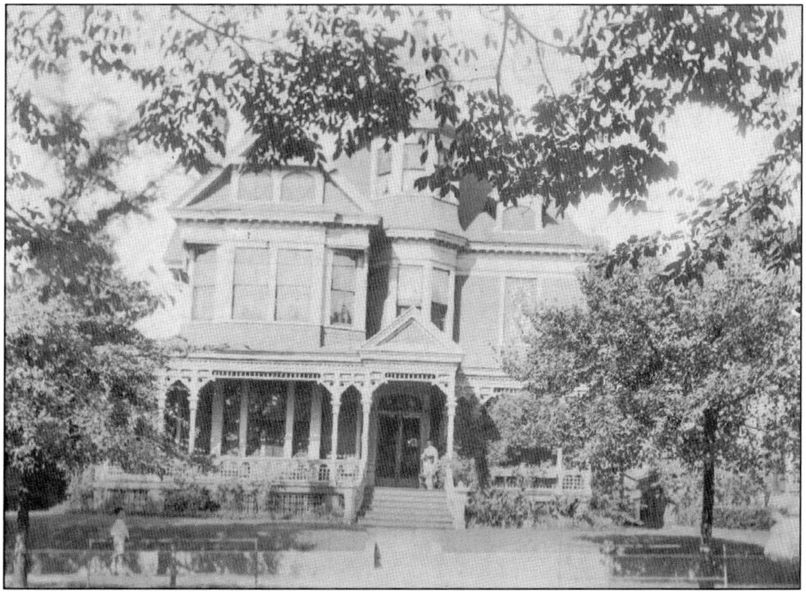

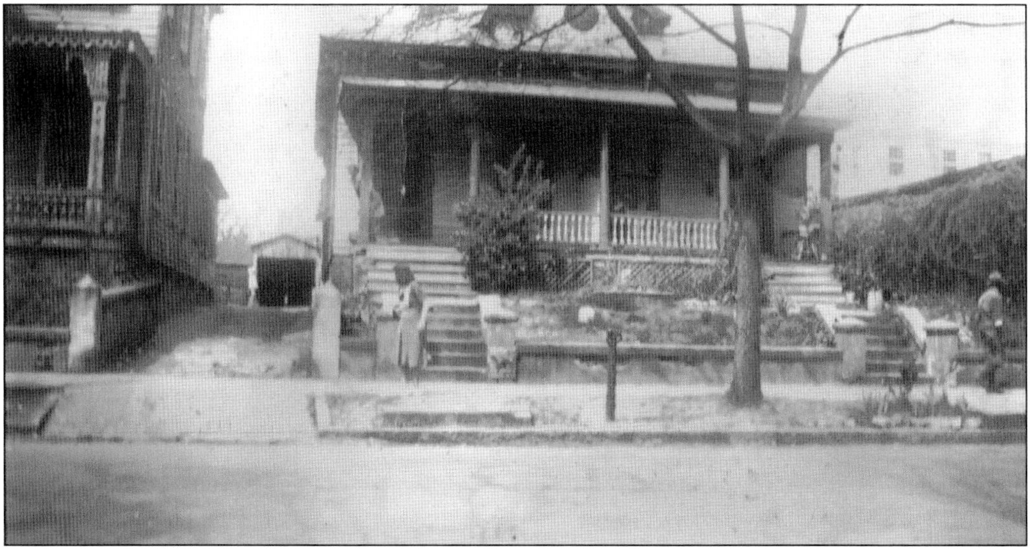

This photograph shows Camille Smith's home at 20 South Hilliard Street. (Courtesy Frazier family collection.)

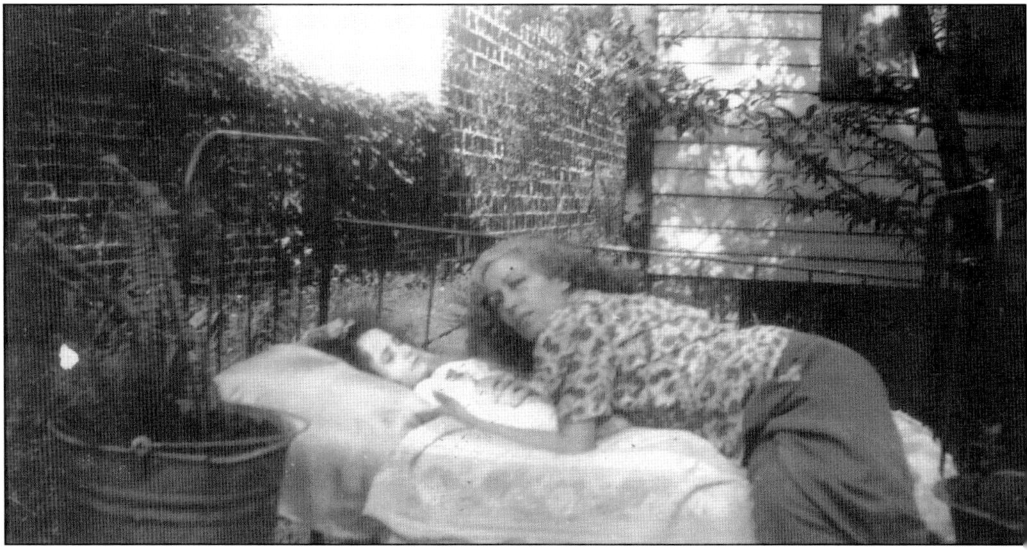

In 1940, Camille Smith and her daughter, Margaret, lived at 20 South Hilliard Street. As a baby, Margaret had fallen from a high wall that rose next to the house and was permanently injured (Courtesy Frazier family collection.)

Two

COTTAGE HILL

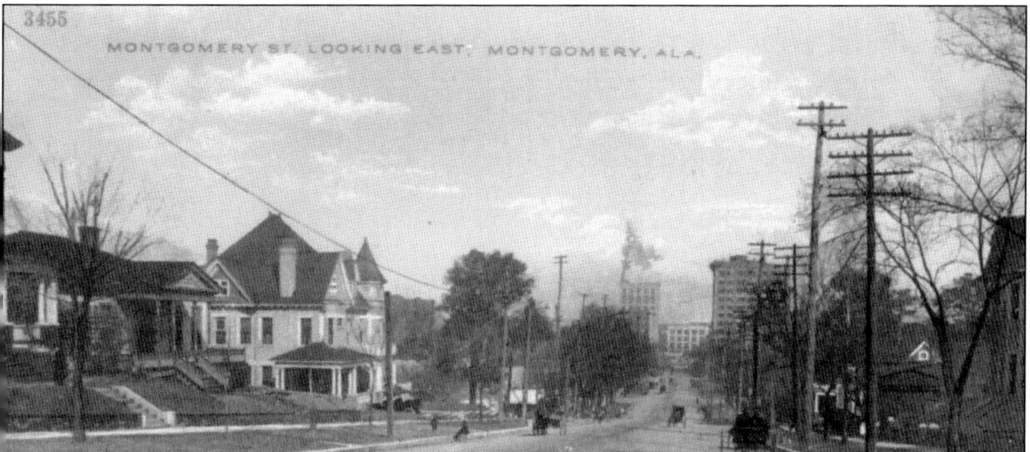

Cottage Hill takes its name from the first public school in the district. The area is located on a rise overlooking the Alabama River to the north and downtown Montgomery to the east. This postcard of one of Cottage Hill's streets shows the neighborhood's proximity to Montgomery's downtown area. The view is from the crest called Five Points. Looking toward downtown, the first skyscrapers are visible. The First National Bank Building and the Bell Building were constructed in 1907. (Courtesy James Bozeman.)

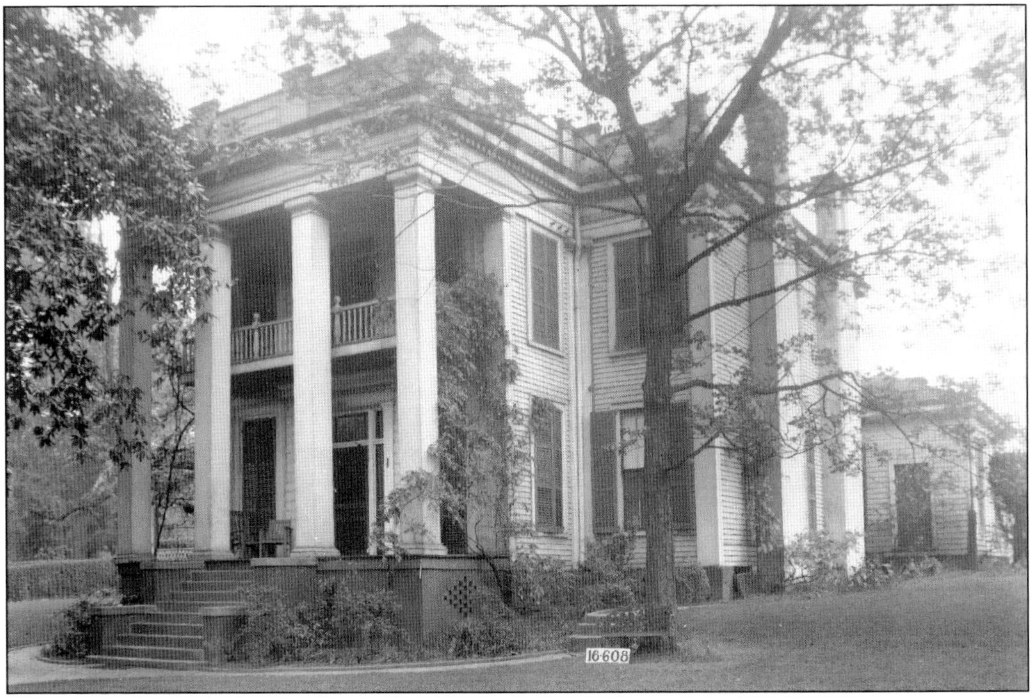

The McBryde-Screws-Tyson House was built around 1854 at 433 Mildred Street, at the head of Goldthwaite Street. Recently widowed Ann Allen McBryde bought the 2-acre lot and married Benjamin Thesis; together, they built the house when Cottage Hill was a new neighborhood. (Courtesy Fred Bush and HABS 1934.)

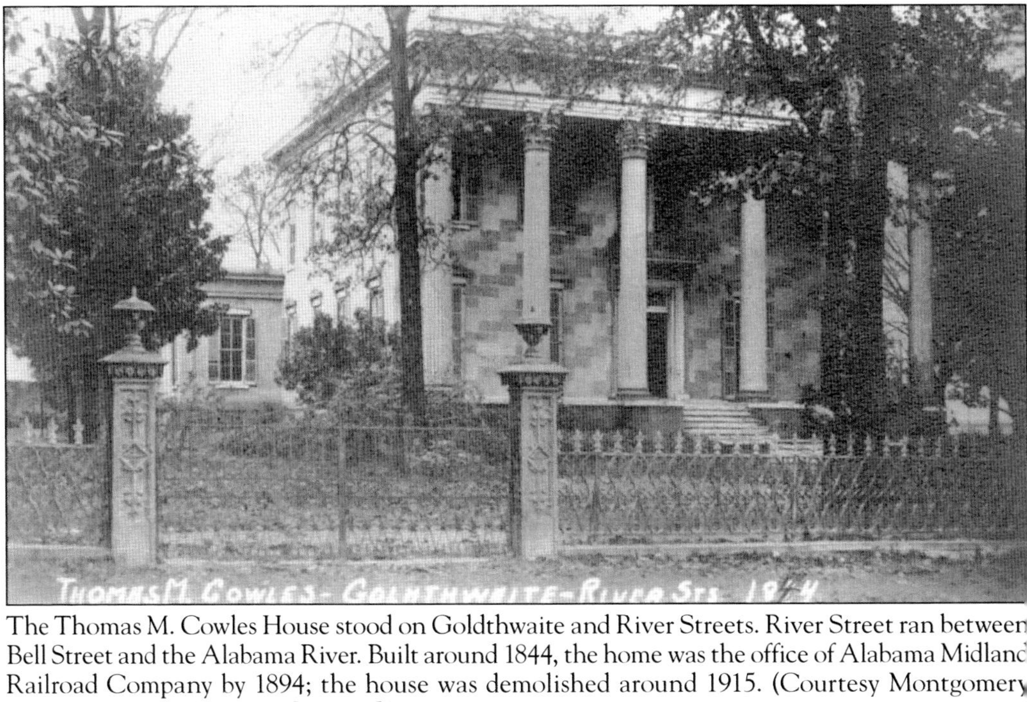

The Thomas M. Cowles House stood on Goldthwaite and River Streets. River Street ran between Bell Street and the Alabama River. Built around 1844, the home was the office of Alabama Midland Railroad Company by 1894; the house was demolished around 1915. (Courtesy Montgomery County Historical Society [MCHS].)

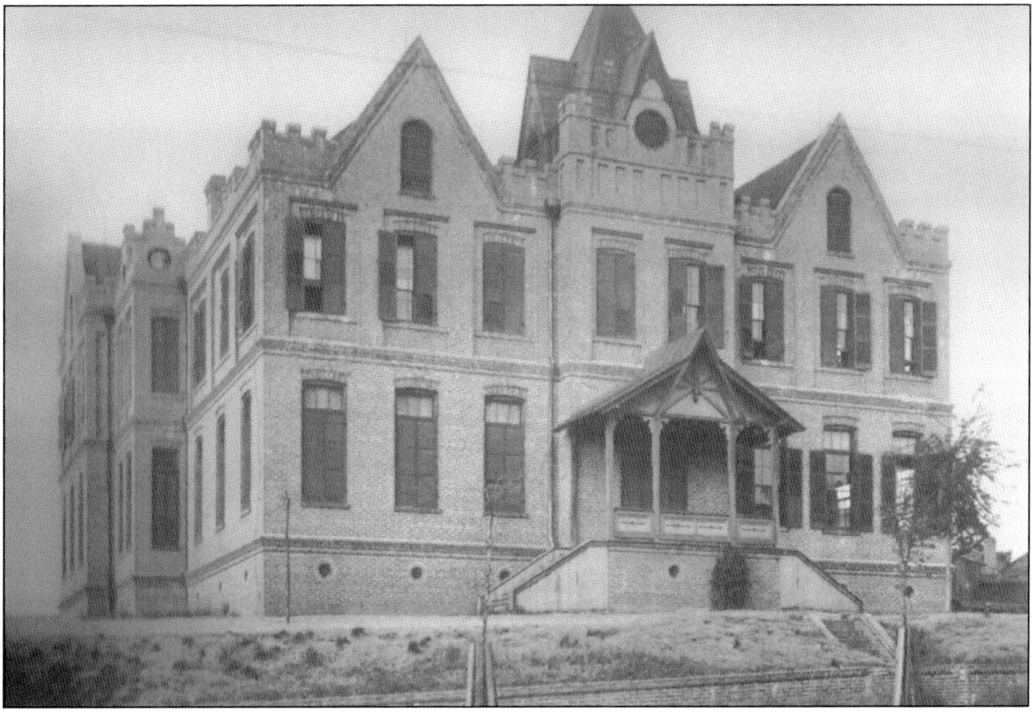

Cottage Hill School was included in a series of 1894 photographs of important places in Montgomery. The school opened in April 1891 and is the namesake of the Cottage Hill neighborhood. (Courtesy Art Work Collection.)

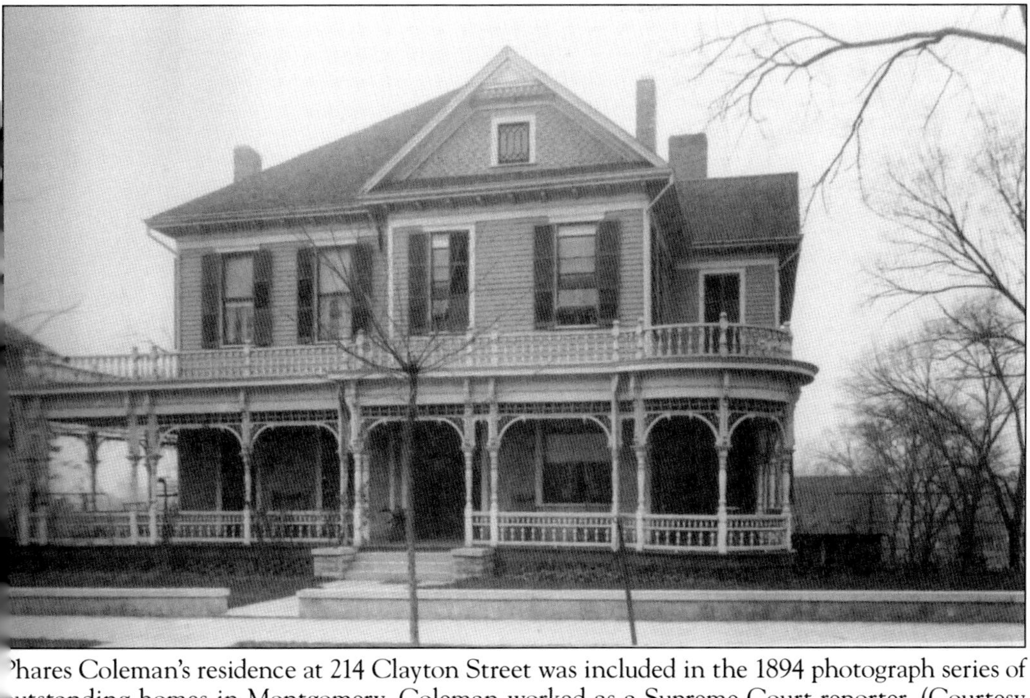

'hares Coleman's residence at 214 Clayton Street was included in the 1894 photograph series of ›utstanding homes in Montgomery. Coleman worked as a Supreme Court reporter. (Courtesy \rt Work Collection.)

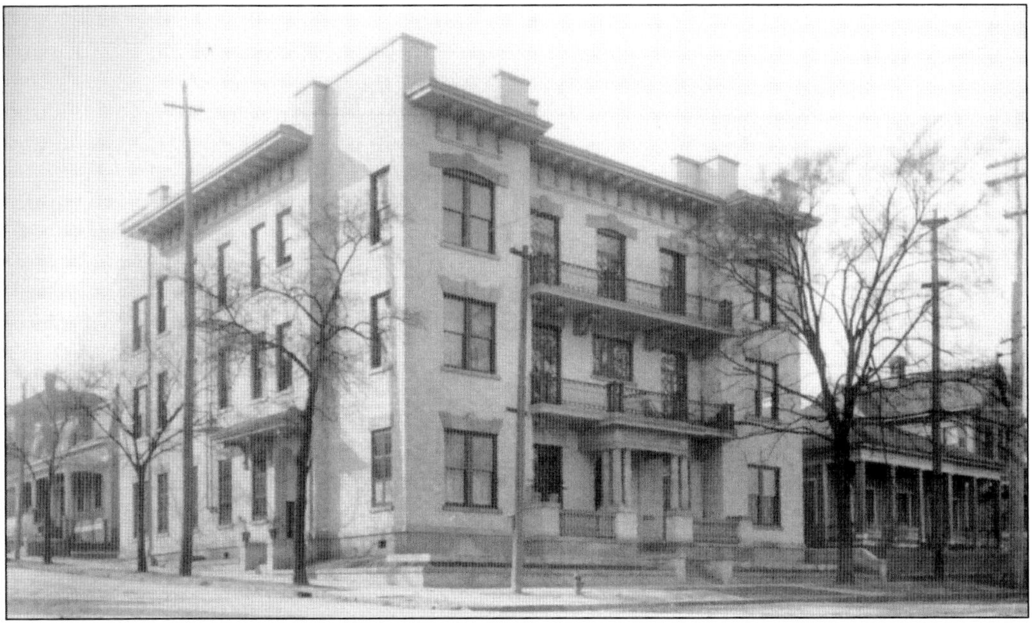

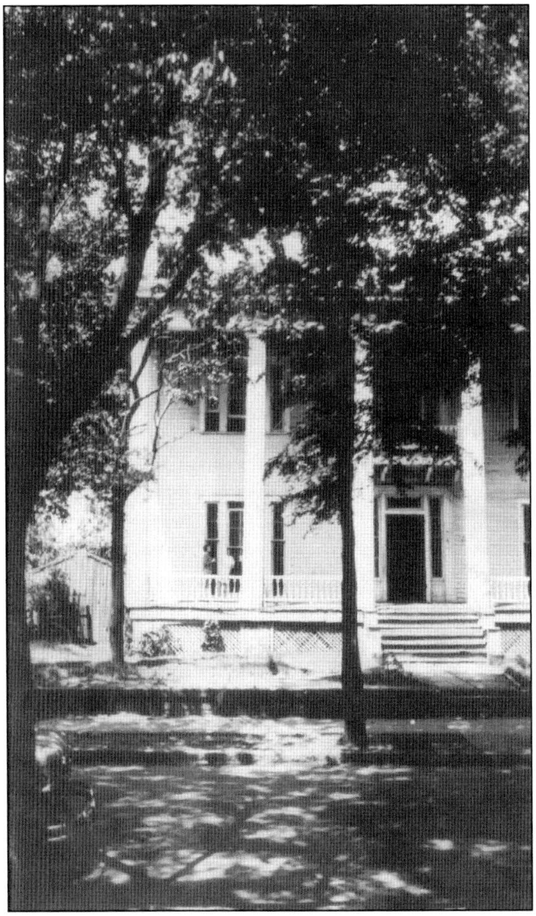

This gravure photograph of the Gay-Kirkland Flats was included in the 1894 series of outstanding buildings in Montgomery. The building, one of the first upscale apartment buildings in Montgomery, stood adjacent to Cottage Hill on Clayton and Holcomb Streets. (Courtesy Art Work Collection.)

The Gunter family home on Clayton Street housed several generations. Family history records that after their wedding in 1899, newlyweds Julia Campbell Scott Gunter and William (Will) Adams Gunter Jr. moved into the home on Clayton Street with Will's father, Colonel Gunter, and Will's two brothers, Charles and Gaston. Multiple generations under one roof was a common practice in the early 1900s. (Courtesy Fairlie Haynes.)

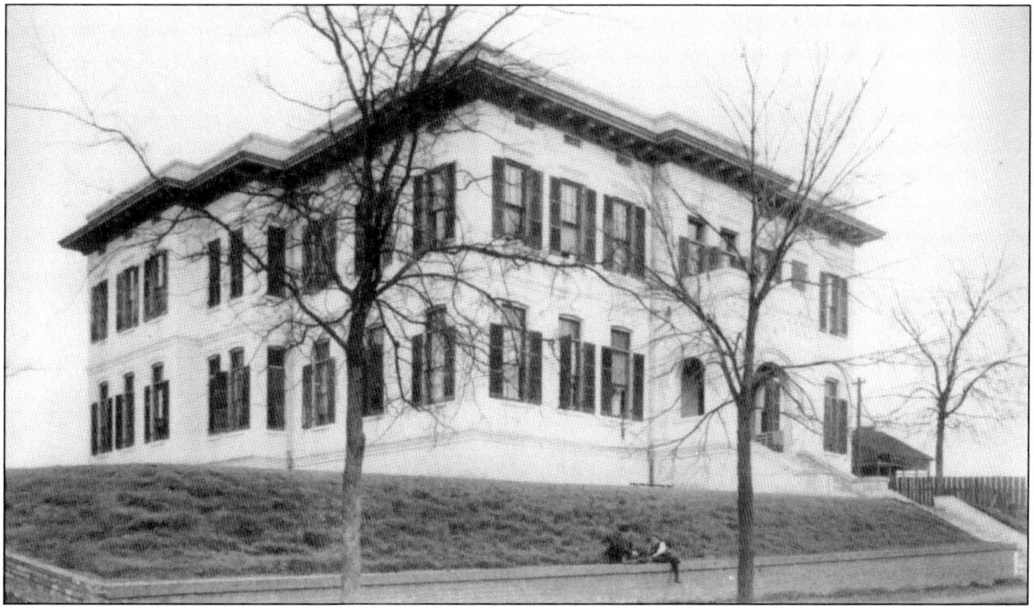

Herron Street School, at 2001 Herron Street, was included in the 1907 series of photographs of important Montgomery landmarks. At the time of this photograph, Virginia Hereford was principal. (Courtesy Art Work Collection.)

The Winter Place consists of two homes connected by a breezeway. Col. Joseph Samuel Prince Winter and his wife, Mary Elizabeth Gindrat, built the houses in 1858. This photograph shows the front of both houses: to the left is the house in the Second Empire style, and on the right is the Italianate. (Courtesy Bob Thorington.)

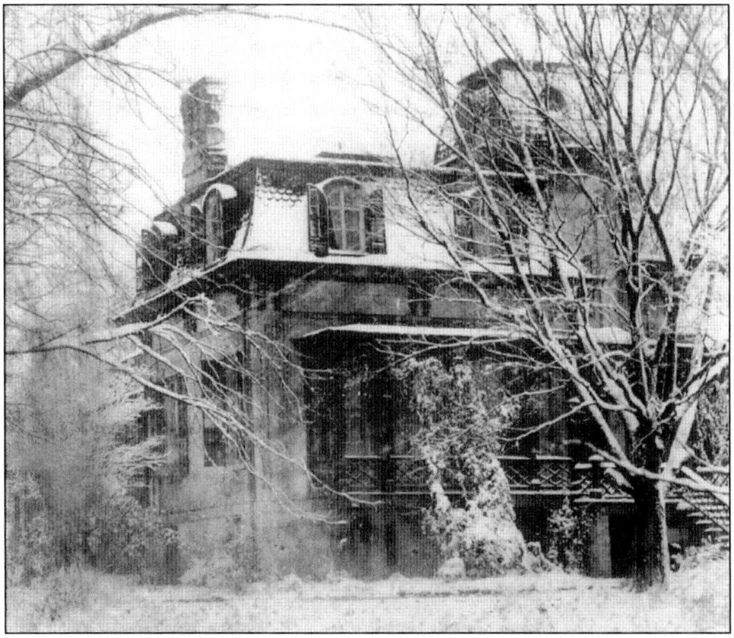

In this 1914 photograph, the Second Empire–style Winter home stands surrounded by trees and snow. The two homes, with 18 major rooms and 23 smaller rooms, were built to house the entire Winter family, including 11 grandchildren. During the Civil War, the first officers of the Confederate army lived in the houses. Currently owned by Craig Drescher, Winter Place is undergoing an impressive renovation. (Courtesy Bob Thorington.)

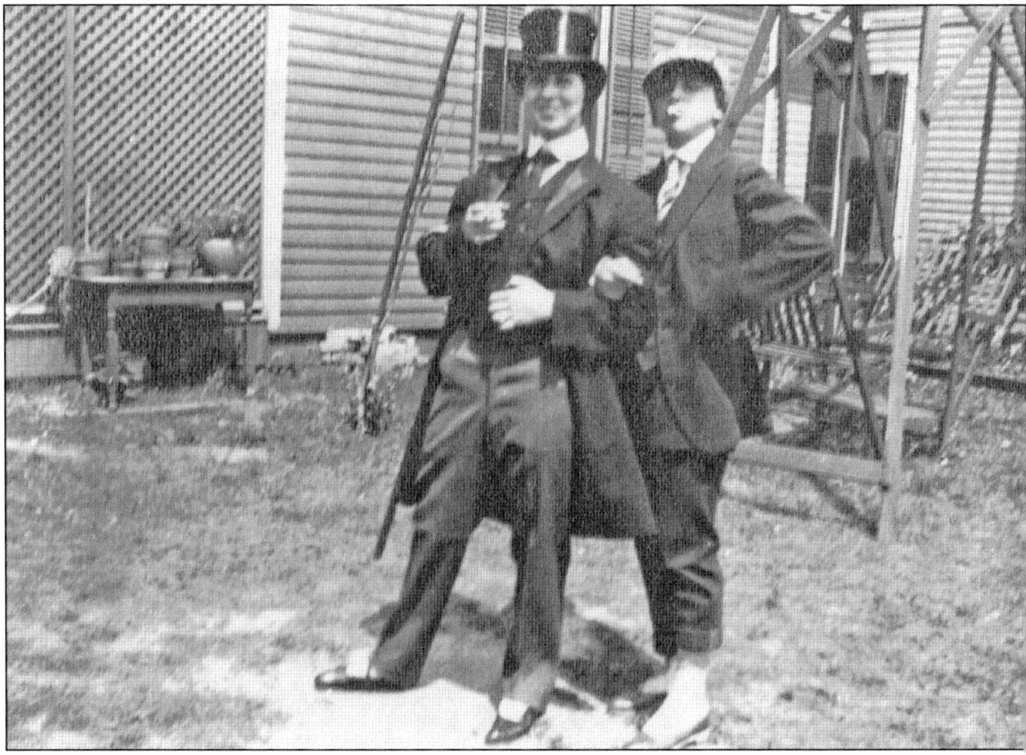

Pageants were popular events. Here Marion Weil (left) and Emily Ligon are dressed as masters of ceremonies for an event at Margaret Booth's school. (Courtesy Ball family collection.)

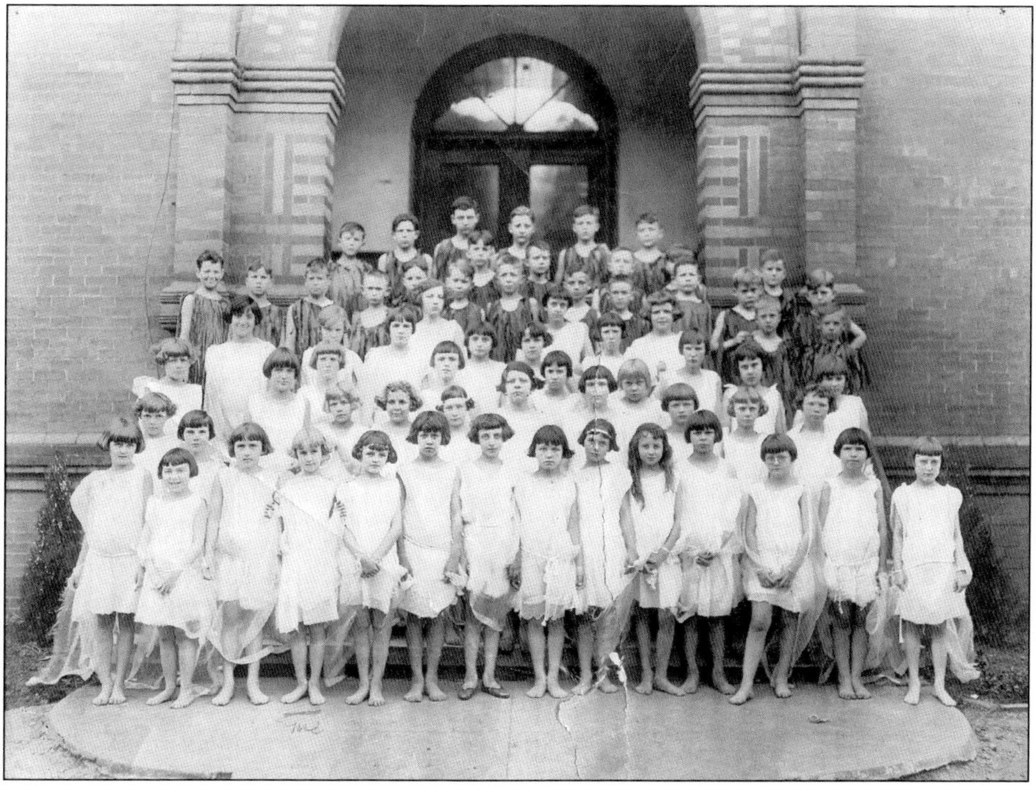

At the Spirit of the South pageant, students at Sayre Street School performed "The Winds" in May 1926. The pageant was part of the Montgomery observance of Alabama Homecoming Week, a statewide celebration that included a downtown parade. (Courtesy MCHS.)

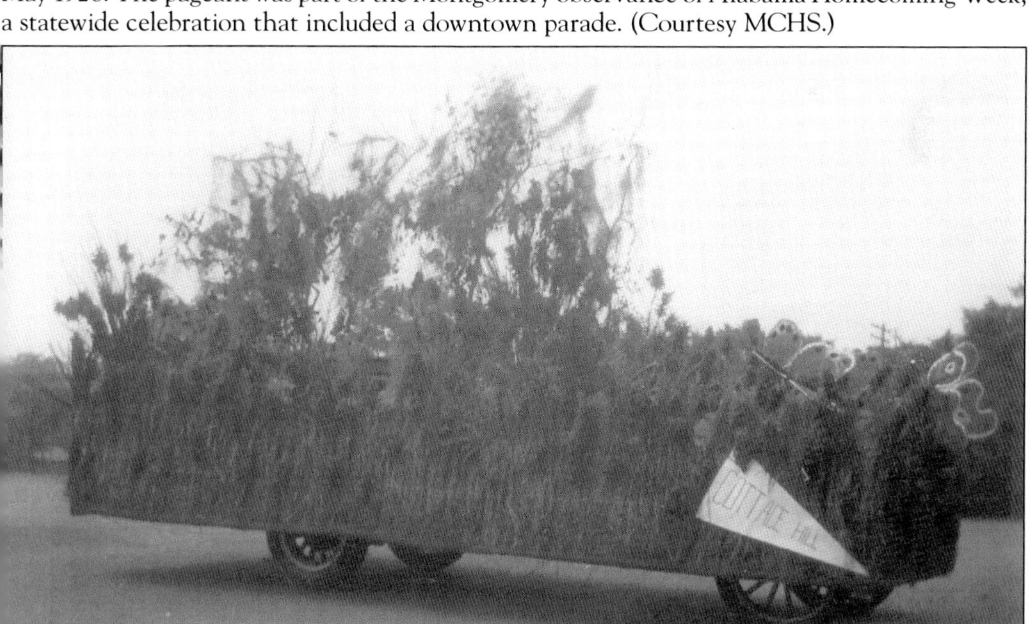

Parades were popular events. This photograph shows a float ready to represent the Cottage Hill neighborhood in 1927. (Courtesy Landmarks Foundation of Montgomery.)

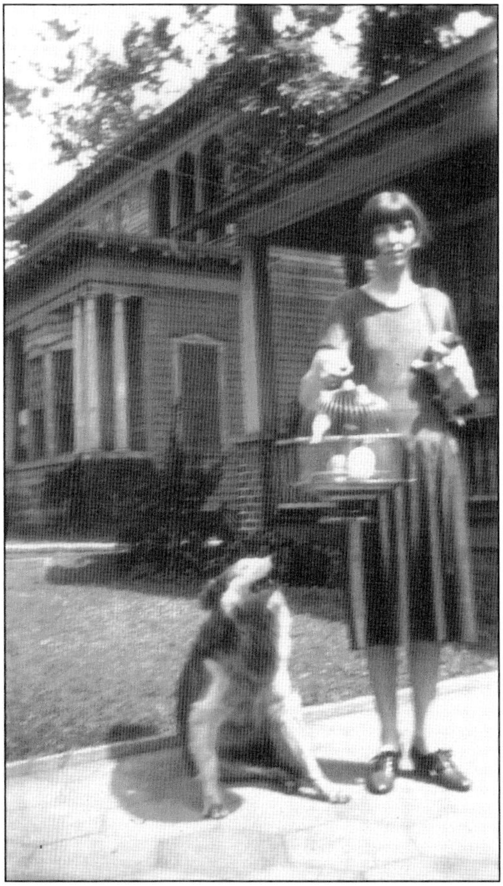

Showing off her dog, a bird in a cage, and a puppy, a young woman stands in front of two houses on Goldthwaite Street. (Courtesy Landmarks Foundation of Montgomery.)

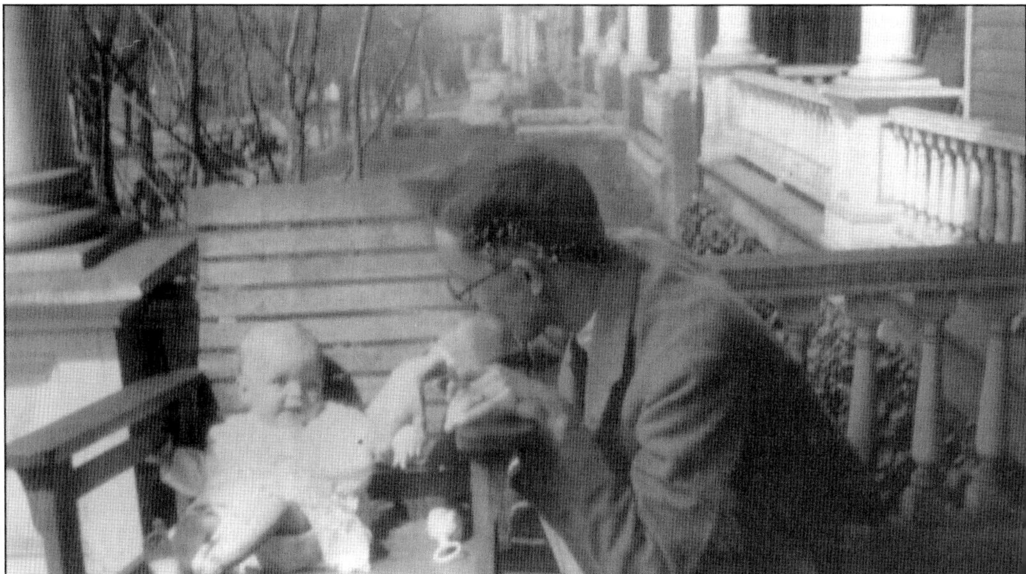

In this photograph, George Marks Woods plays with George Marks Wood Jr. on the porch at 212 Sayre Street in 1926. (Courtesy Sallie Millsap.)

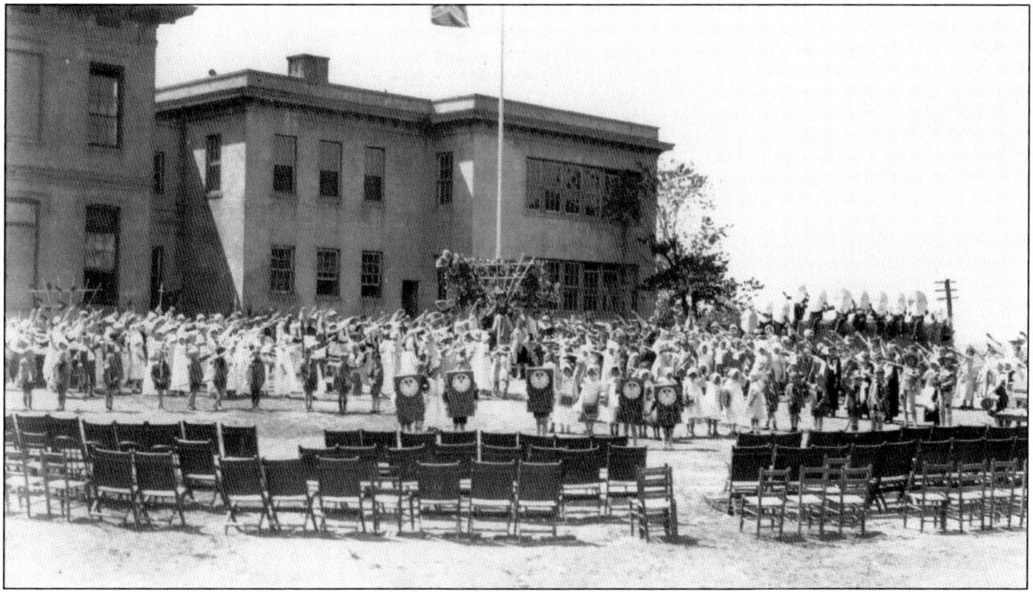

Pageants were popular school events. This is a full view of Cottage Hill School's Mother Goose pageant of what the note on the back of the photograph calls "the whole assembly" on April 22, 1927. Note the Humpty Dumptys on the back wall. (Courtesy Landmarks Foundation of Montgomery.)

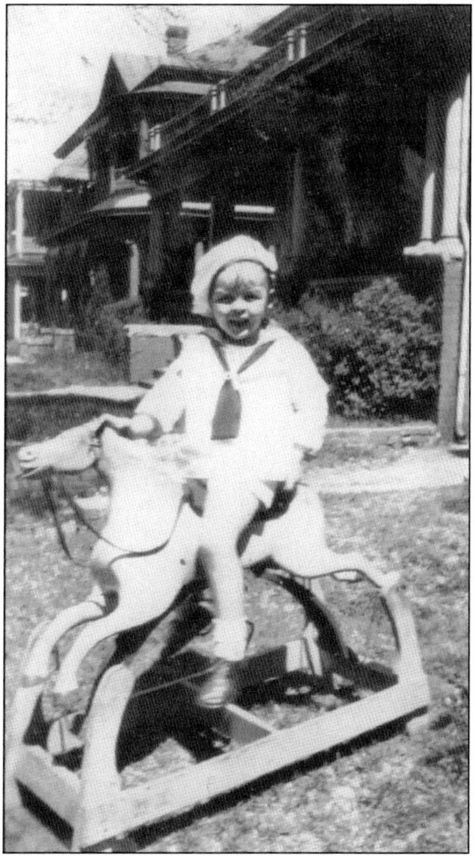

n this 1928 photograph, George Marks Vood Jr. rides a hobbyhorse at his home at 12 Sayre Street. (Courtesy Sallie Millsap.)

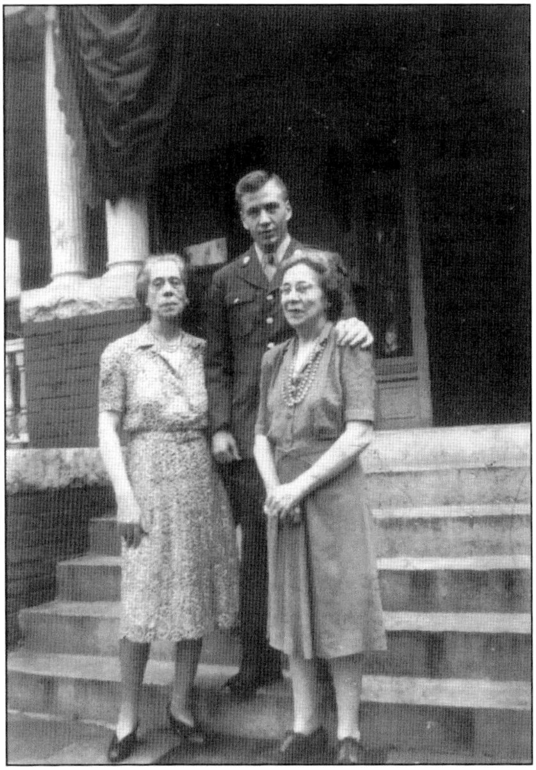

Margaret Booth ran a popular and respected college preparatory school for girls at her residence on Sayre Street. From left to right, Margaret Booth, her nephew Gardiner Parker, and his mother, Nell Parker, pose for a picture during Gardiner's visit while he was on leave from service during World War II in 1944. (Courtesy Sallie Millsap.)

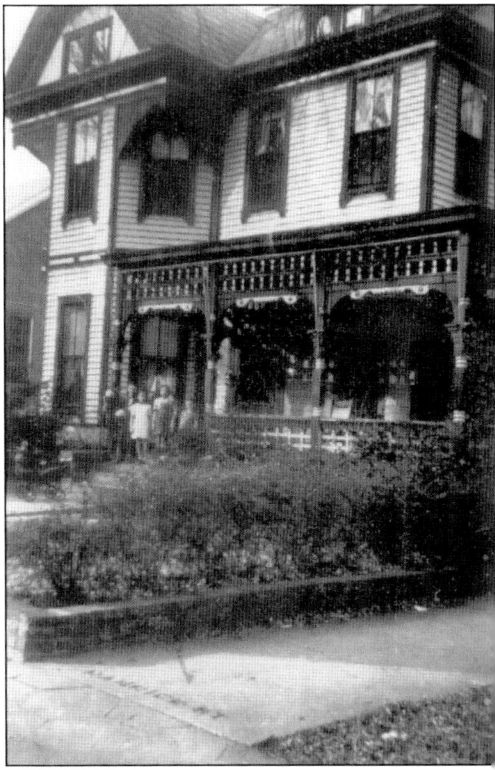

Russell Whigham lived in this house at 602 Clayton Street with his parents, Francis Dix Whigham and Mavis Vickery Whigham, from 1945 to 1949, when Russell was four years old. He remembers the house was divided into apartments, and his family lived upstairs. Mrs. Crawford, the landlady, lived downstairs. Russell Whigham remembers children in the house named Kay, Lindsay, and Herman. However, the children in the photograph are unidentified. (Courtesy Russell Whigham.)

Three

Old Line Street

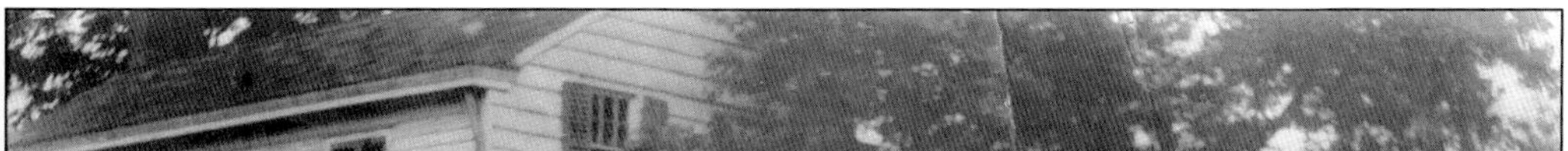

The neighborhood takes its name from Line Street, which ran west of Court Street and was the southern city limit. In the late 1800s, the street was renamed West Jeff Davis Avenue after Jefferson Davis, the president of the Confederacy. The trolley provided service, but by the 1900s, the automobile had arrived. The first automobile in Montgomery, purchased by the Gunter family, left from the Old Line Street neighborhood and traveled to New York in 1908. In the first car sits driver Fred Thompson and, beside him in the front seat, Will Gunter. In the backseat sit Julia Gunter (left) and her sister-in-law, Rosa Gunter Semple. (Courtesy Fairlie Haynes.)

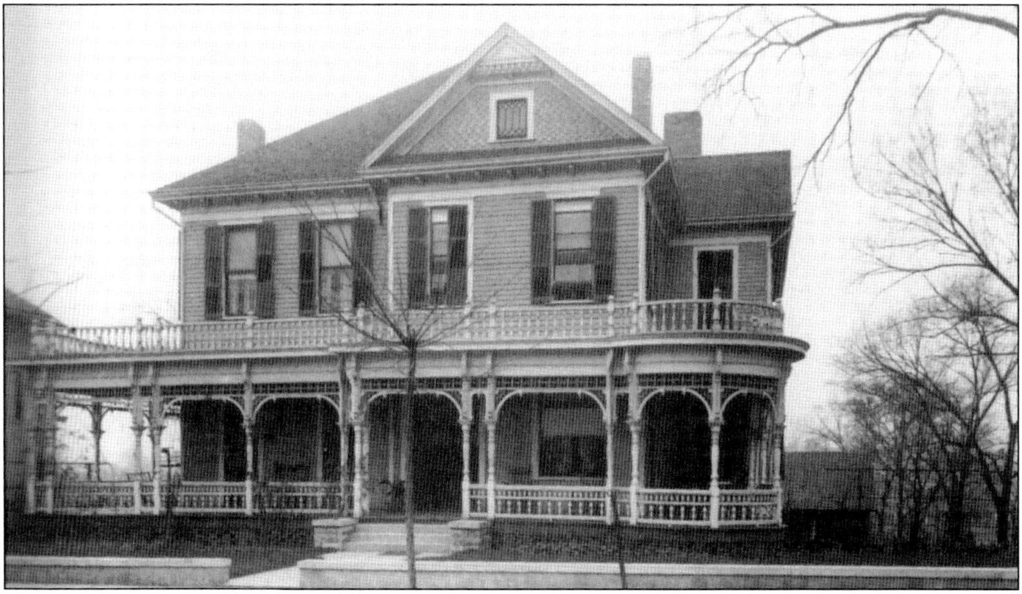

Issac and Pauline Stanton's home stood at 304 Sayre Street. Issac Stanton was vice president and superintendent of Planter's Cotton Oil Company. (Courtesy Art Work Collection.)

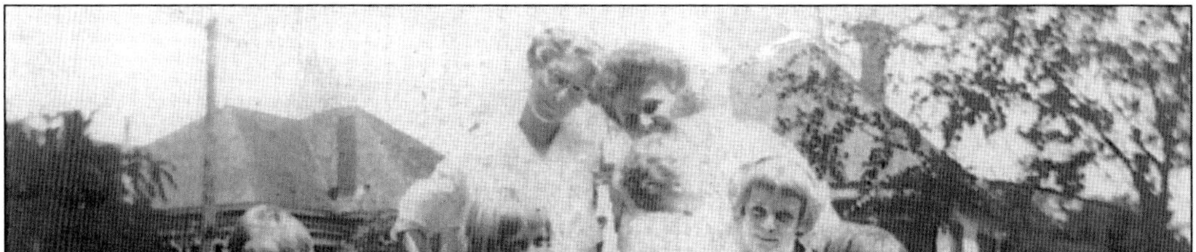

On a June afternoon in 1912, the Gunter girls and their Marks cousins pose in front of the Gunter home at 139 West Jeff Davis Avenue. Kneeling in front is Grace Gunter; behind her, from left to right, are John Marks, Rose Gunter, Ellen Gunter, Kitty Marks holding Mozelle Scott, and Jean Gunter. In the background, Priscilla Marks (left) stands next to her sister, Julia Gunter. (Courtesy Fairlie Haynes.)

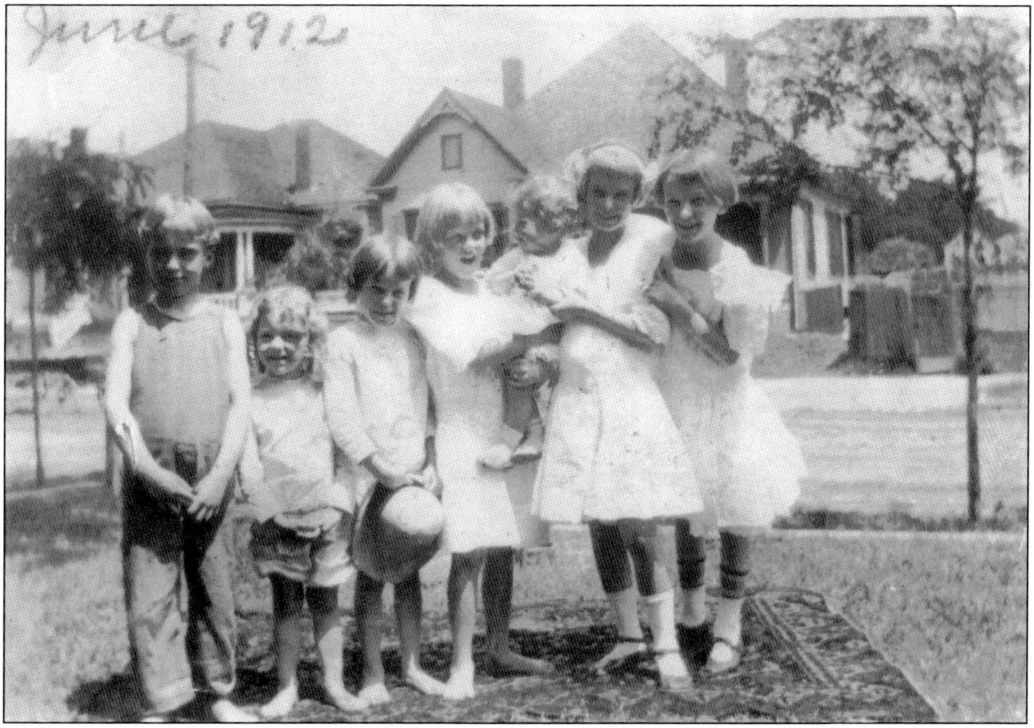

In this photograph, the Marks and Gunter girls include their cousin, John Marks. From left to right pose John Marks, Rose Gunter, Virginia Gunter, Ellen Gunter, Mozelle Scott, Kitty Marks, and Grace Gunter. (Courtesy Fairlie Haynes.)

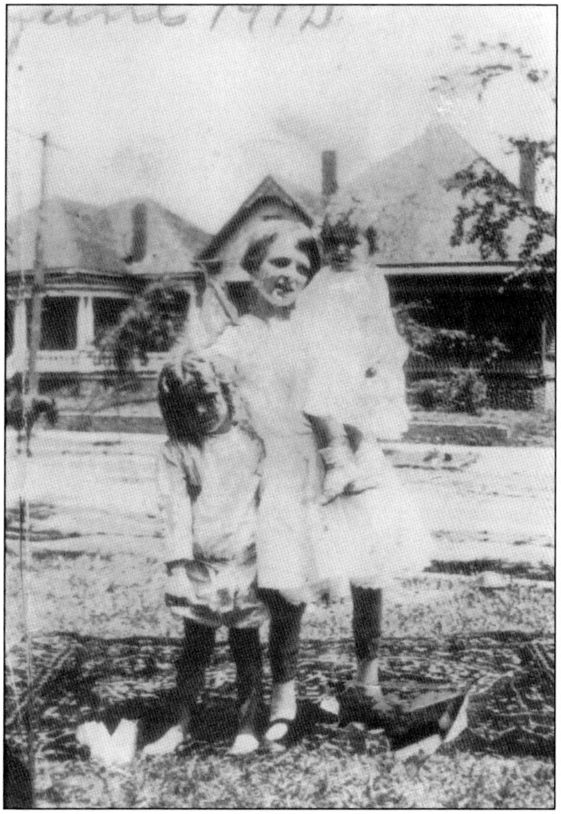

'hotographs are fun when families et together. From left to right, rrace Gunter smiles while her sister, ose Gunter, holds their cousin, lozelle Scott, on West Jeff Davis venue. (Courtesy Fairlie Haynes.)

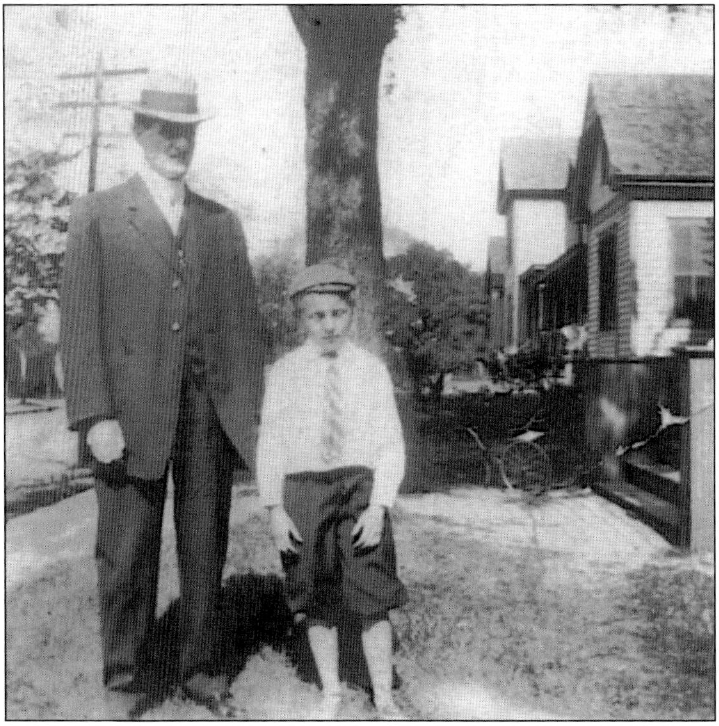

Will Gunter and his son, Bill, pose for this photograph at 139 West Jeff Davis Avenue in 1911—the year Will Gunter campaigned for mayor of Montgomery. (Courtesy Fairlie Haynes.)

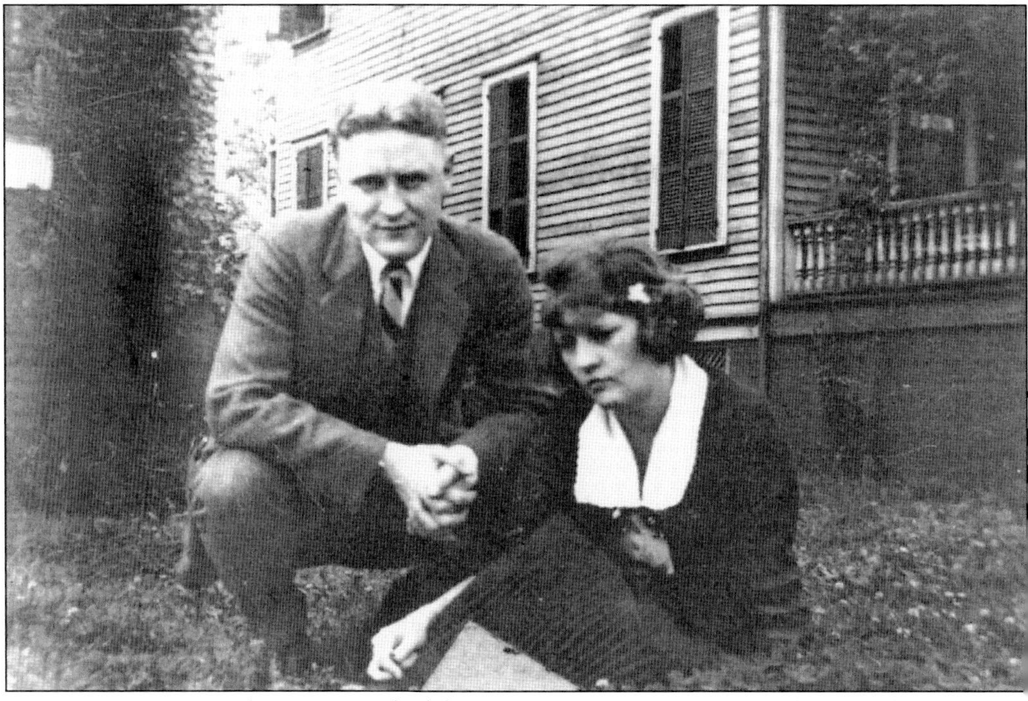

Minerva "Minnie" Machen Sayre and Alabama Supreme Court justice Anthony Dickinson Sayre lived and raised their family, including their daughter Zelda, at 6 Pleasant Avenue. Zelda married F. Scott Fitzgerald in 1920. This photograph of the famous couple was taken during a visit to Zelda's parents in 1921. (Courtesy Linda Wagner-Martin.)

Zelda Fitzgerald is pictured as a young girl around 1914, standing in the yard of her parents' home at 6 Pleasant Avenue. (Courtesy of the *Romantic Egotists.*)

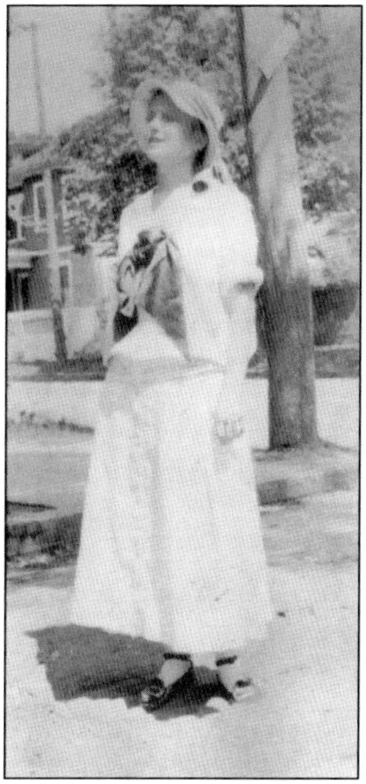

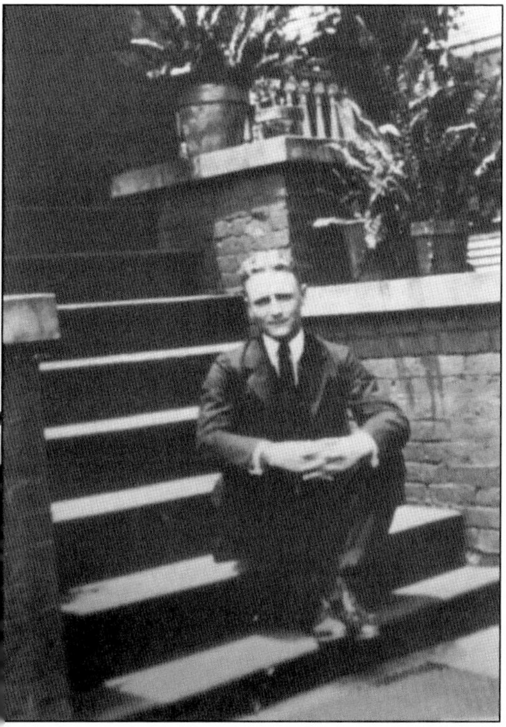

When novelist F. Scott Fitzgerald was stationed in Montgomery during World War I, he met and later married Zelda Sayre. Here in 1921, during a visit to her parents, Minerva Machen Sayre and Judge Anthony Dickinson Sayre, F. Scott Fitzgerald sits on the front porch steps of their home at 6 Pleasant Avenue. (Courtesy the *Romantic Egotists.*)

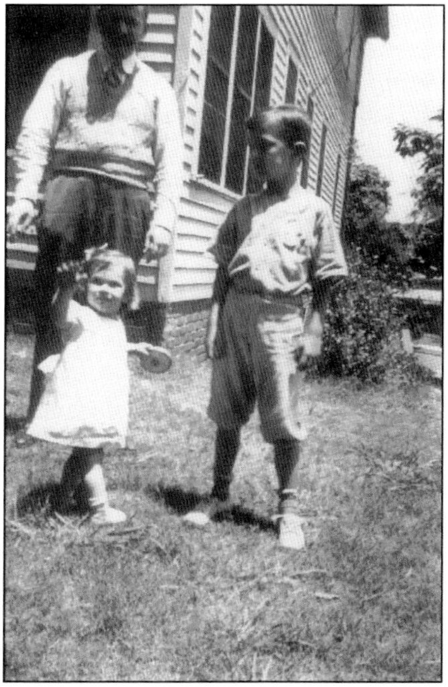

)n May 6, 1942, from left to right, Vaughan nd Marilyn Williford and Jackie Salter ose in the yard at 234 Pleasant Avenue. Courtesy Pearson family collection.)

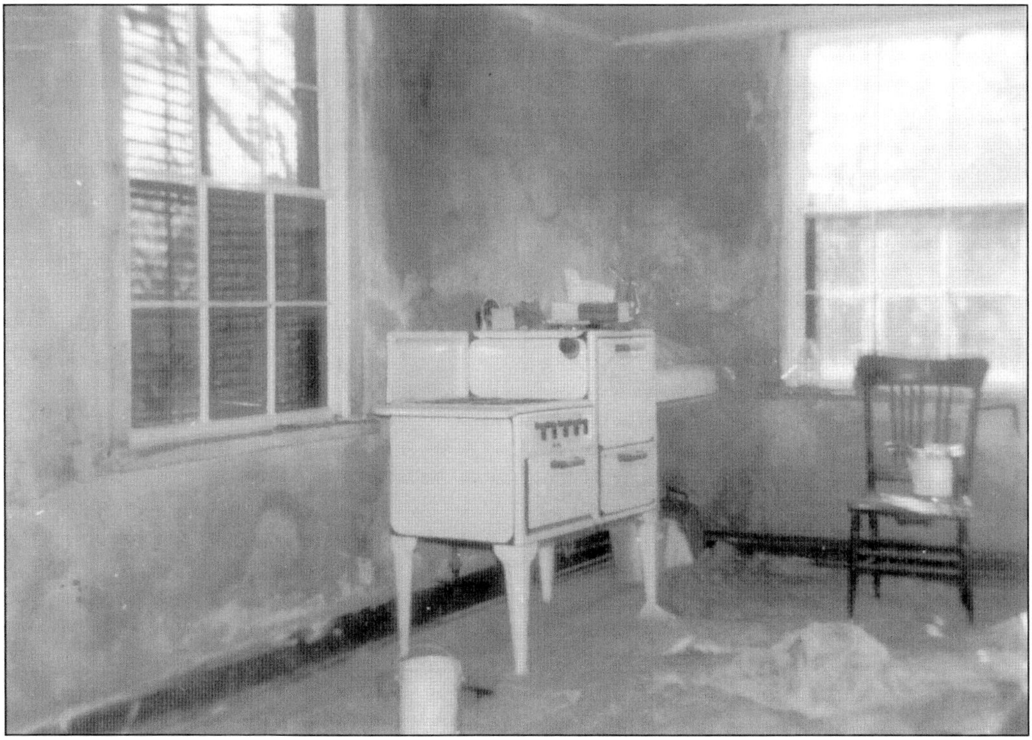

In 1955, newlyweds Sallie and Gene Millsap moved into the Opp Cottage, an antebellum home named for its second owner, Valentine Opp. Sallie and Gene immediately went to work renovating. (Courtesy Sallie Millsap.)

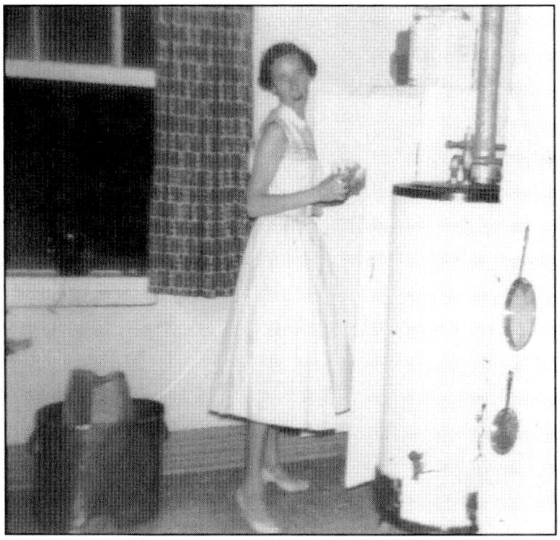

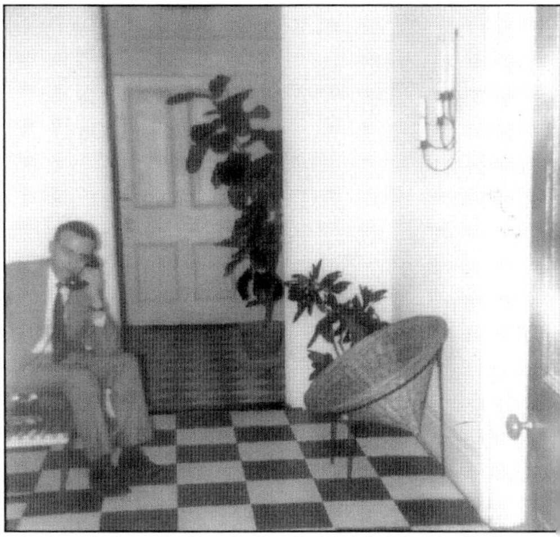

On the left, Sallie Millsap stands in the kitchen in the Opp Cottage at 33 West Jeff Davis Avenue Her mother's note on the back of the photograph reads, "Sallie in her kitchen." On the righ is Sallie and Gene Millsap's newly renovated hall in the Opp Cottage in 1955. (Both courtesy Sallie Millsap.)

Four

Highland Park

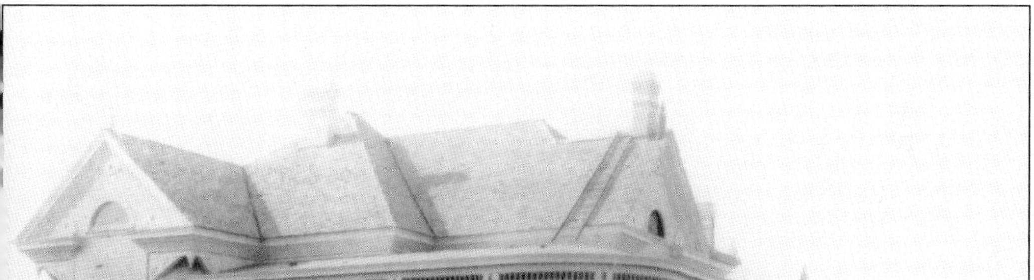

'orbes Liddell constructed this impressive home on Highland Avenue around 1900. He was a uccessful wholesale electrical and mill supply dealer downtown. The structure was later moved round the corner and relocated on Forest Avenue. This photograph is part of the 1907 photograph eries of impressive homes in Montgomery. (Courtesy Art Work Collection.)

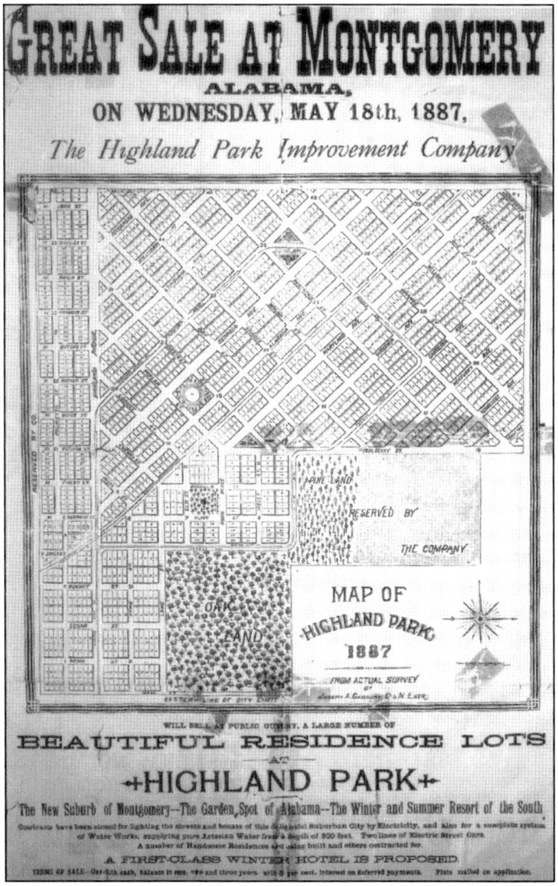

An 1887 advertisement shows an early map of Highland Park. Highland Park was a stop for both the Montgomery trolley and the Central of Georgia Railroad. Joseph A. Gaboury surveyed and laid the streets in the diagonal manner parallel to the railroad. By the time homes were being built, J. A. Garrett had resurveyed the areas and straightened the streets. (Courtesy Landmarks Foundation of Montgomery.)

In 1937, paper routes were popular ways for young boys to make money. Here a group of enterprising young men meet at the *Alabama Journal* (the evening paper) substation No. 2 at the corner of Highland Avenue and South Capitol Parkway to pick up their newspapers so they can make their daily deliveries. (Courtesy Ruth Ott.)

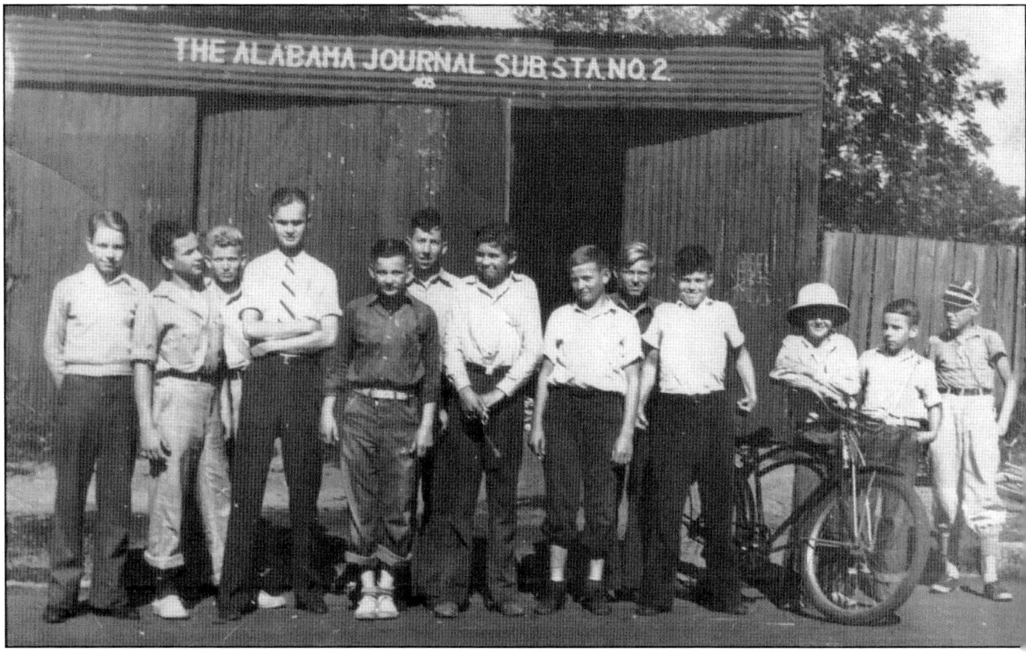

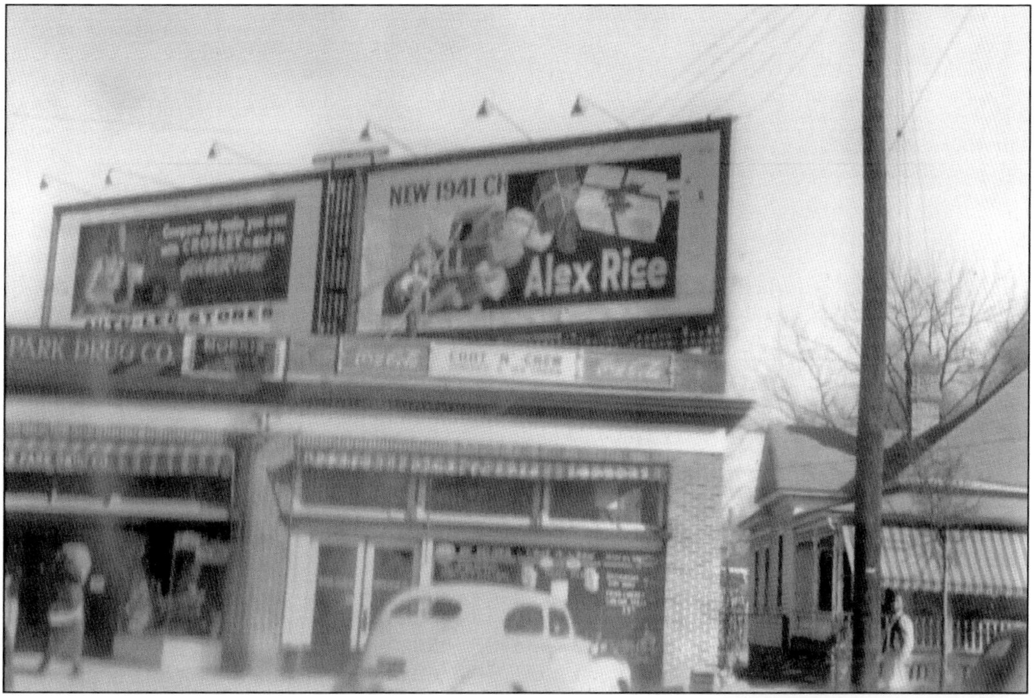

Popular business establishments such as the Chat and Chew Café were right around the corner from Highland Avenue on Forest Avenue in 1941. (Courtesy Frazier family collection.)

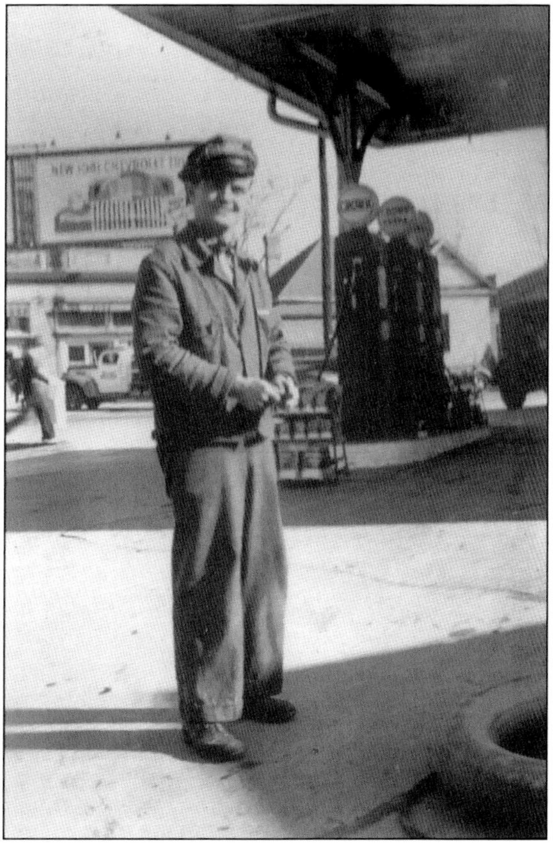

A smiling attendant stands in front of the Crown Gasoline Station in 1941. (Courtesy Frazier family collection.)

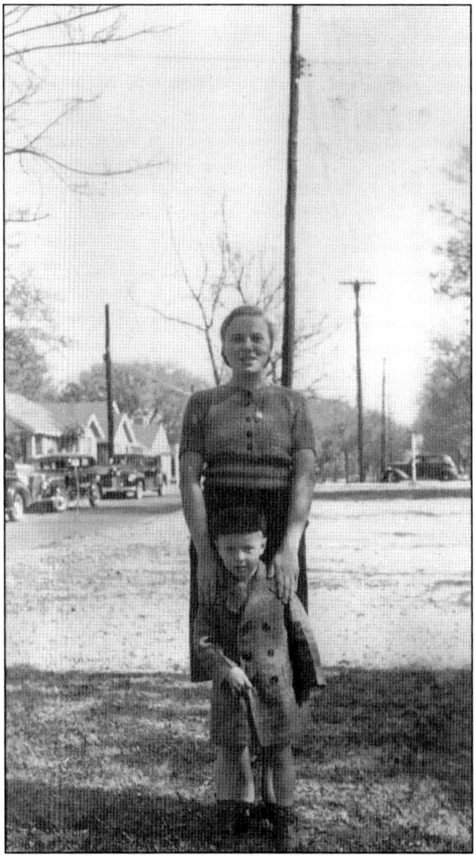

Two members of the Frazier family pose for a photograph on Highland Avenue. (Courtesy Frazier family collection.)

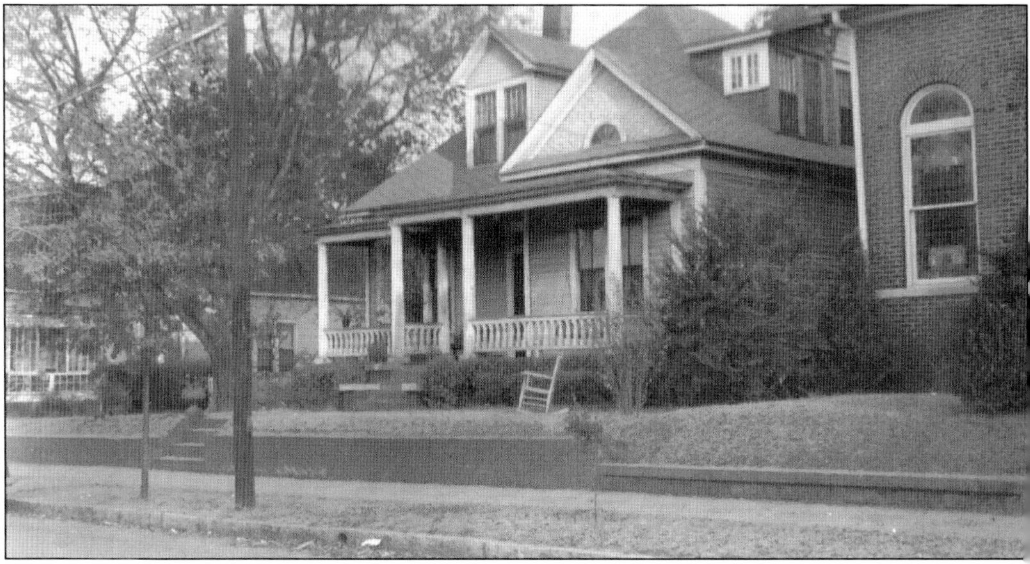

The Frazier family home stood at 907 Highland Avenue beside the Highland Avenue Baptist Church. The home was built early in Highland Park's history by Lafayette and Della Reese Nelson Rollins. Lafayette Rollins owned a lumber mill, and family history relates that he used the very best lumber to build his family's home. (Courtesy Frazier family collection.)

George Edgar Frazier stands beside Annie Bell, who rocks comfortably in the side yard of 907 Highland Avenue around 1916. Note Highland Avenue Baptist Church in the background. (Courtesy Frazier family collection.)

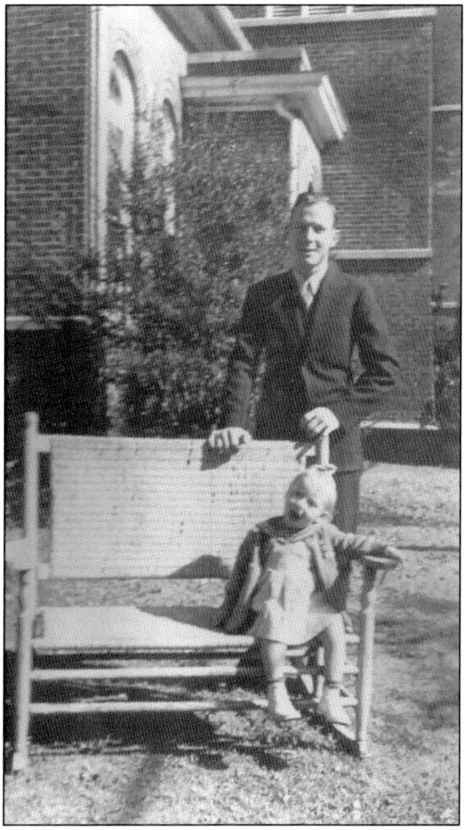

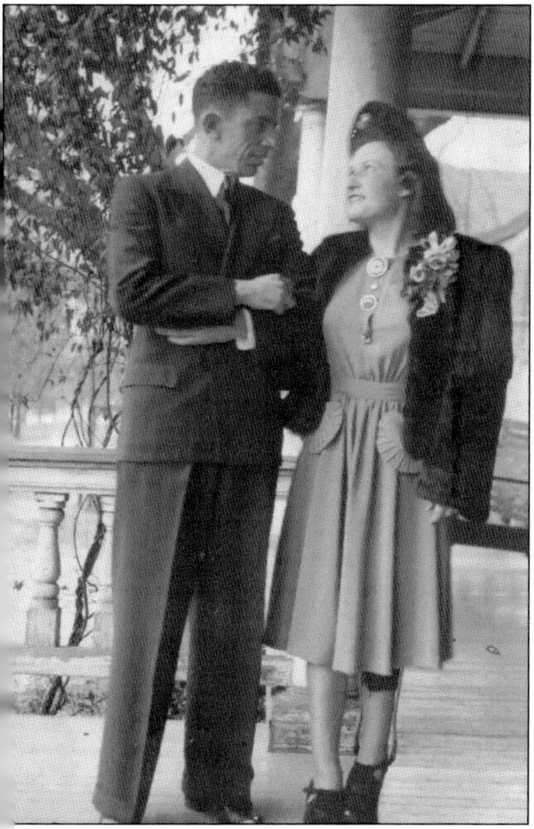

On their wedding day in the late 1930s, Louise Nelson Frazier and Aubrey R. Rogers pose on the porch at 907 Highland Avenue. Louise Frazier had polio as a child and suffered permanent damage to her leg. However, her family through the years remembers her bravery and her success in enjoying an active life. (Courtesy Frazier family collection.)

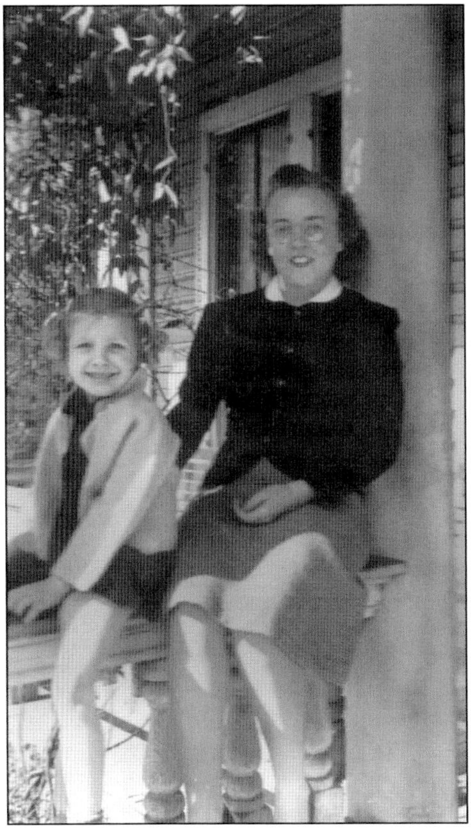

An unidentified child (left) and Ethel Mae Rollins Jernigan lean against the porch pillar at 907 Highland Avenue around the 1920s. (Courtesy Frazier family collection.)

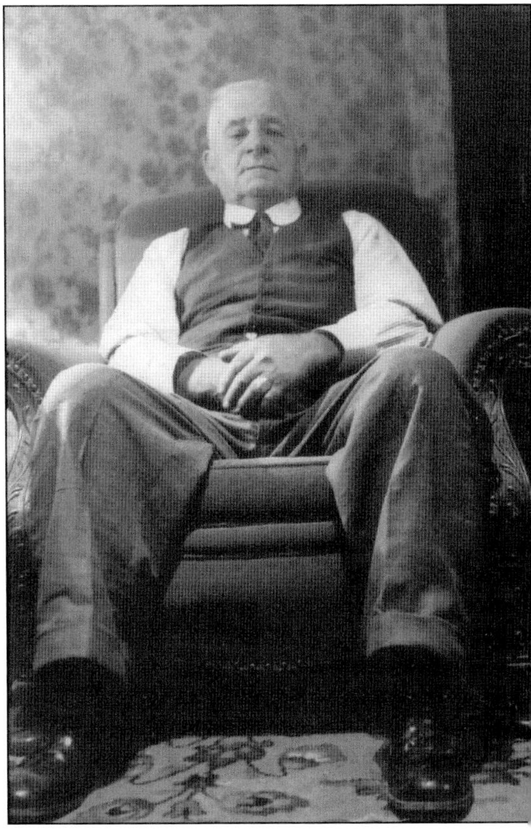

A Frazier family member rests in the living room in 907 Highland Avenue. (Courtesy Frazier family collection.)

Margaret Meriwether gets ready to go inside on a summer's day on South Capitol Parkway in 1946. (Courtesy Alica Tompkins Varner.)

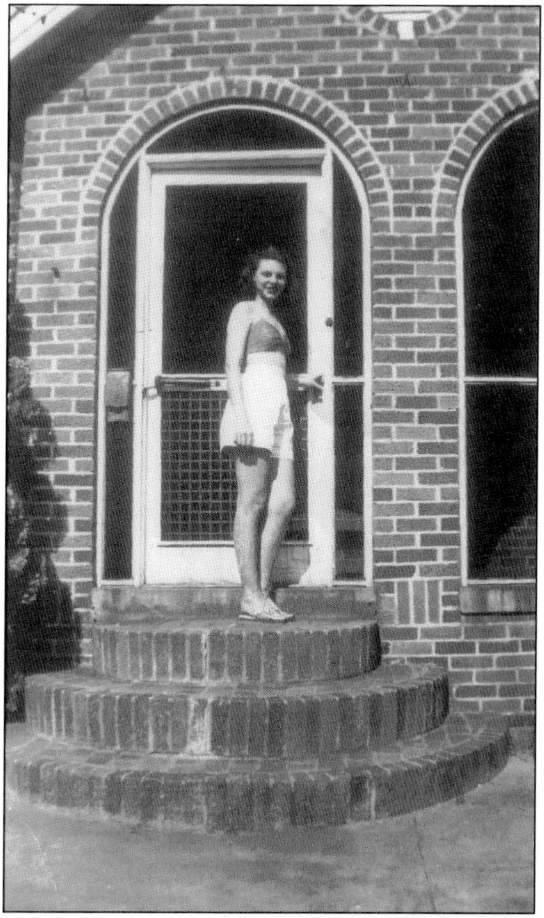

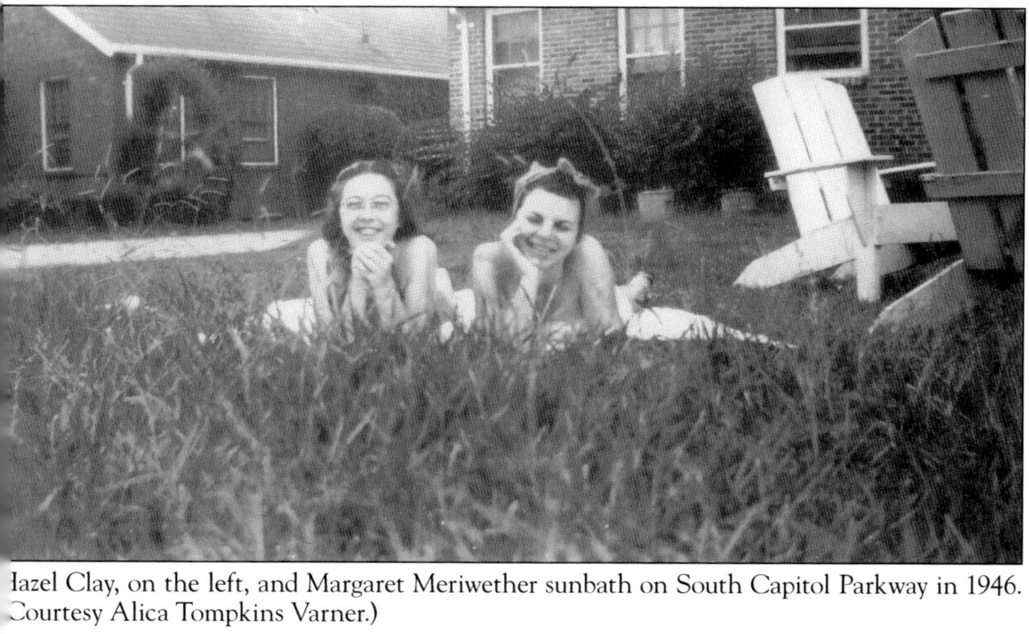

Hazel Clay, on the left, and Margaret Meriwether sunbath on South Capitol Parkway in 1946. (Courtesy Alica Tompkins Varner.)

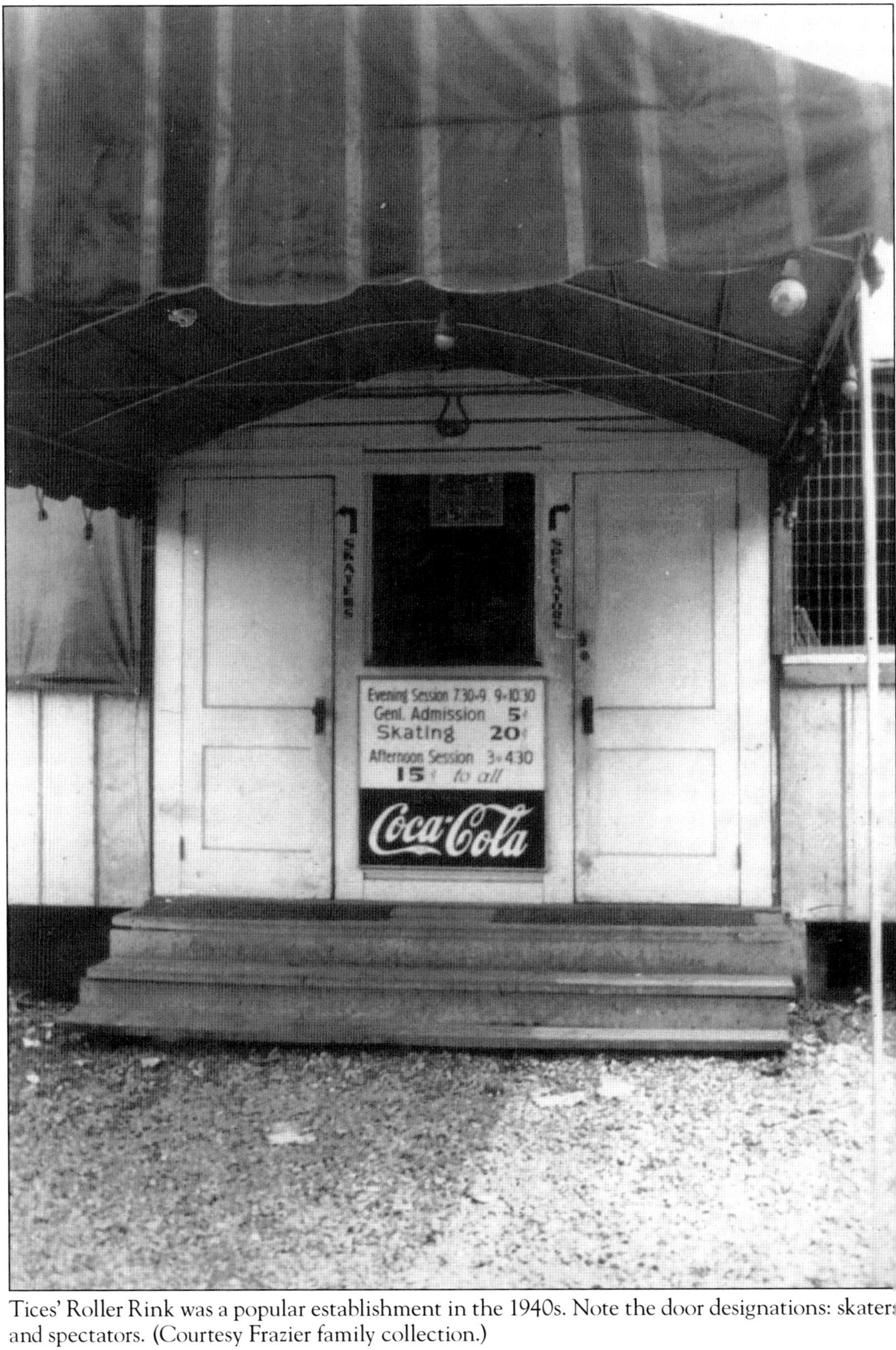

Tices' Roller Rink was a popular establishment in the 1940s. Note the door designations: skaters and spectators. (Courtesy Frazier family collection.)

Five

Centennial Hill

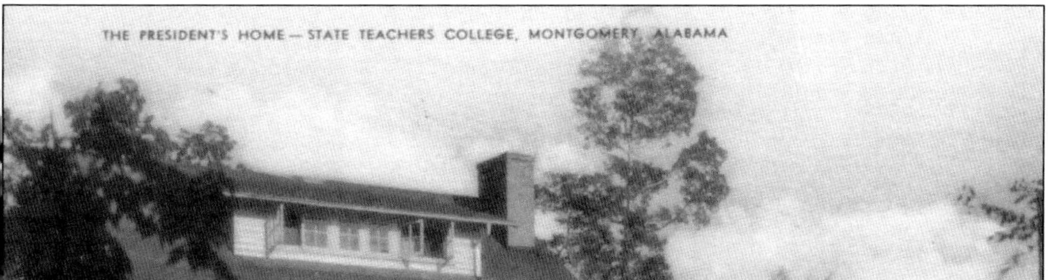

Centennial Hill was named for the nation's celebration in 1876. The area developed when, after the Civil War, African Americans built homes, churches, and schools close to downtown. Many of the residents of Centennial Hill were active in the civil rights movement. Alabama State University, a descendant of one of the oldest institutions of higher learning for black Americans, stands adjacent to Centennial Hill. In 1878, William Paterson, the founder of Alabama State University, became president. President for 37 years, Paterson was the driving force in the school's relocation to Montgomery from Marion in 1887. The president's home of Alabama State University stands on the campus. (Courtesy James Bozeman.)

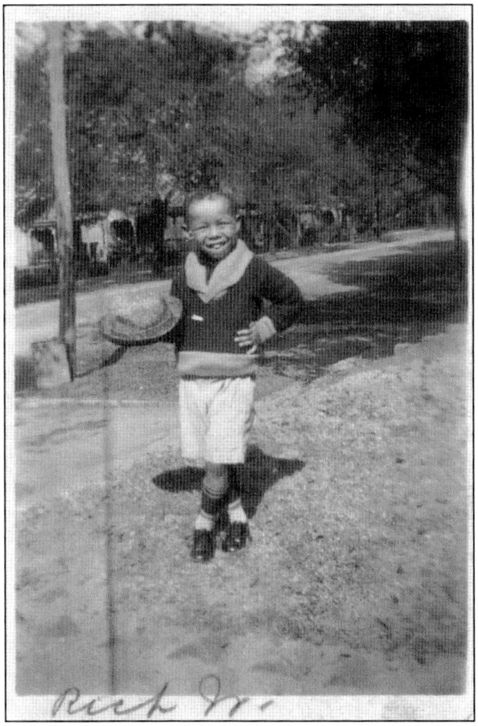

Richard Harris Jr. stops along South Jackson Street to pose for this photograph on his way to Sunday school on October 29, 1923. (Courtesy Dr. Richard Harris Jr. family.)

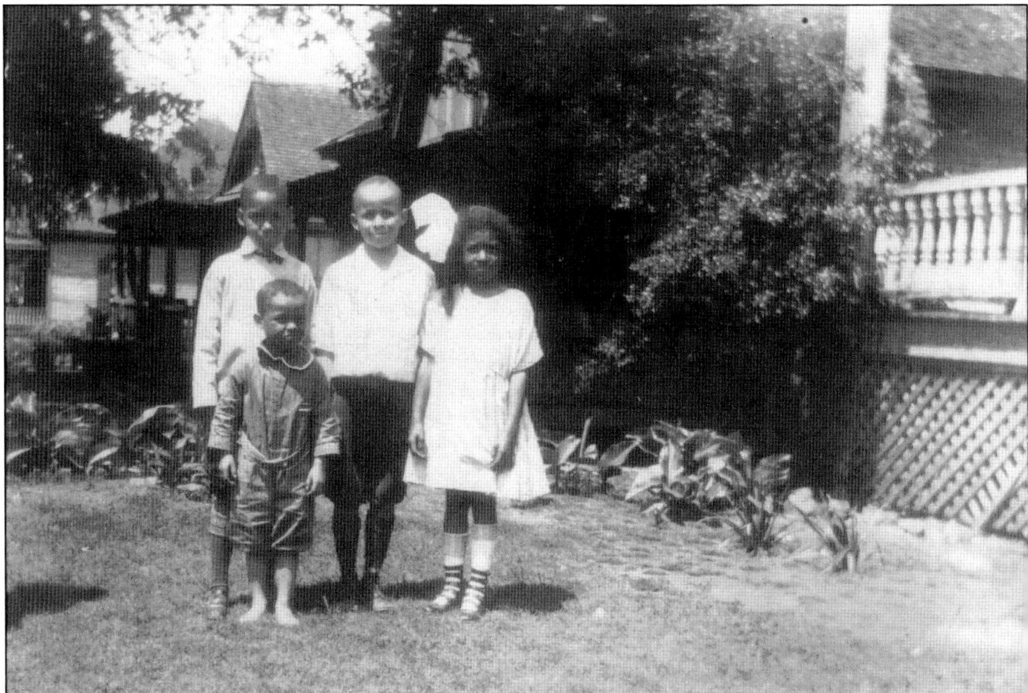

Gathered for a photograph in front of 326 South Jackson Street in 1928, from left to right, are (first row) Richard Harris Jr.; (second row) unidentified, William Washington, and unidentified (Courtesy Richard Harris Jr. family.)

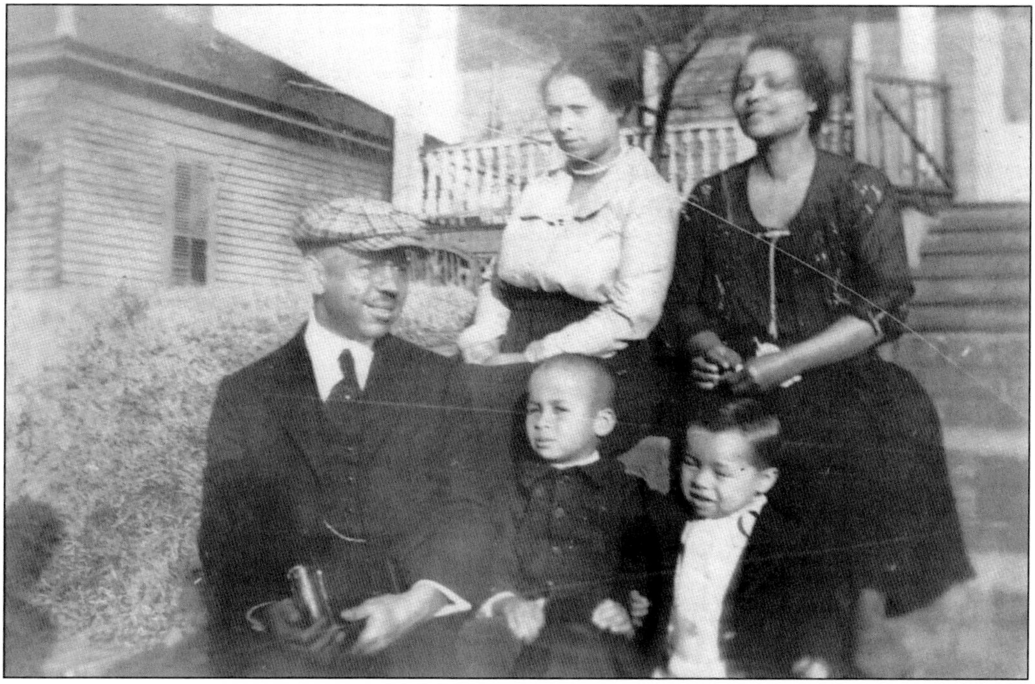

Family members gathered for a photograph in 1920 at 326 South Jackson Street are, from left to right, (first row) Dr. William Washington, Richard Harris Jr., and William Washington; (second row) Evelyn Jones Harris and Ruby Jones Washington. (Courtesy Richard Harris Jr. family.)

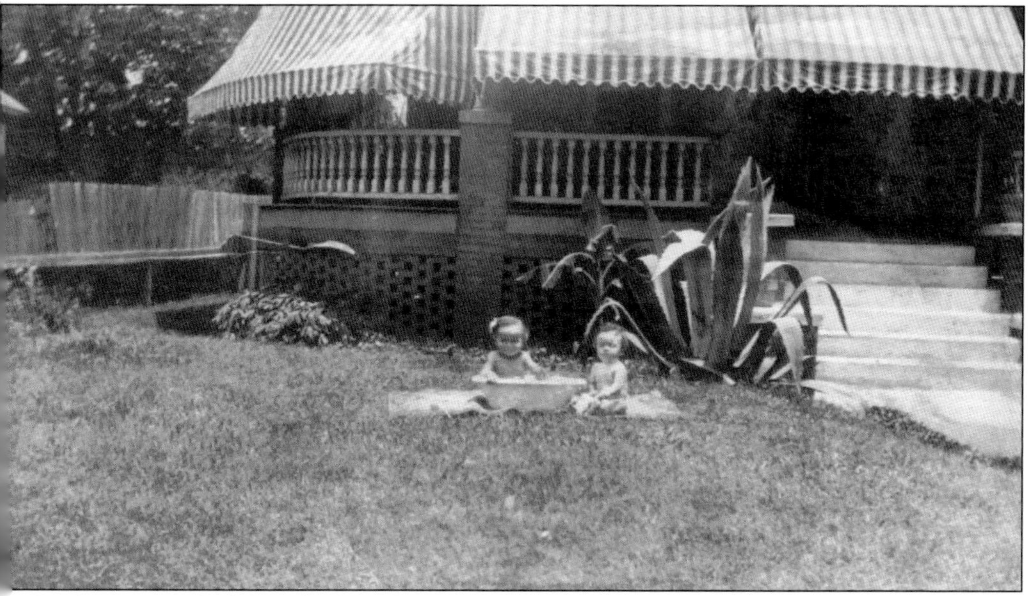

ichard Harris Jr. (right) and a friend play in a tub of water at 327 South Jackson Street in 1918. Courtesy Richard Harris Jr. family.)

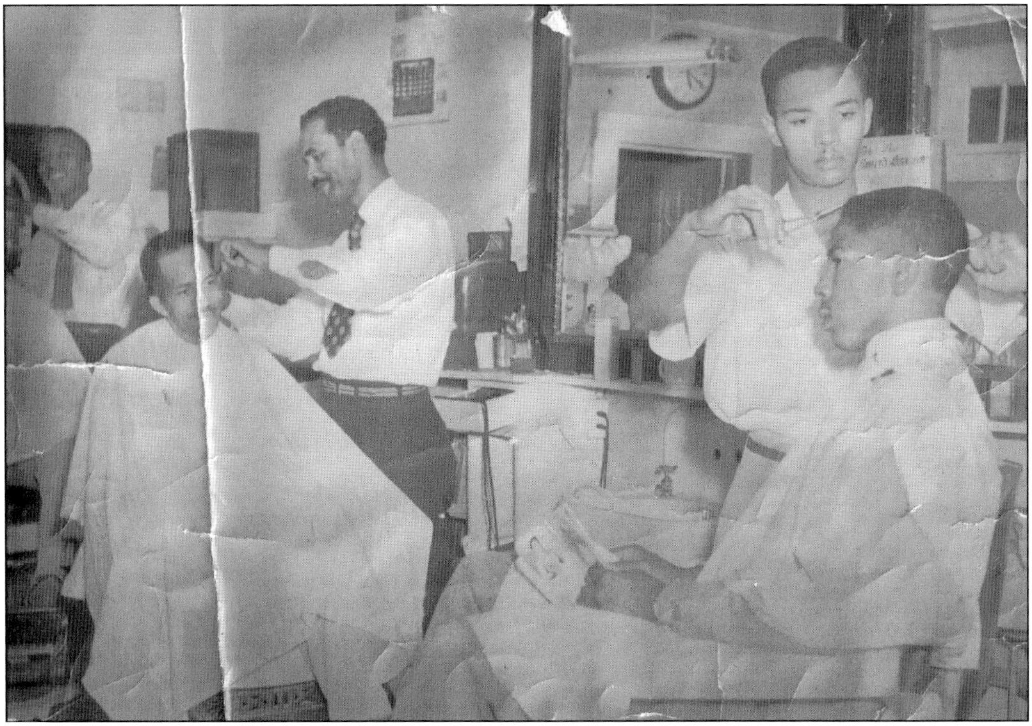

Nelson Malden is in the foreground giving a haircut in this busy scene in the Malden Brothers Barbershop shortly after it opened. The popular establishment has operated since 1958 at 407 South Jackson Street. (Courtesy Nelson Malden.)

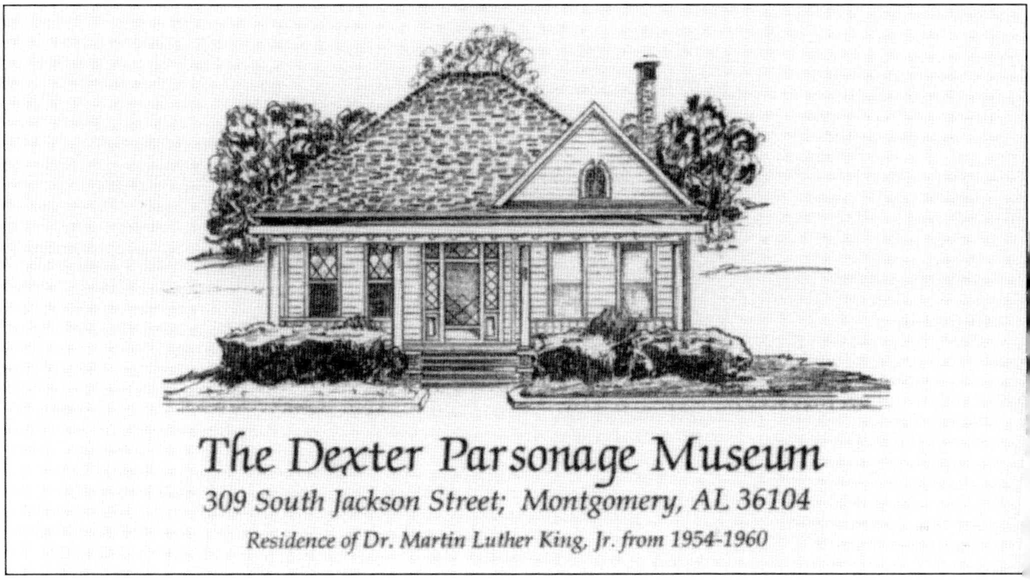

Dr. Martin Luther King lived in the Dexter Avenue Baptist Church parsonage from September 1954 to February 1960. King was a leader in the 1955–1956 Montgomery bus boycott. On January 30, 1956, the parsonage was bombed; no one was hurt. The bombing focused national attention on the bus boycott and Dr. King's non-violent movement. The parsonage is now a museum. (Courtesy John Fagen.)

Six

Garden District

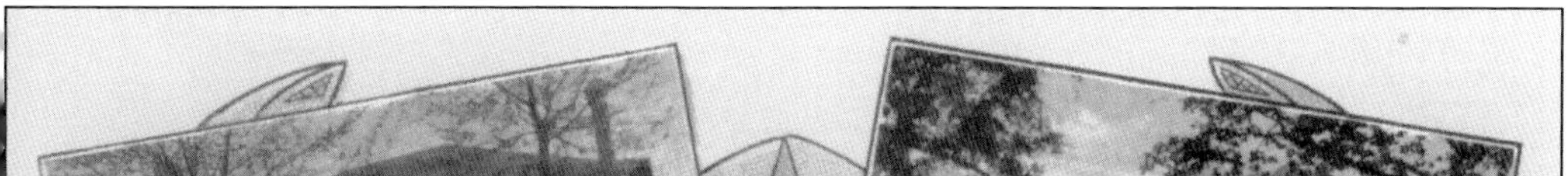

Many fashionable and prestigious homes were built along South Perry Street as the new residential areas outside of the downtown area grew popular. In the early 1900s, Montgomery was proud of the new suburban neighborhoods. Popular postcards featured outstanding houses. The neighborhood's name, Garden District, was not adopted until the area applied for historic designation in the current era. (Courtesy Landmarks Foundation of Montgomery.)

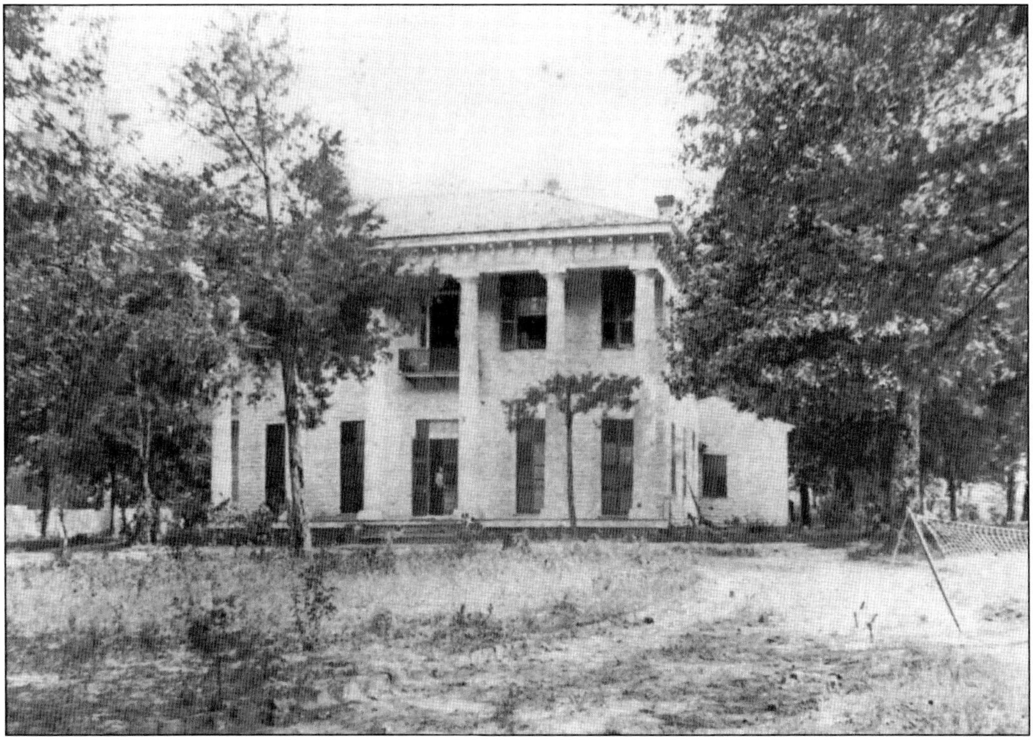

The Clanton-Elsberry-Thorington House was built around 1850 on what is now the corner of Hull Street and Felder Avenue. The house became the home of the Elsberry and Thorington families for many years. The home burned in 1910, but the columns, the iron balcony, and the stairway were used in a new house that stands at 1846 South Hull Street. (Courtesy Edward Pattillo.)

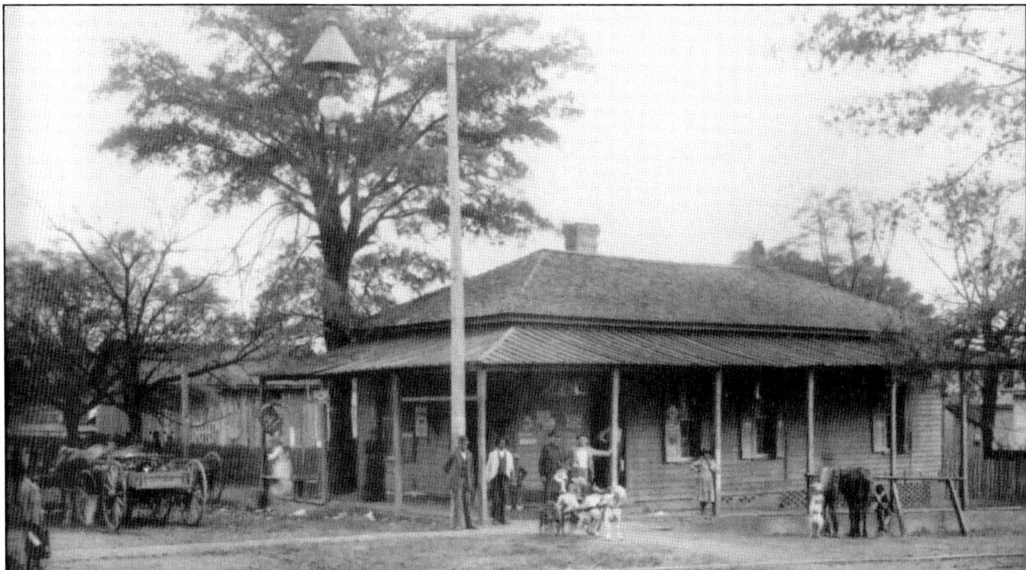

The Corner Grocery stood on the corner of South Hull Street and Julia Street in 1890. Note trolle tracks in the foreground. This photograph was part of the 1894 collection of gravure photograph taken of notable Montgomery buildings. (Courtesy Art Work Collection.)

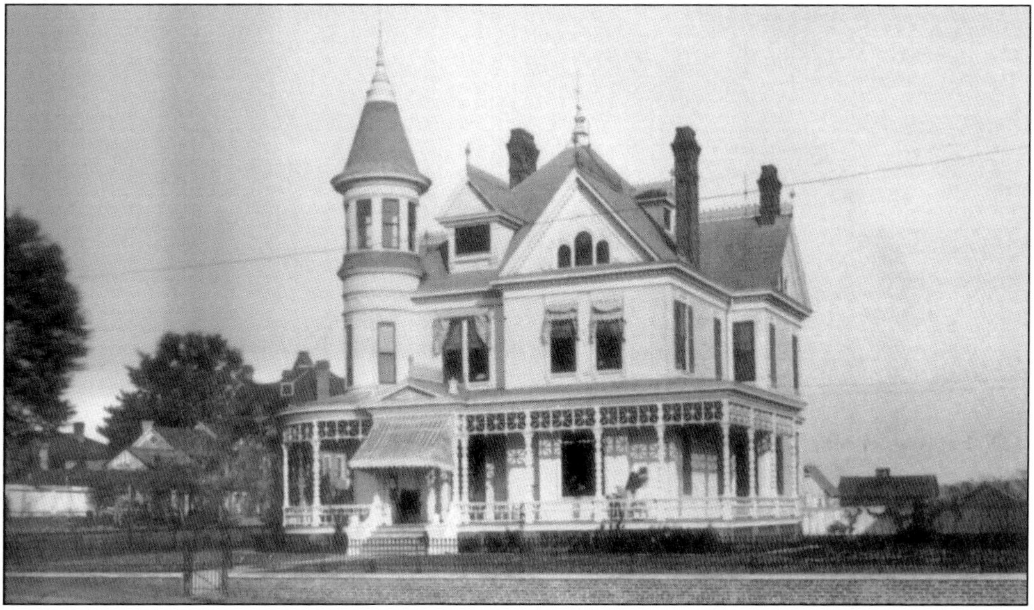

Arthur Pelzer lived at 723 South Perry Street. He was president of Alabama Machinery and Supply Company, which is still operating today. This gravure photograph of his home was part of the 1894 collection taken of outstanding homes in Montgomery. (Courtesy Art Work Collection.)

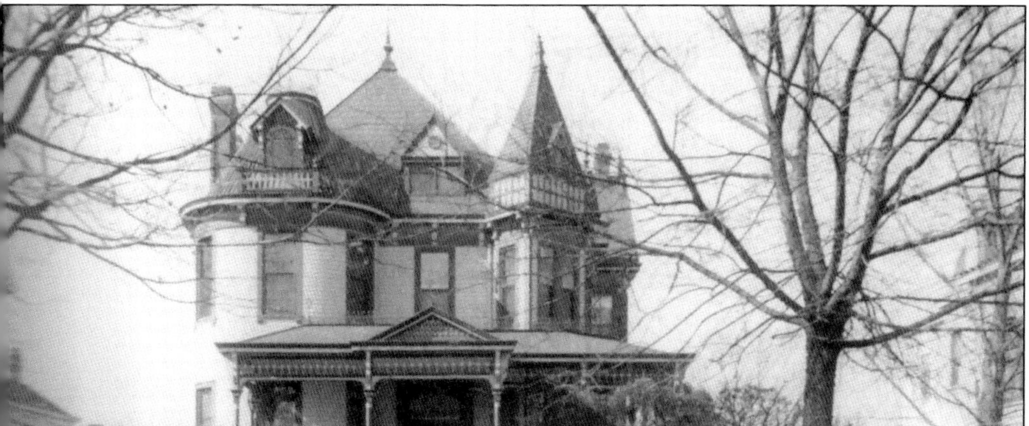

William K. and Elizabeth Pelzer lived at 714 South Perry Street. William Pelzer was the treasurer for Alabama Machinery and Supply Company, which is still operating today. This gravure photograph of their home was part of the 1907 collection taken of outstanding homes in Montgomery. (Courtesy Art Work Collection.)

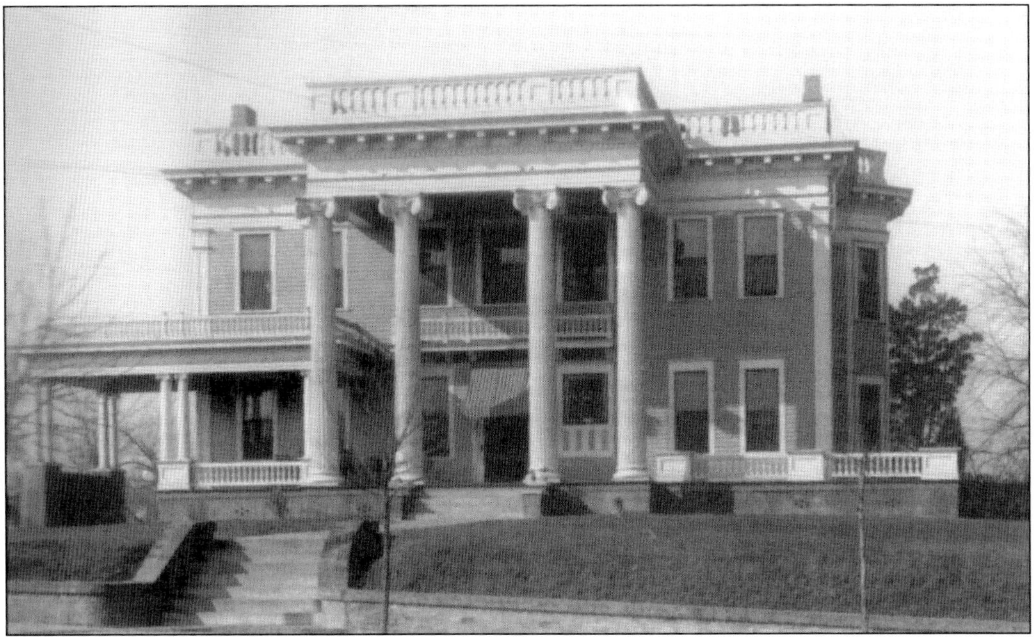

Dr. Charles A. and Daisy C. Thigpen's residence at 1200 South Perry Street was included in the 1907 Art Work Collection of gravure photographs taken of outstanding homes in Montgomery. Dr. Thigpen saw patients in his downtown office at 13 South Perry. (Courtesy Art Work Collection.)

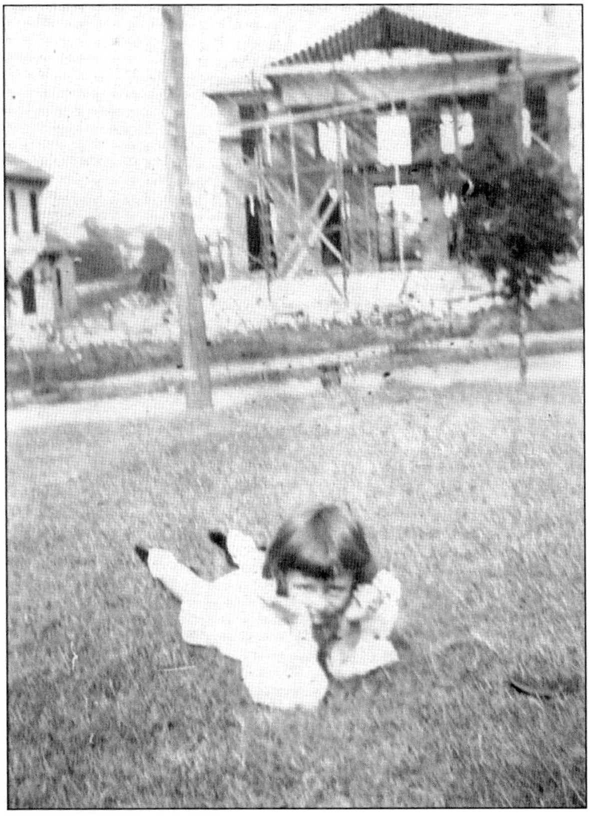

An unidentified child lounges on the lawn of Dr. Charles A. Thigpen on South Perry at Clanton Street. Note that in the background, the Thigpen House is undergoing construction. (Courtesy MCHS.)

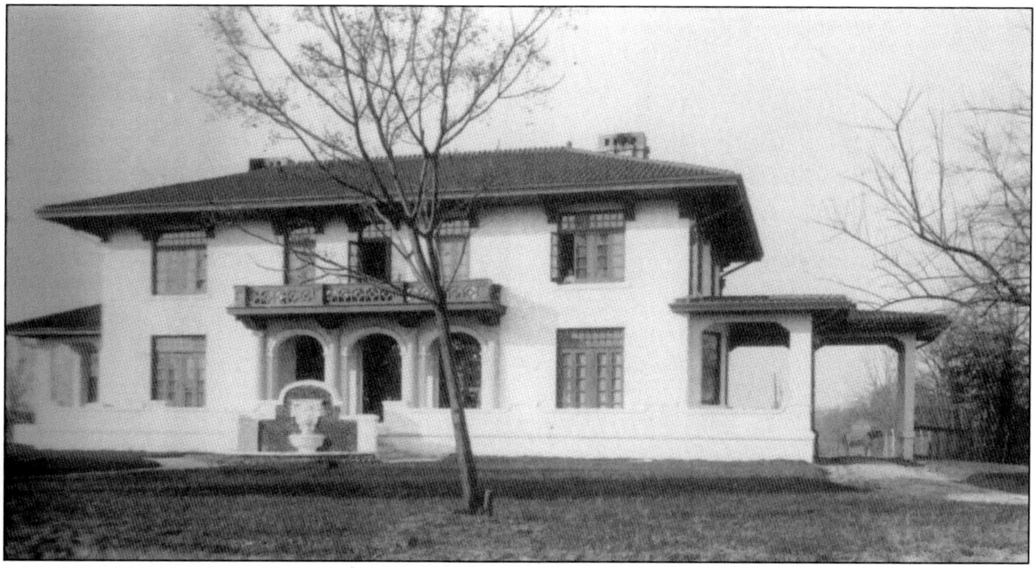

John C. and Emma T. Virden's residence at 326 Felder Avenue was included in the 1907 series of gravure photographs. John Virden worked at Verder and Company. (Courtesy Art Work Collection.)

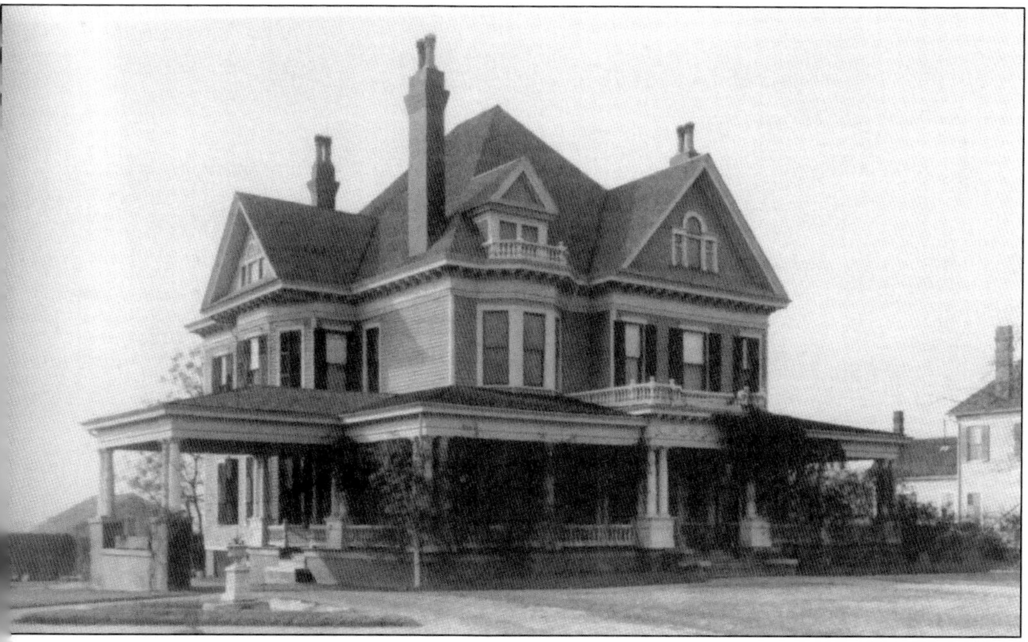

Villiam A. and Mary W. Gayle's residence at 408 Felder Avenue was included in the 1907 series f gravure photographs as well. William Gayle worked for Marks and Gayle Company. (Courtesy art Work Collection.)

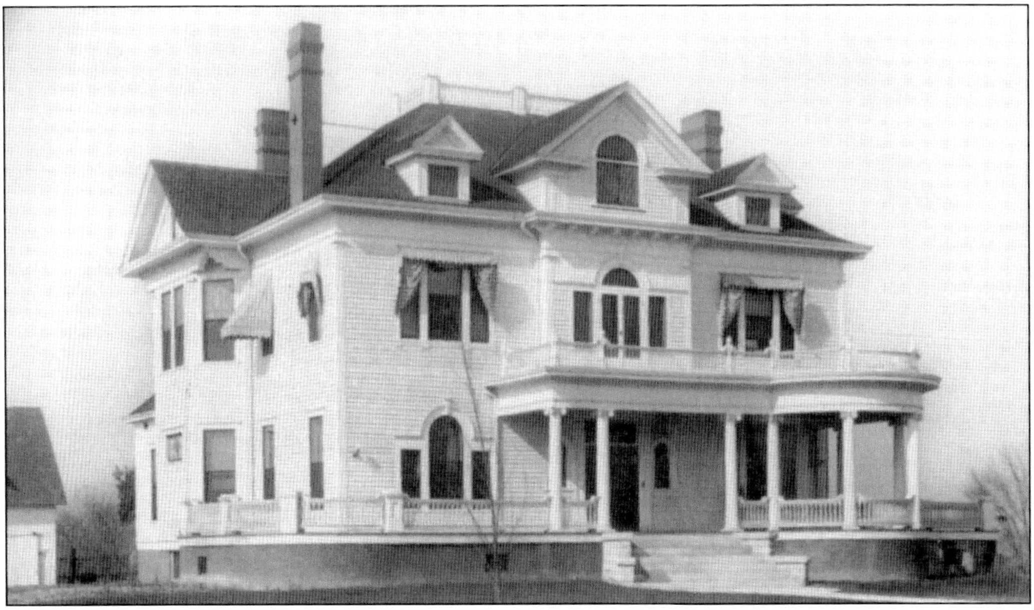

Fred S. Ball and his wife, Florence C., lived at 1504 South Perry Street. Ball was an attorney. This gravure photograph of their home was part of the 1907 series. (Courtesy Art Work Collection.)

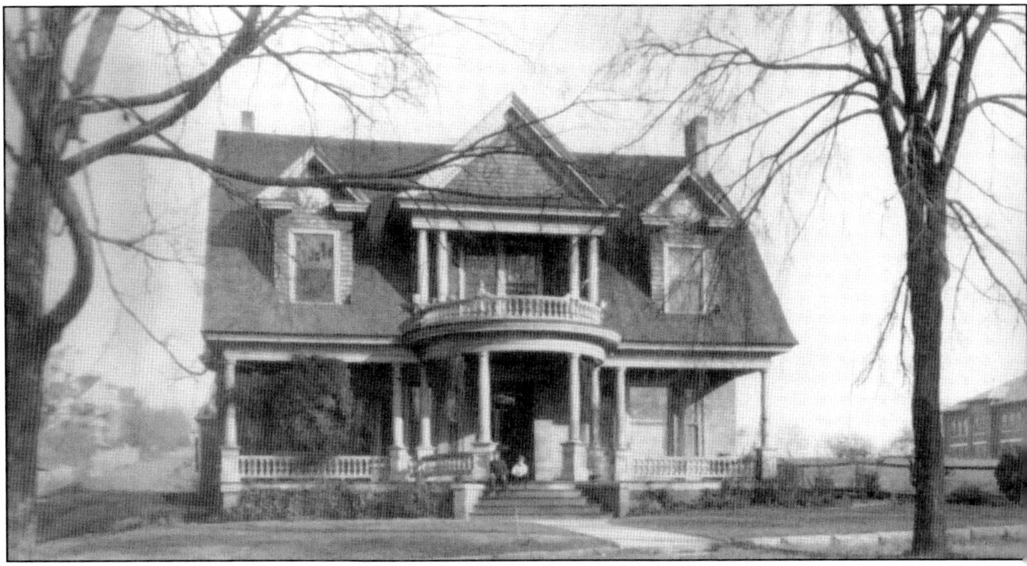

Benjamin B. Smith lived at 1019 South Perry Street, across from the Ligon home. Smith, a popula architect, worked with architect T. Weatherly Carter. This gravure photograph of their hom was part of the 1907 series of photographs of outstanding Montgomery buildings. (Courtesy Ar Work Collection.)

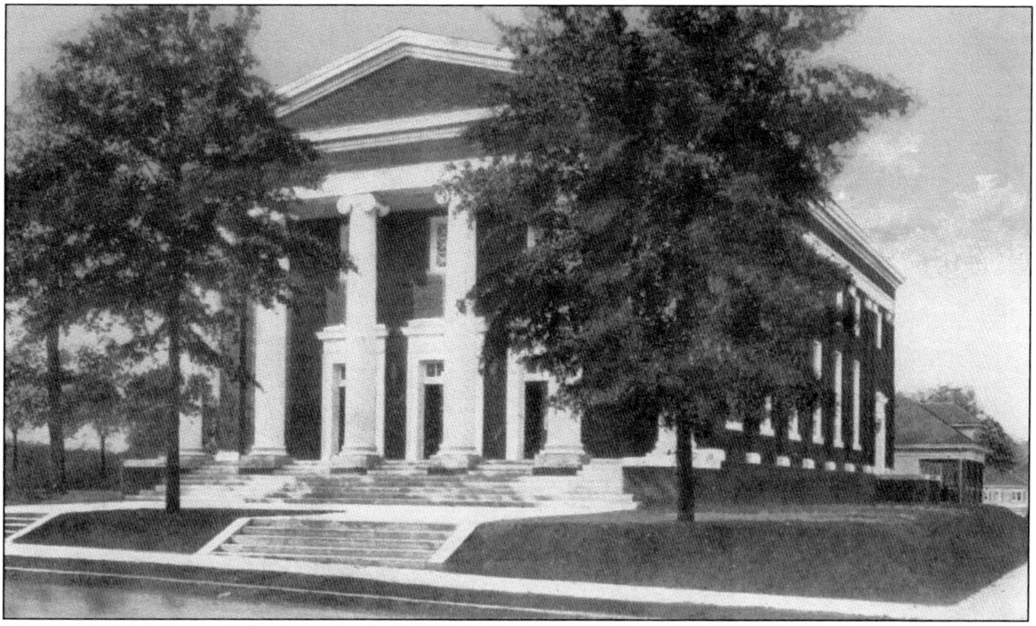

Trinity Presbyterian Church, at the corner of Hull Street and Felder Avenue, was finished in 1913. Much of the original structure burned in 1951, but the church was rebuilt and stands at 1728 South Hull Street. (Courtesy James Bozeman.)

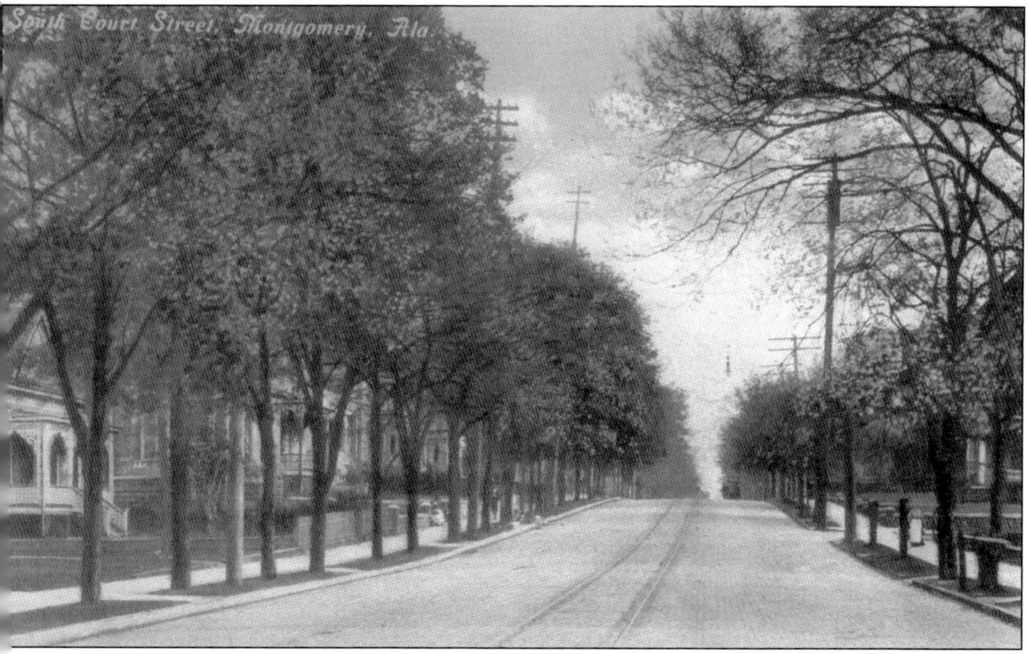

As the trolley tracks expanded from downtown southward, residential areas blossomed. In this vintage postcard, the trolley tracks are visible. (Courtesy David Smith.)

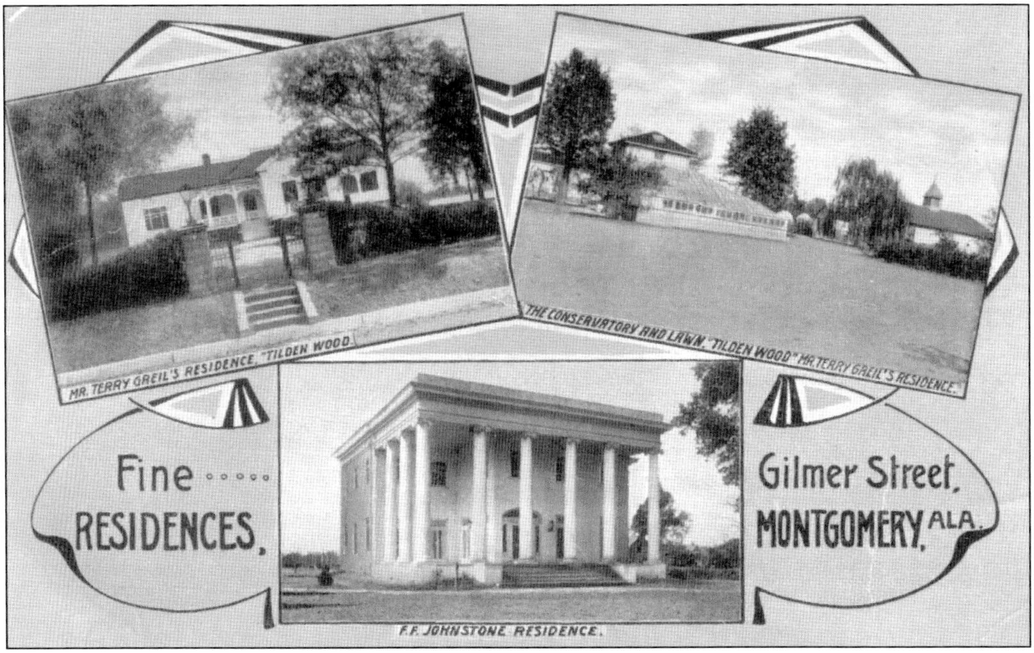

Gilmer Avenue is named for the Gilmer family, who settled in the area before the Civil War. As the new residential areas beyond the city grew, new streets were formed, paved, and named after old families. (Courtesy James Bozeman.)

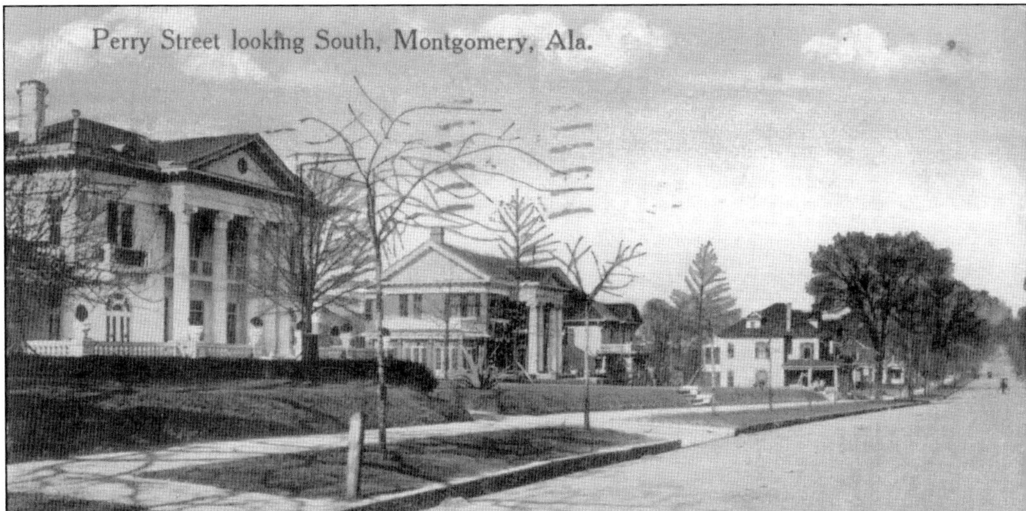

This postcard show a view of Perry Street featuring the Ligon mansion, which now serves as the Alabama Governor's Mansion, and next to it the Hill House. (Courtesy James Bozeman.)

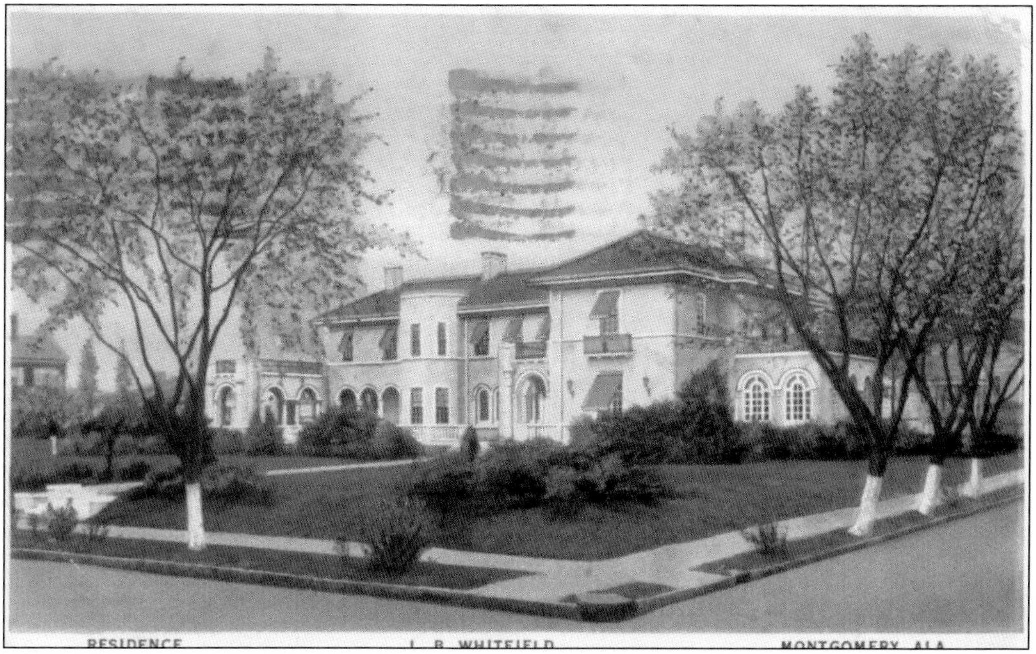

The Whitfield-McGregor Mansion was built between 1918 and 1920 by the L. B. Whitfield family. The home is affectionately known as the Pickle Palace, because Whitfield made a fortune manufacturing the "pickle with the perfect pucker." Frank Lockwood, one of Alabama's leading architects, designed the home. Milton and Pat McGregor bought and renovated the home in the 1980s. (Courtesy David Smith.)

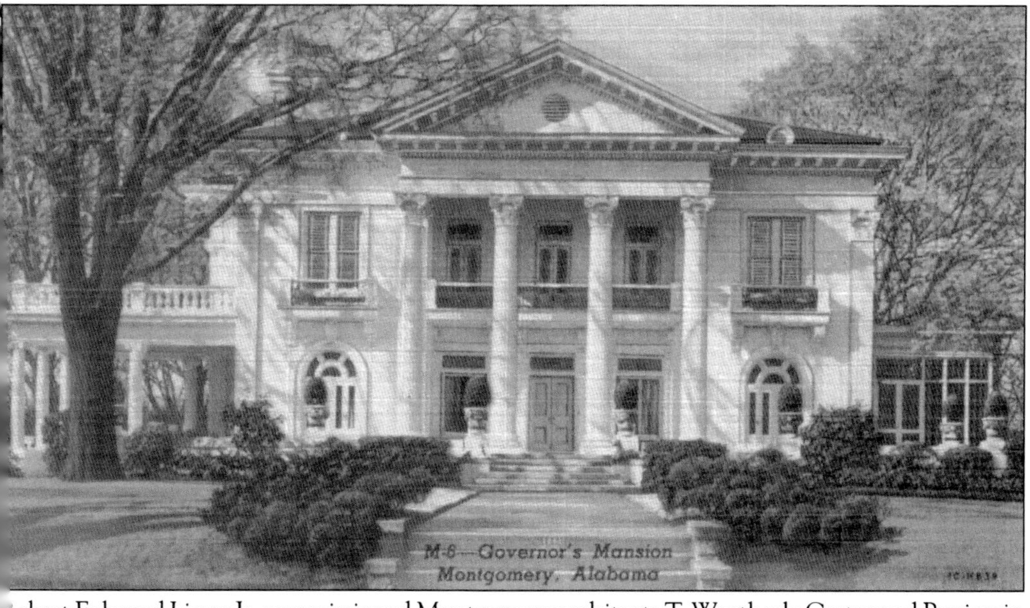

Robert Fulwood Ligon Jr. commissioned Montgomery architects T. Weatherly Carter and Benjamin Smith to build his family's home at 1142 South Perry Street in 1907. The Ligon family resided there until 1951, when Emily Ligon Foley sold it to the State of Alabama (following her mother's wishes) for the governor's mansion. Gov. Gordon Persons was the first governor to live in it. (Courtesy James Bozeman.)

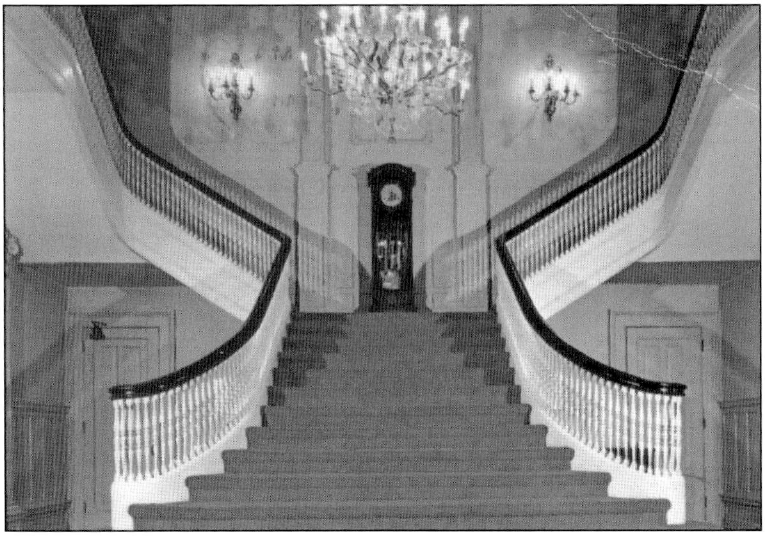

The formal staircase in the entry hall of the Ligon Mansion remains an elegant feature of the home. The Emily Ligon wedding party (next photograph) posed for photographs on these stairs. (Courtesy James Bozeman.)

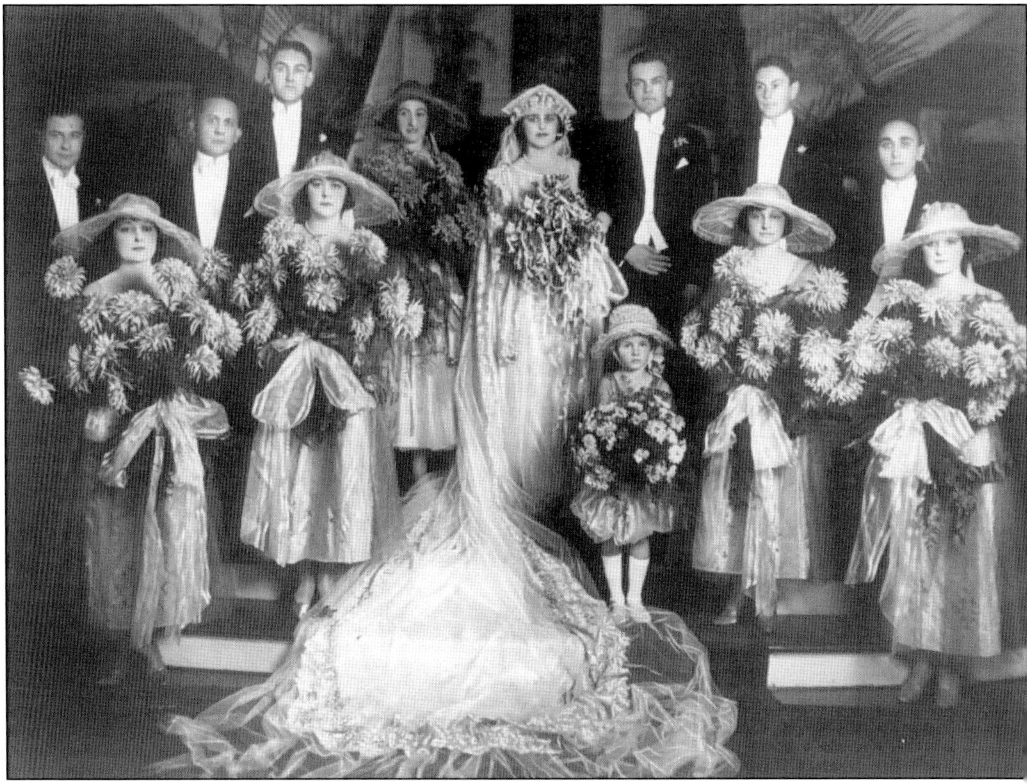

Emily Castleton Ligon and George Temple Bowdoin's wedding party poses on the staircase o Emily's family home at South Perry Street on September 19, 1919. Groomsmen are, from left tc right, Junius Morgan, two unidentified, George Temple Bowdoin (the groom), Irving Kingsford and unidentified. Bridesmaids are, from left to right, unidentified, Jette-Aileen Bandy, unidentified Emily Castleton Ligon (the bride), flower girl Marion Oates, Majory Allen, and unidentified (Courtesy MCHS.)

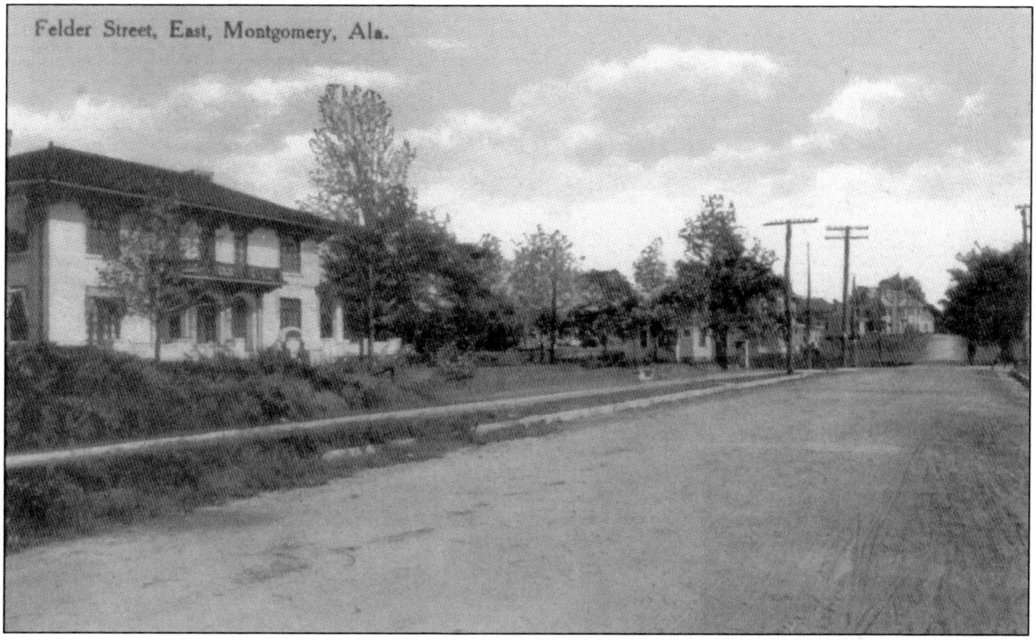

Felder Avenue, named for an early landowner in the area, runs in both Cloverdale and the Garden District. (Courtesy James Bozeman.)

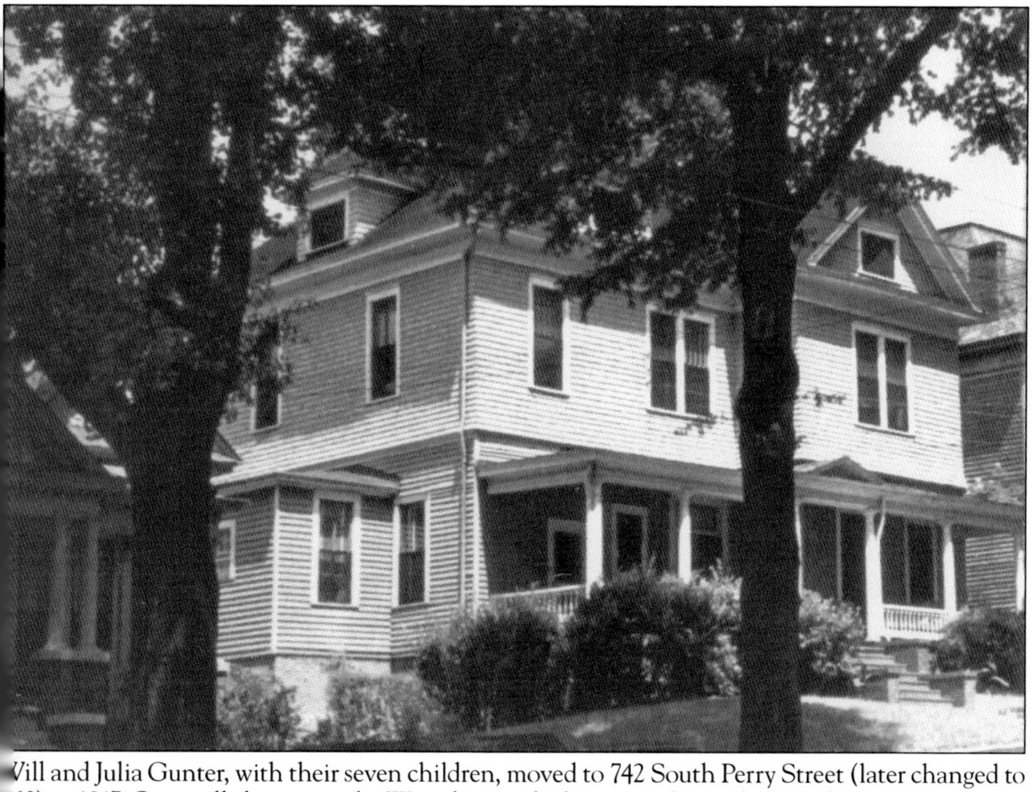

Vill and Julia Gunter, with their seven children, moved to 742 South Perry Street (later changed to 60) in 1917. Originally known as the Watts house, the home was located across the street from Perry ark. The house remained in the Gunter family for many years. (Courtesy Fairlie Haynes.)

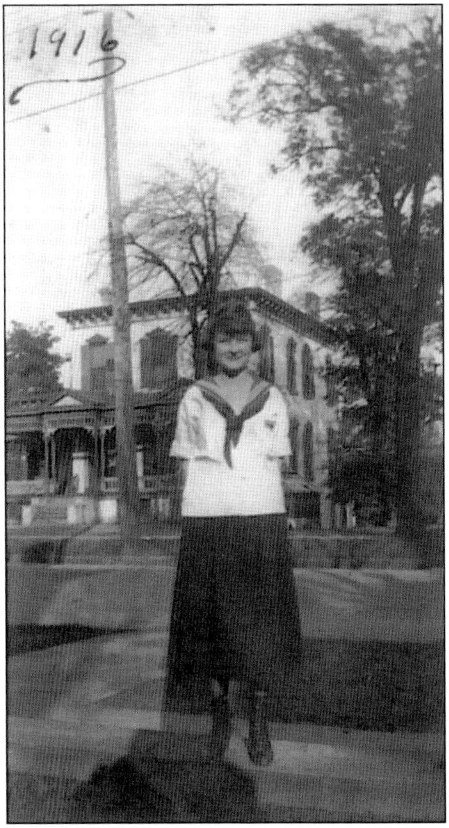

In 1916, Grace Gunter stands at the top of the Perry Street hill. In the background is Myrtle Johnson's house. (Courtesy Fairlie Haynes.)

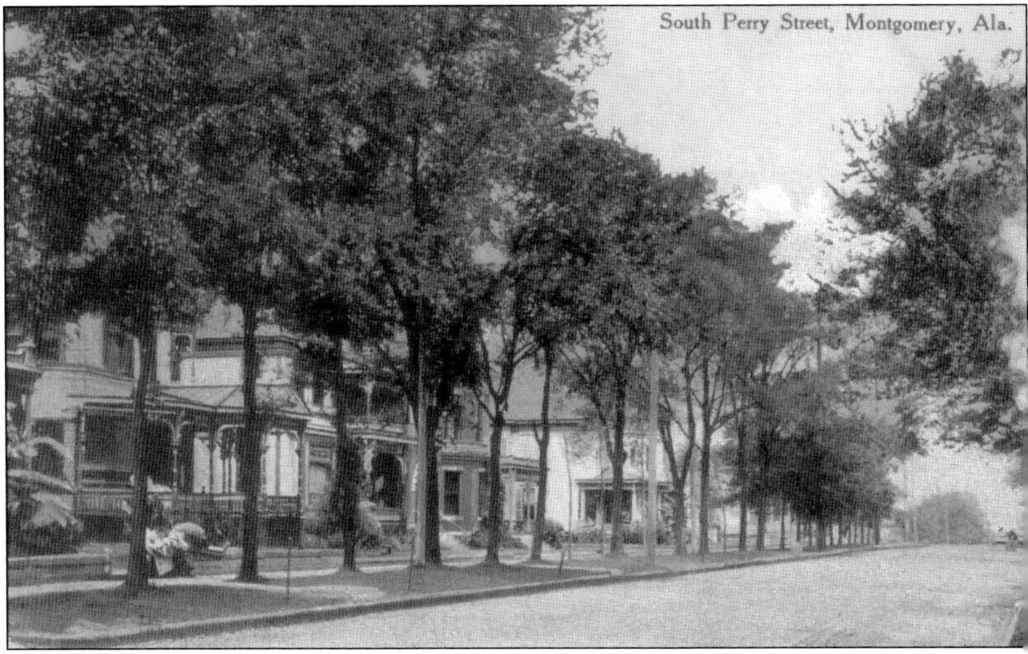

This postcard shows a view of homes on South Perry Street that are all lost to the interstate (Courtesy David Smith.)

In the Ligon family home on South Perry Street (currently the governor's mansion), the family gathers for a portrait. Pictured are, from left to right, George Temple Bowdoin, Aileen Means Ligon, Emily Ligon Bowdoin holding Helen Hamilton Bowdoin, Robert F. Ligon, and (seated on the floor) Aileen Ligon Bowdoin. (Courtesy MCHS.)

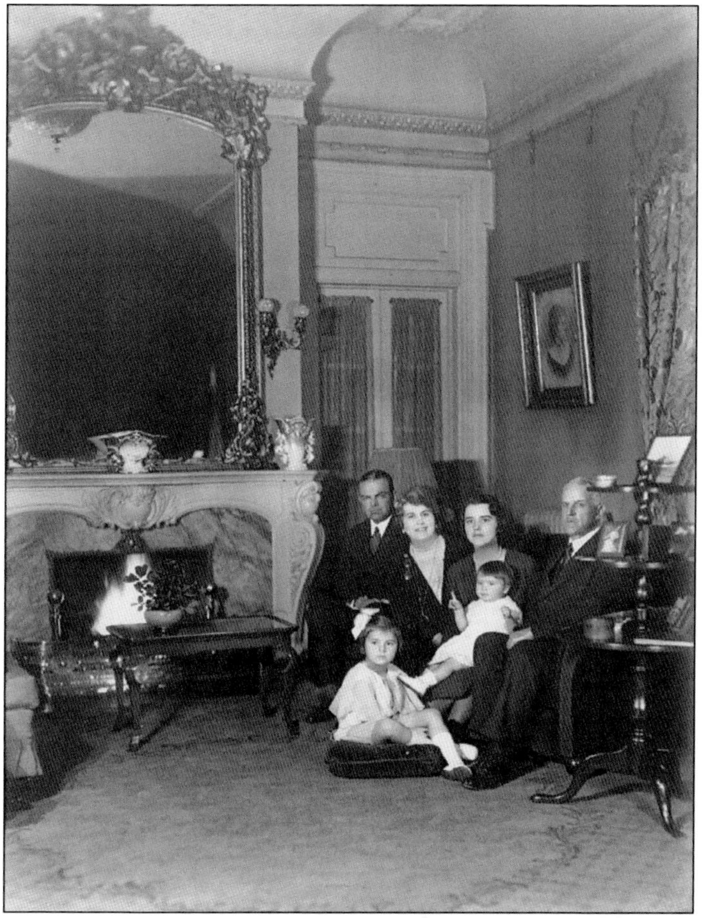

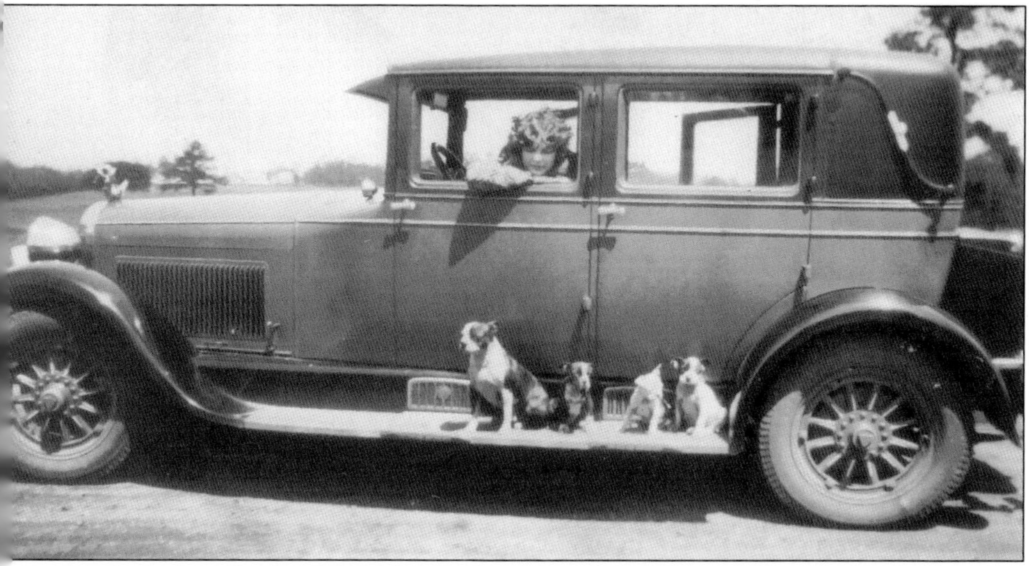

ı 1927, Jule Gunter, the driver here, let the family dogs hitch a ride on the running board of the ›unter family's Hudson. (Courtesy Fairlie Haynes.)

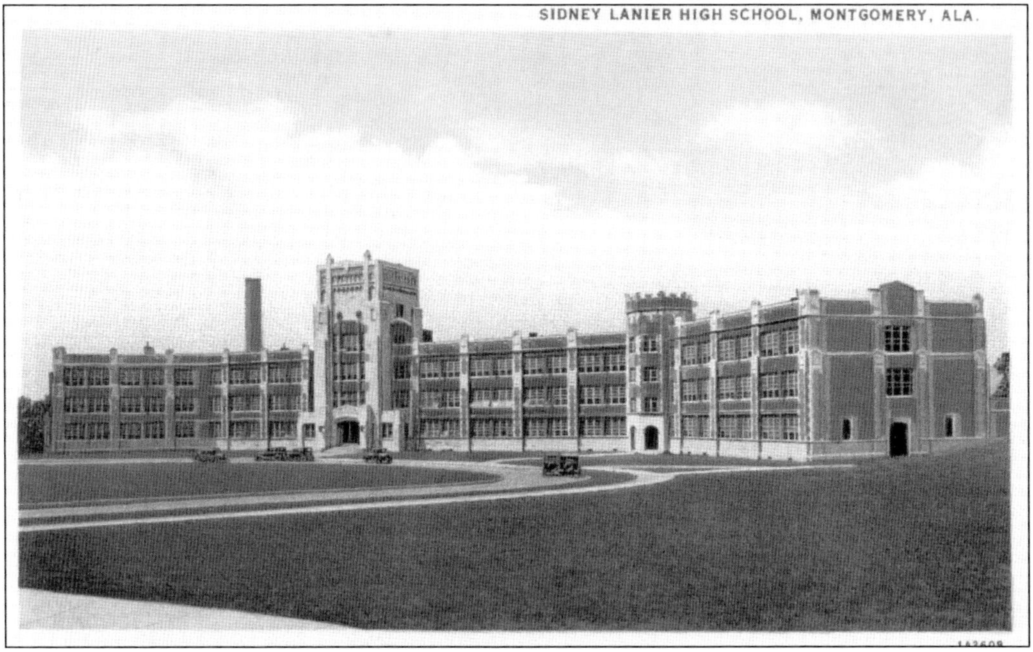

Sidney Lanier High School was named after a Southern poet who lived in Montgomery following the Civil War. The consolidated school, designed by Frederick Ausfeld and built by Algernon Blair, opened in September 1929 and is still open. (Courtesy James Bozeman.)

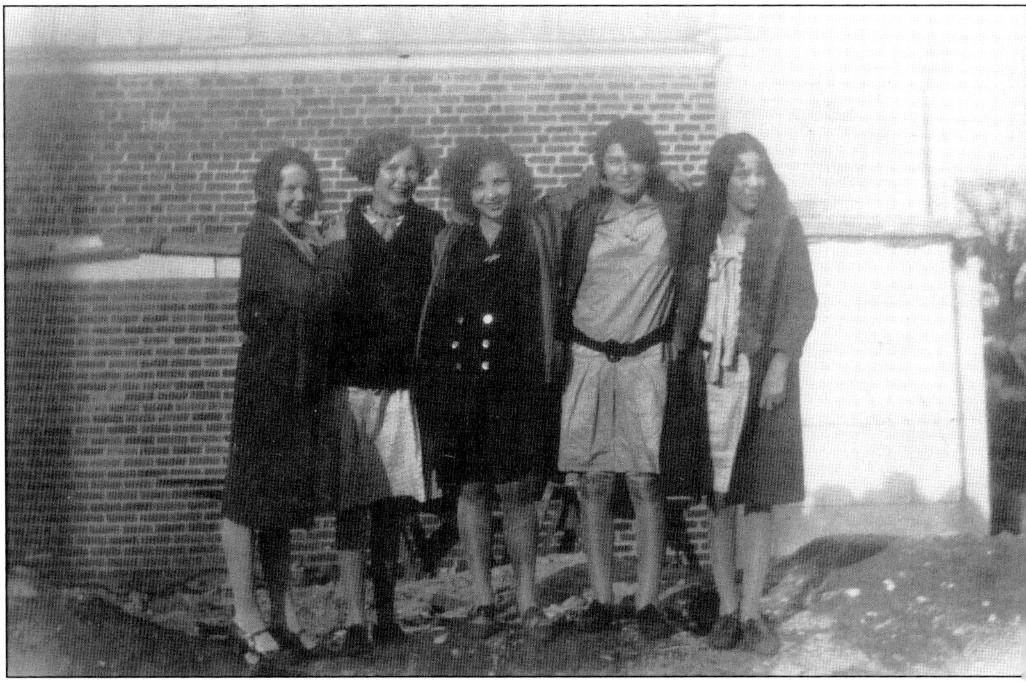

The note on the photograph reads, "Woody, me [Margaret], Jo, Jimmy, and Bill by the new Lanier. Obviously some of the girls go by male nicknames. (Courtesy Mastin family collection.)

Peter Paul Bartholomew Brooke, a popular physics teacher at Lanier High School in 1932, was known to his students as "P^2B^2." (Courtesy Mastin family collection.)

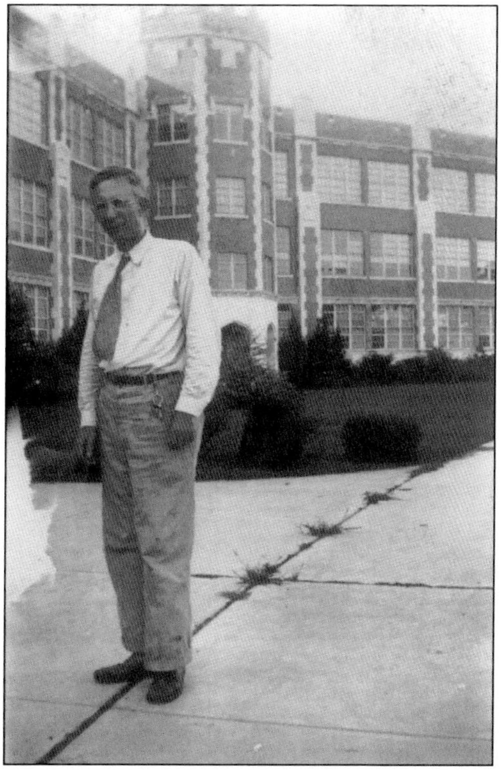

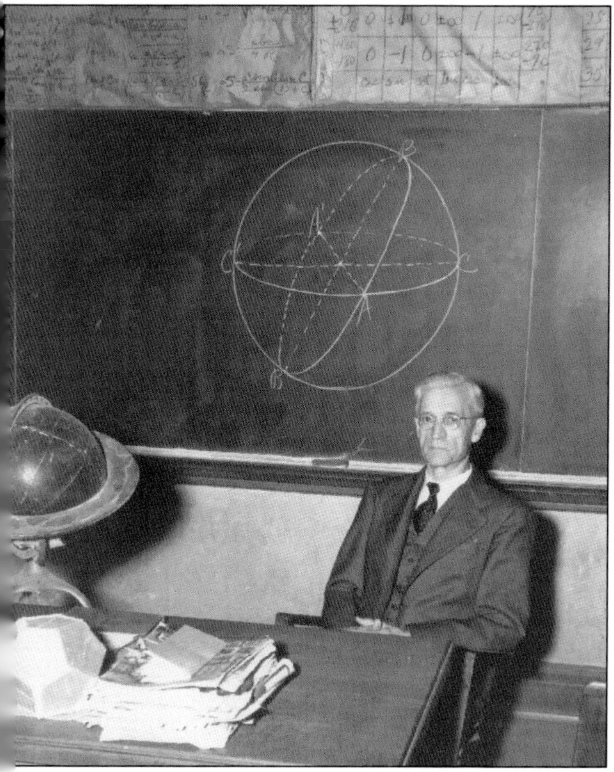

Marvin Hunter Pearson sits in his classroom during his last year teaching at Lanier High School. He retired in the late 1940s after teaching for over 40 years. (Courtesy Pearson family collection.)

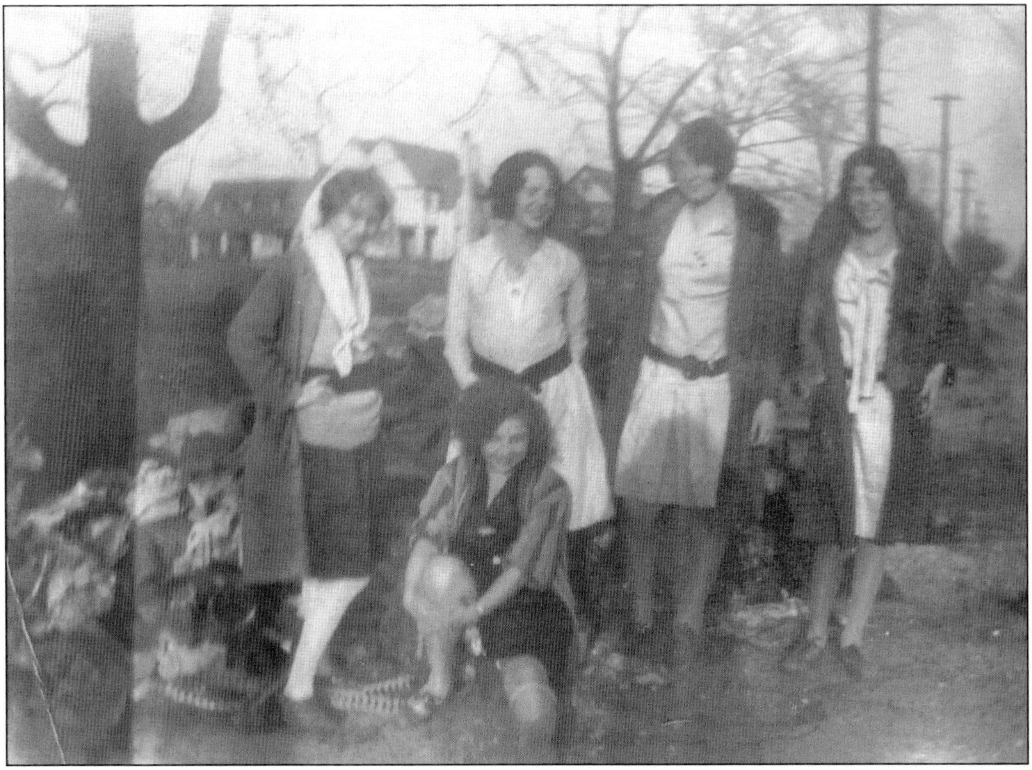

The same group of girls who posed in front of Lanier High School then posed on Fairview Avenue at what the note on the photograph calls "the dump." Note the Rice-Jones and the Brewbaker houses in the background. (Courtesy Mastin family collection.)

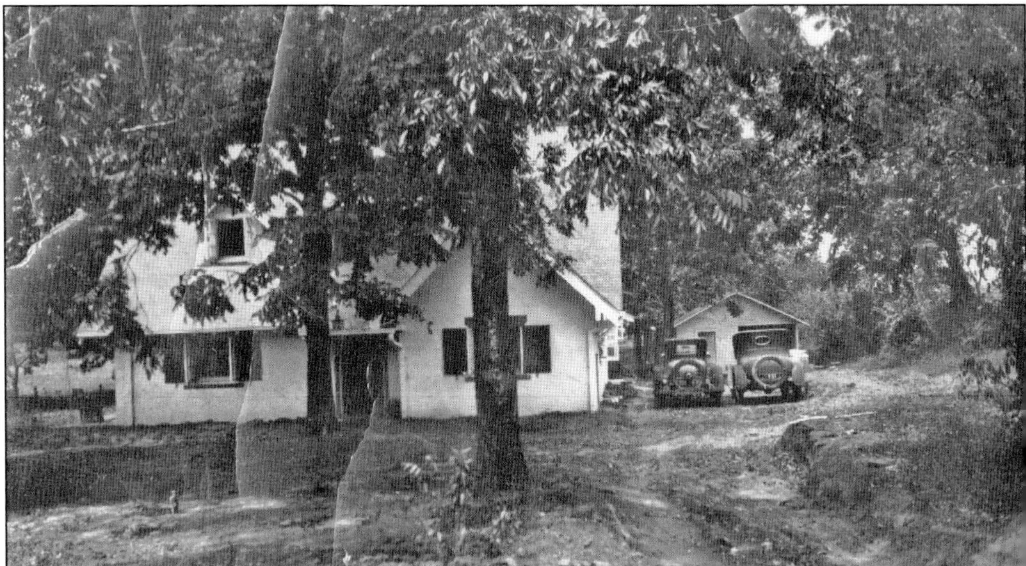

After Caroline Lee Davidson and Fred Ball Jr. married in 1924, they moved to this cottage. Famil[y] history tells that Fred Ball Jr.'s father built the home especially for the newlyweds in an area know[n] as "the Grove" near the Ball home on Perry Street. (Courtesy Ball family collection.)

During their courtship, Colquitt Lane gave Grace Gunter her dog, Major. Family stories tell the tale that Major derived his name because he resembled a neighbor. Here Grace and Major sit on the wall beside the Gunter home at 742 South Perry Street. (Courtesy Fairlie Lane.)

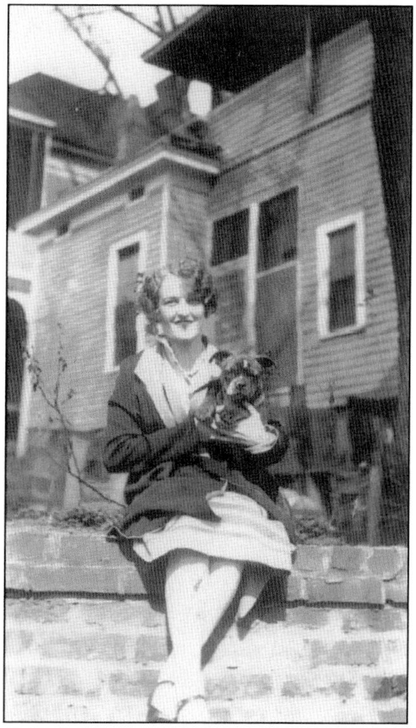

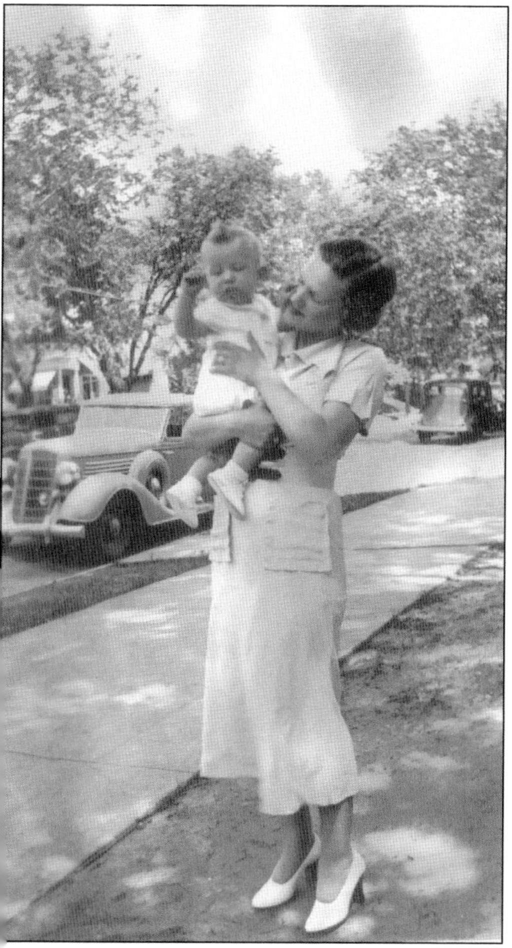

Eleanor Clements Pruett poses with her son, James D. Pruett, in front of Colonial Court Apartments on Felder Avenue in 1936. (Courtesy James Pruett family.)

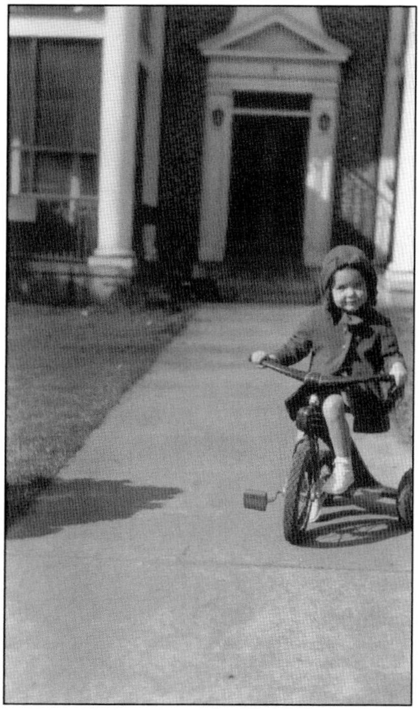

Joanne Dubose rides her bicycle in front of the Colonial Court Apartments on Felder Avenue in 1938. (Courtesy Joanne Dubose Morgan.)

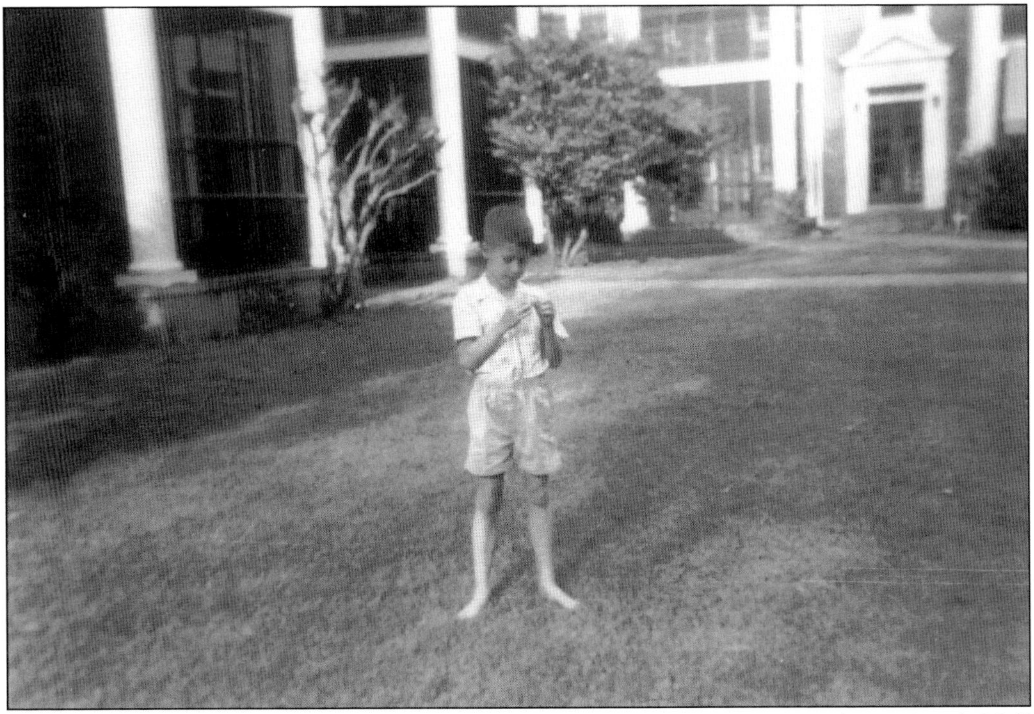

James G. Pruett stands in the courtyard of the Colonial Court Apartments facing South Hull Street. (Courtesy Joanne Dubose Morgan.)

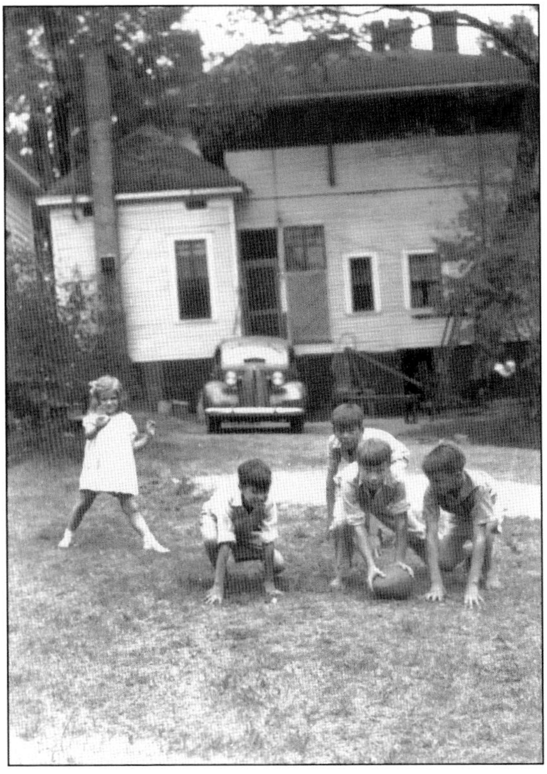

During a 1939 football game in the backyard of 742 South Perry Street, from left to right, Ellen Rogers prepares to receive the pass and Bobby Haas takes the snap while their cousins wait on the play. (Courtesy Fairlie Haynes.)

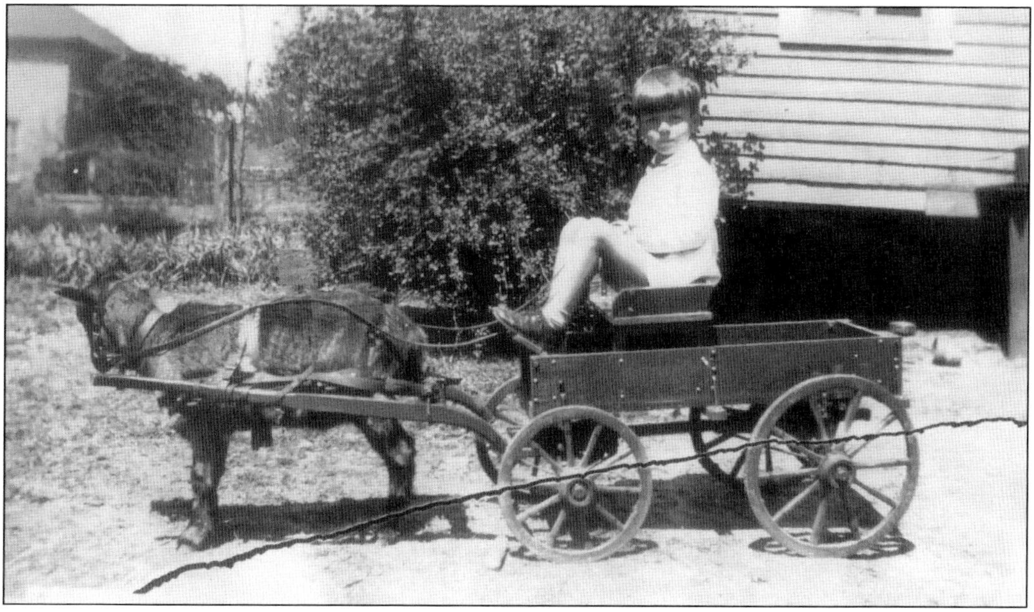

Bobby Haas travels around the neighborhood in his goat cart in 1935. (Courtesy Fairlie Haynes.)

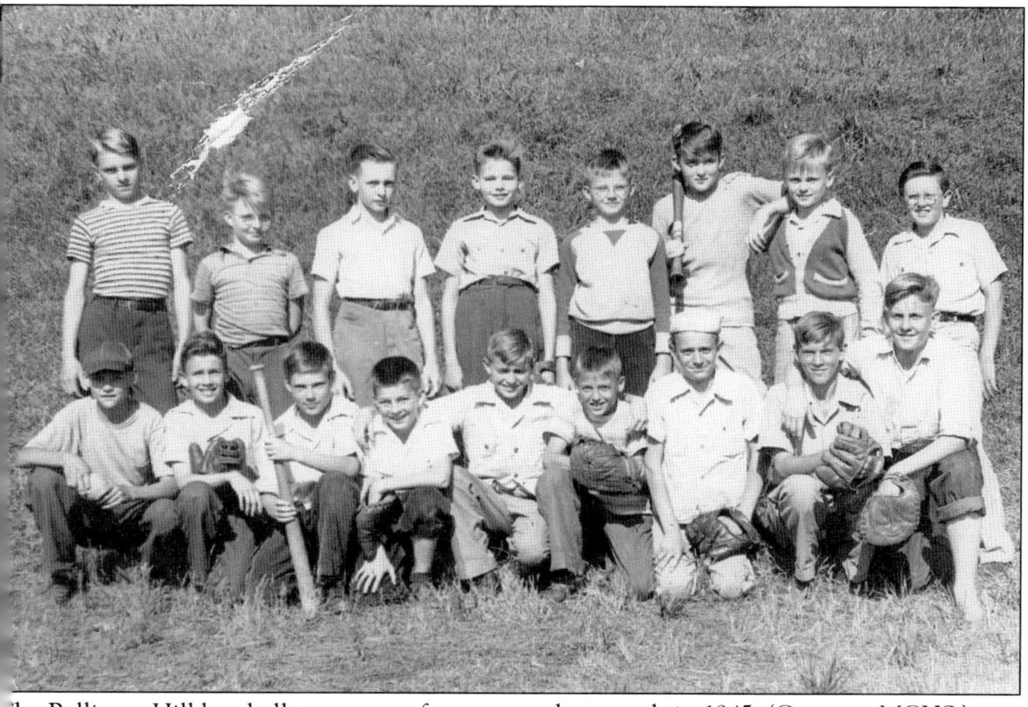

'he Bellinger Hill baseball team poses for a group photograph in 1945. (Courtesy MCHS.)

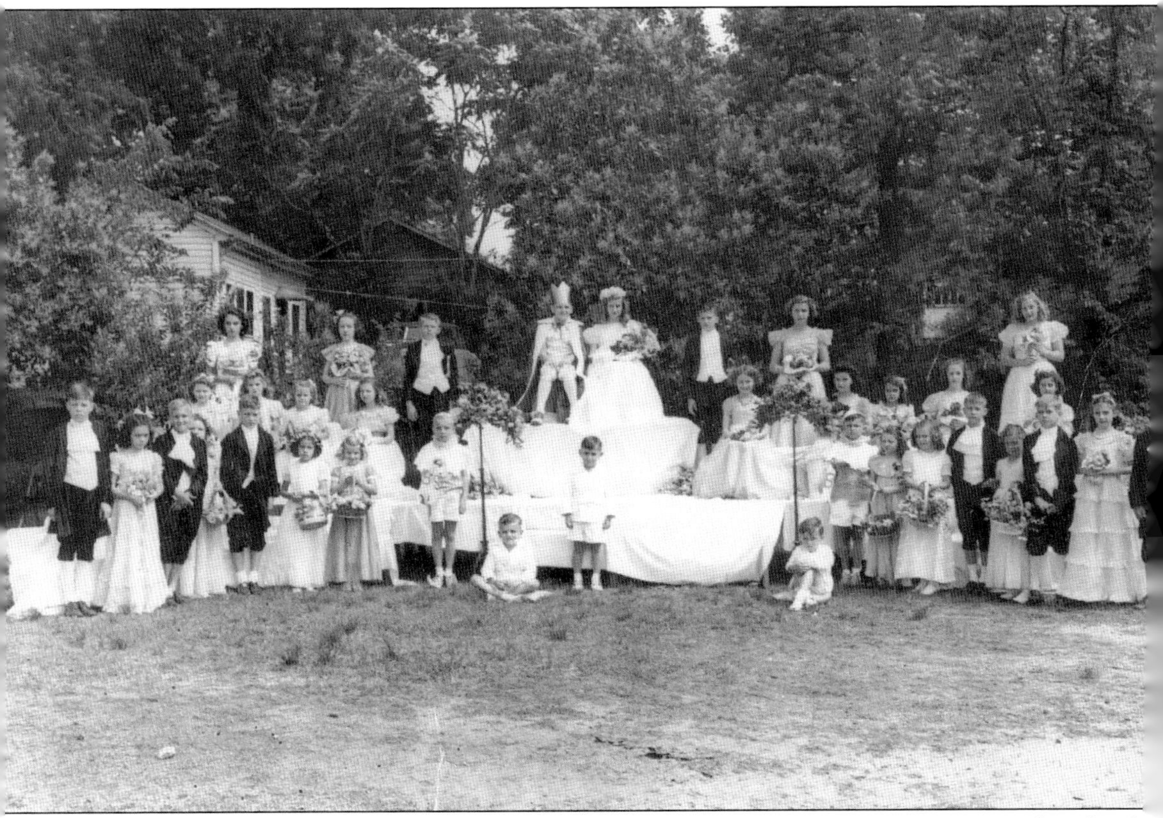

The Bellinger Hill School held Play Day on May 3, 1944. The May Day Court poses on the school steps. On the first row stand, from left to right, Burns Patterson, Joanne DuBose, Gary Waller, unidentified, Bill Brewbaker, three unidentified, Burke Sylvest (seated), unidentified, Paul Watson (seated), Frank Tatone, two unidentified, Warren Goodwyn, Francis Fowler Holding, David Davis, Judi Rushin, and Lee Paulk; (second row) Marian King, Ellen Rogers, Cornelia Bear, Gene Langhon, Elizabeth Hastings, Caroline Owens, Marian Thorington, Janet Humphrey, and Patsy Smith; (third row) unidentified, Patsy Yelverton, unidentified, King Peter Brock, Queen Ann Bowman, unidentified, Merle Watkins, and Dora Stephens. (Courtesy MCHS.)

Seven

Cloverdale

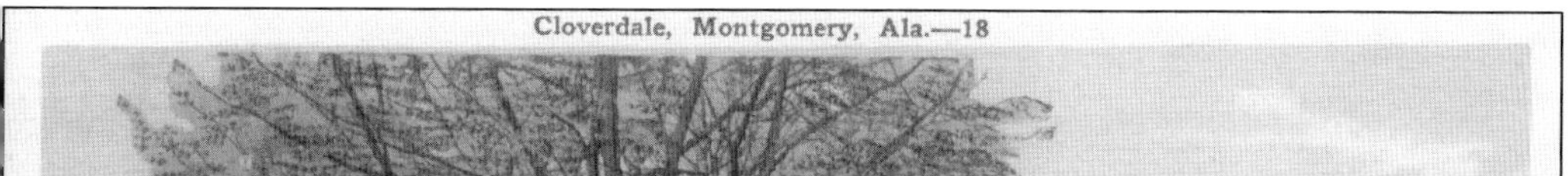

Cloverdale was developed from the area known as Graham's Woods. These woods were predominately pine trees, so the area was also called the Pines. According to local lore, in these wooded areas were open meadows with an abundance of clover that inspired the development's name. By the 1900s, the woods were giving way to fashionable homes. This postcard features Felder Avenue, named after Adam Felder, an early resident. (Courtesy James Bozeman.)

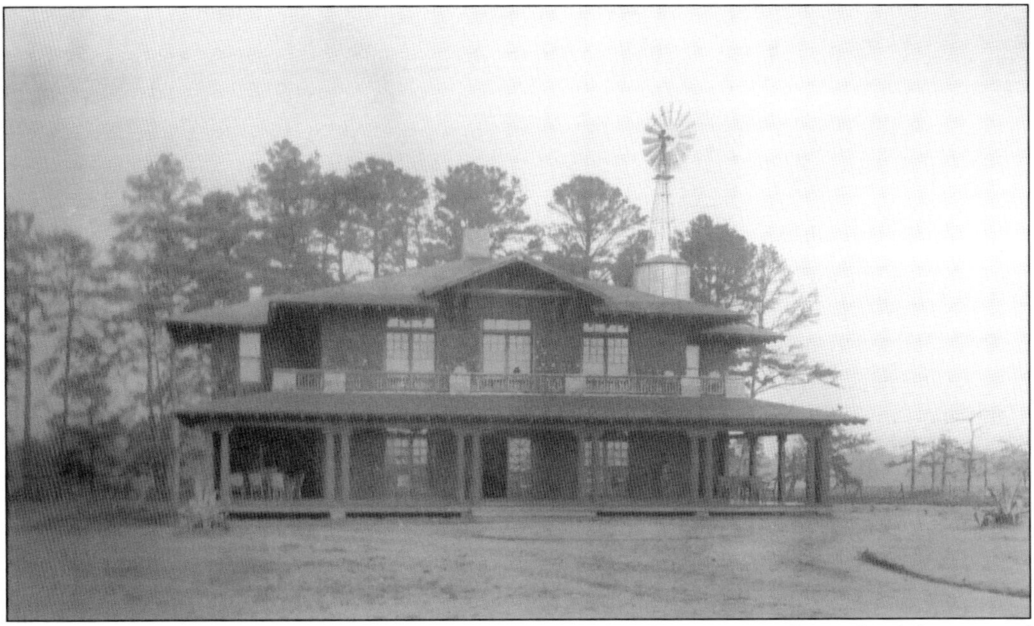

The first Montgomery Country Club was built in 1903 close by Carter Hill Road, Clubview, and Mulberry Street. On February 15, 1925, the building burned to the ground. In her book *Save Me the Waltz*, Zelda Fitzgerald claimed the cause of the fire was "the fiery explosion of a gallon of moonshine stored in a locker." (Courtesy MCHS.)

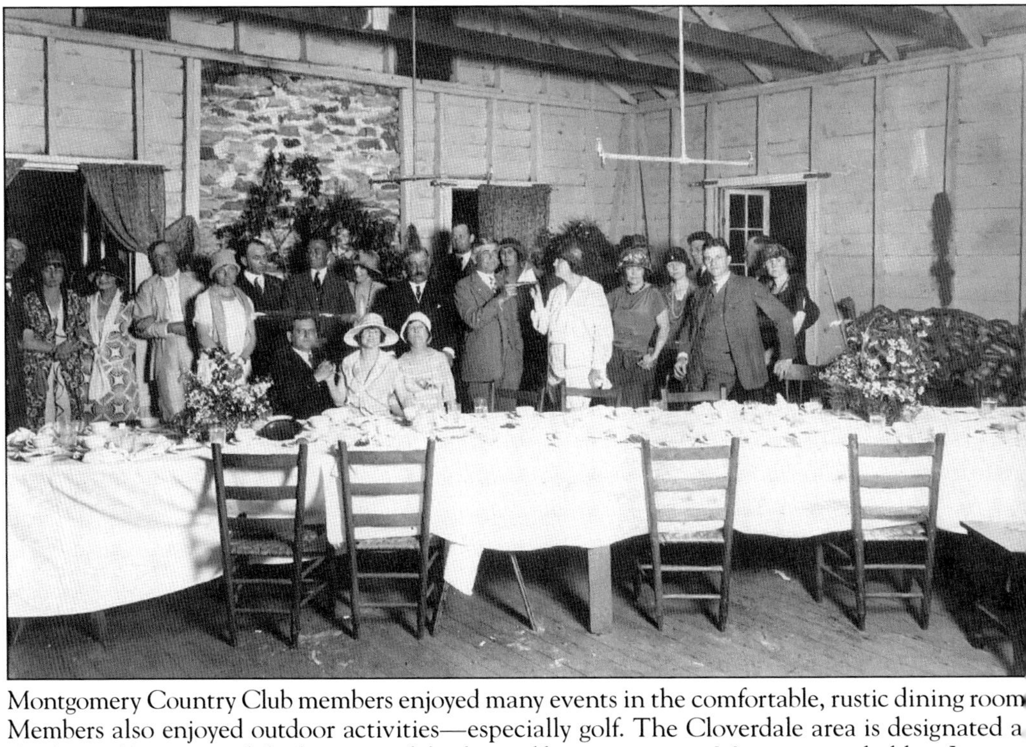

Montgomery Country Club members enjoyed many events in the comfortable, rustic dining room. Members also enjoyed outdoor activities—especially golf. The Cloverdale area is designated a the first golf course and the location of the first golf tournament in Montgomery, held on Januar 1, 1898. (Courtesy MCHS.)

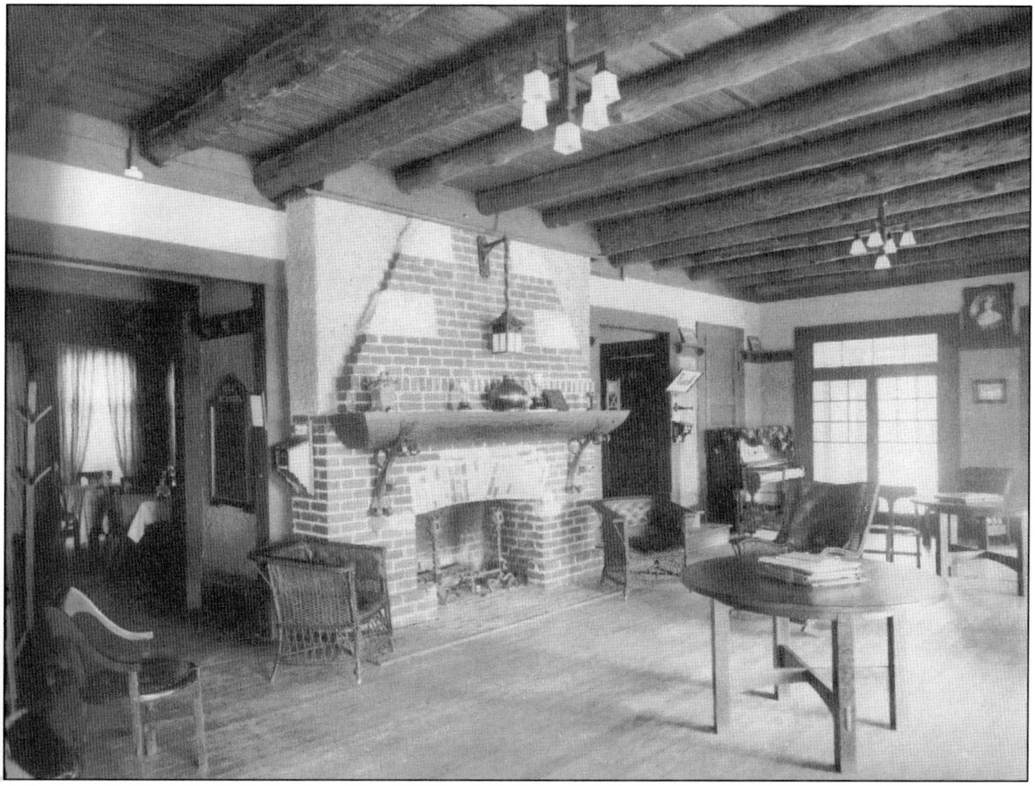

This interior portrait of the first Montgomery Country Club was included in the 1907 collection of gravure photographs taken of outstanding buildings in Montgomery. Zelda Sayre and F. Scott Fitzgerald met at a dance at the country club. (Courtesy Art Work Collection.)

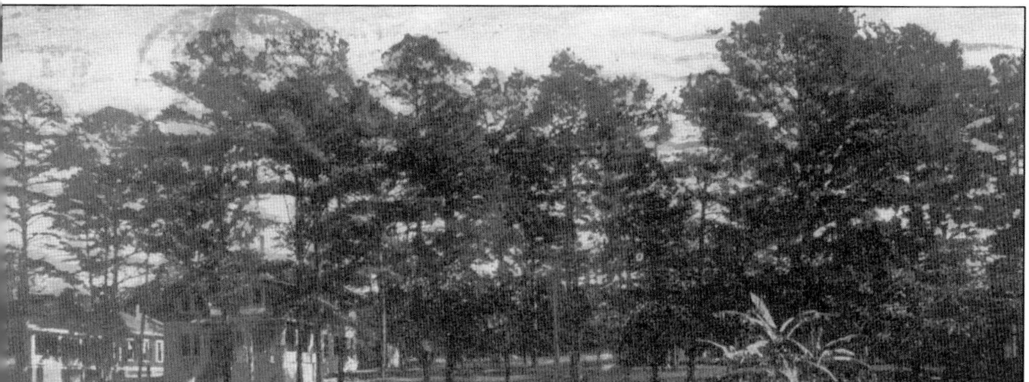

efore Cloverdale was developed into a residential area, its woods were known as the Pines. This ostcard view shows the junction of what became Cloverdale Road and Galena Avenue. The riangle area, which has remained a park, was the location for the famous mermaid fountain and currently dedicated to Milo Barrett Howard Jr., a historian and archivist. (Courtesy MCHS.)

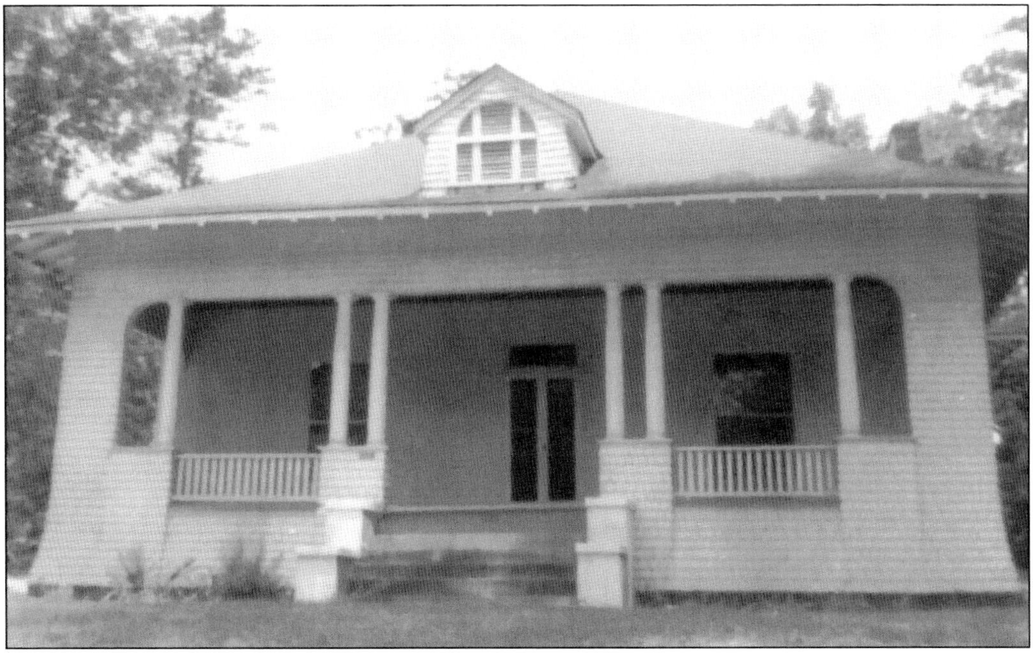

This photograph shows the house at 663 Cloverdale Road as it appeared in the early 1900s. The house at that time belonged to Robert and Alice Smith. (Courtesy Lee Frazer.)

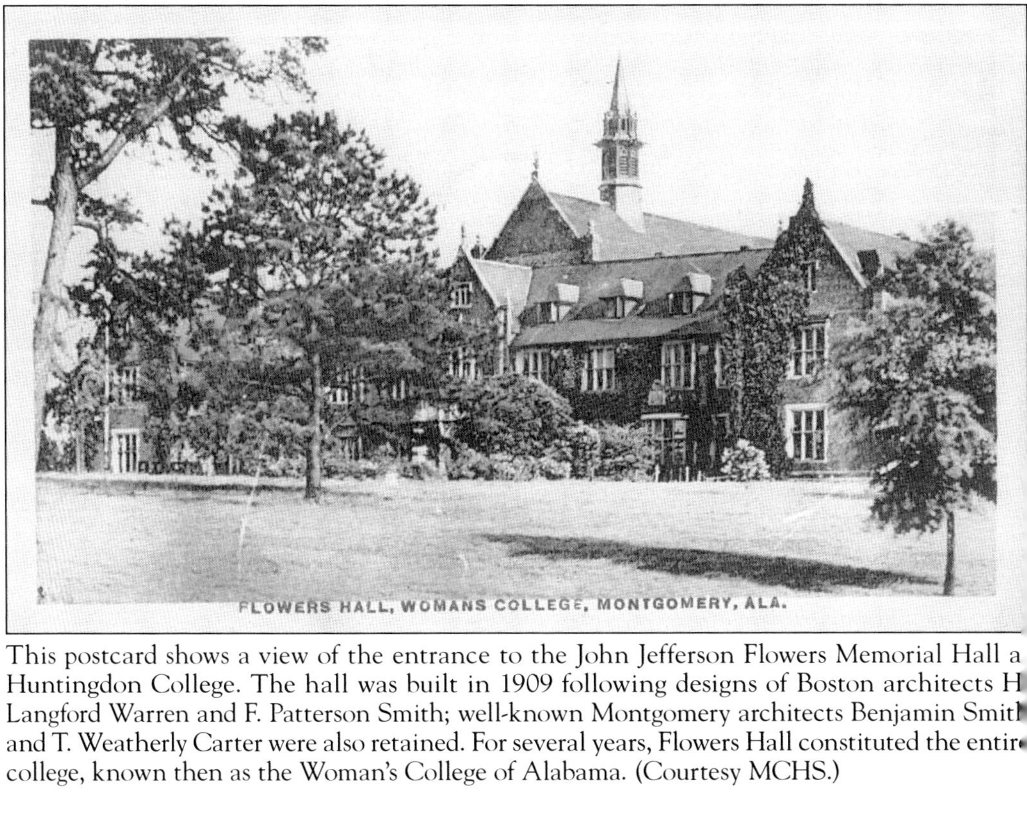

This postcard shows a view of the entrance to the John Jefferson Flowers Memorial Hall a Huntingdon College. The hall was built in 1909 following designs of Boston architects H Langford Warren and F. Patterson Smith; well-known Montgomery architects Benjamin Smit and T. Weatherly Carter were also retained. For several years, Flowers Hall constituted the entir college, known then as the Woman's College of Alabama. (Courtesy MCHS.)

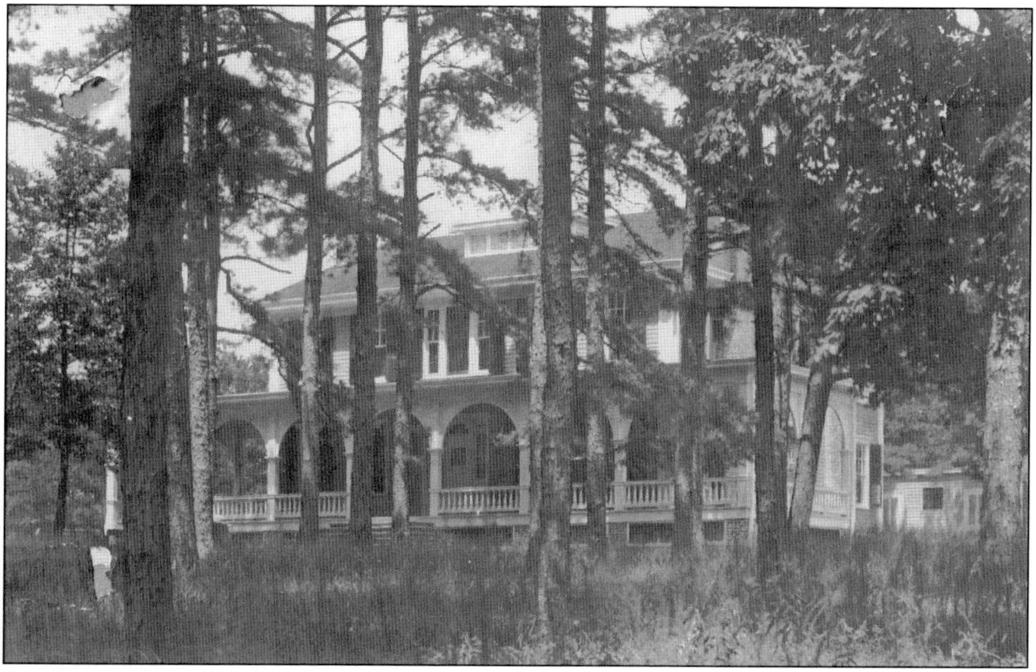

Caroline C. Davidson bought property at the corner of Park Avenue and Cloverdale Road in 1907 and built a large house. In 1909, she married Nicholas B. Marks, and they lived in the home until 1918, when Nick Marks died. Caroline then sold the house to William and Mary Elmore Bellingrath. After Caroline Davidson sold the house, it was known as the Bellingrath House and also as Somerset. (Courtesy Ball family collection.)

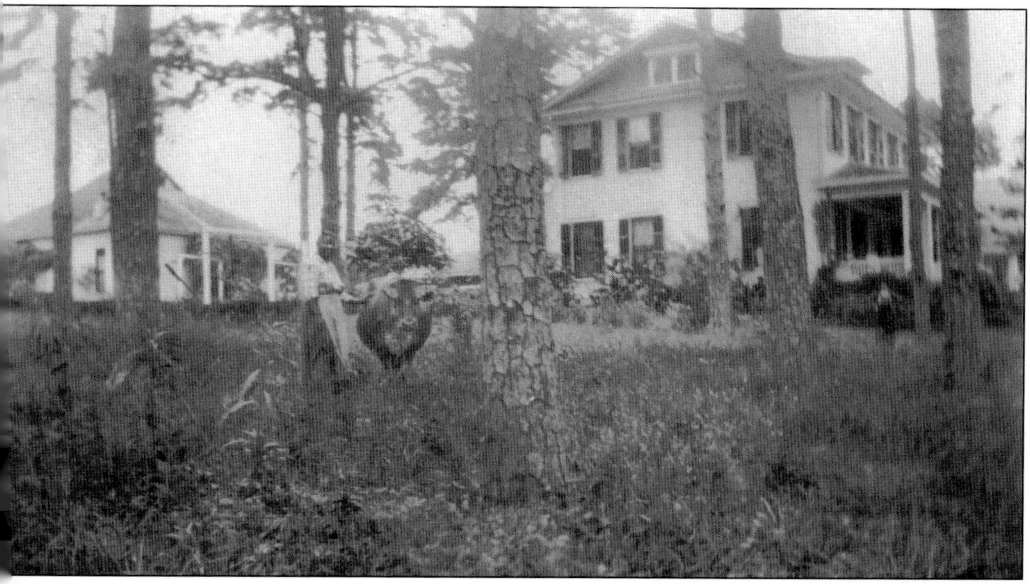

n this c. 1918 photograph, the Mertins family nurse stands beside a cow in the side yard of the lertins home. The smaller building in the back, the carriage house, was torn down in the 1980s. Courtesy Frances Durr.)

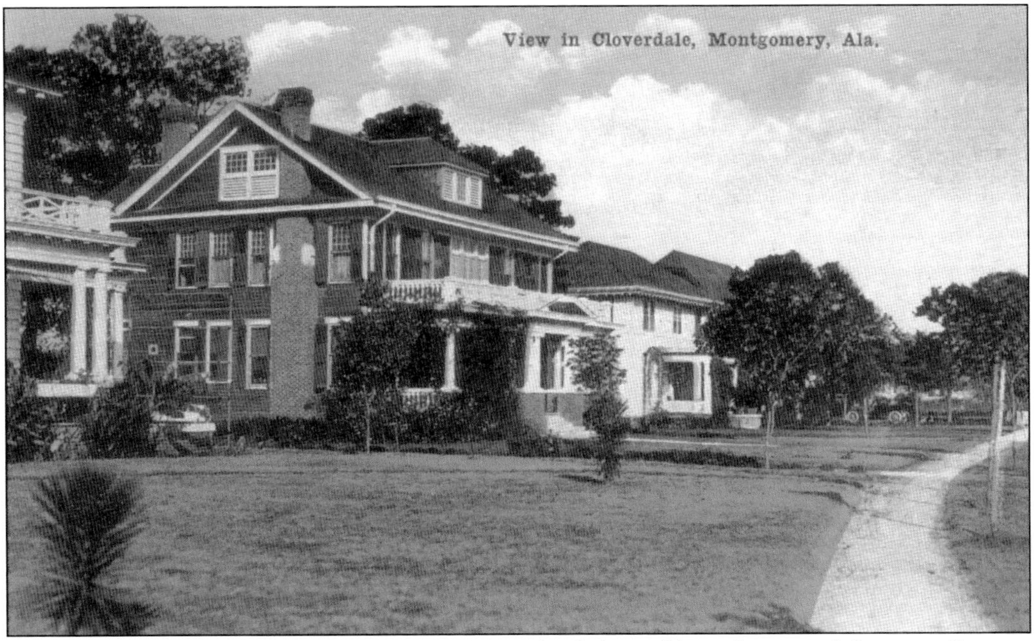

Titled "View in Cloverdale," this postcard shows the fashionable architectural designs of houses built in Cloverdale in the 1900s. The house in the foreground was built by William and Harriet Cromwell in 1910. (Courtesy Hudson family collection.)

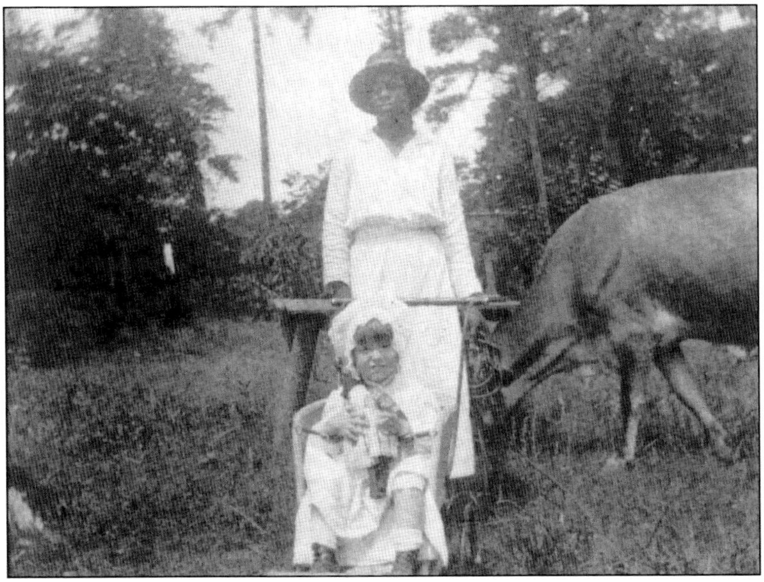

When it was first developed, Cloverdale was considered to be out in the country. Residents kept chickens, goats, horses, and cows. William and Harriet Cromwell built their home on 805 Felder Avenue around 1910. This photograph is dated 1918 and shows their baby daughter, Nancy, her nurse, Sally, and a cow. (Courtesy Hudson family collection.)

Jane Mertins sits with her grandmother, Jennie Mertins, enjoying the shade under the Cloverdale pines. (Courtesy Frances Durr.)

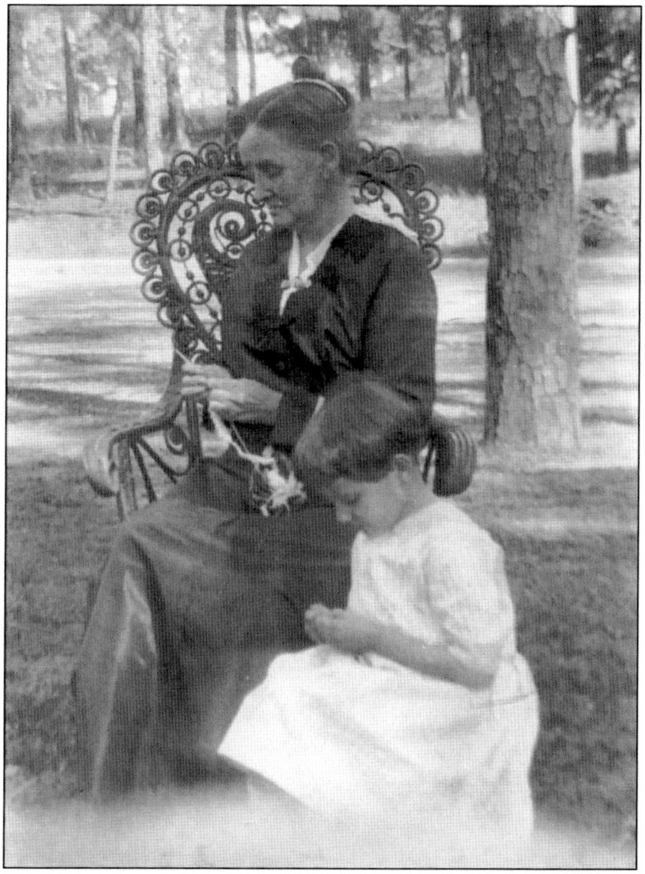

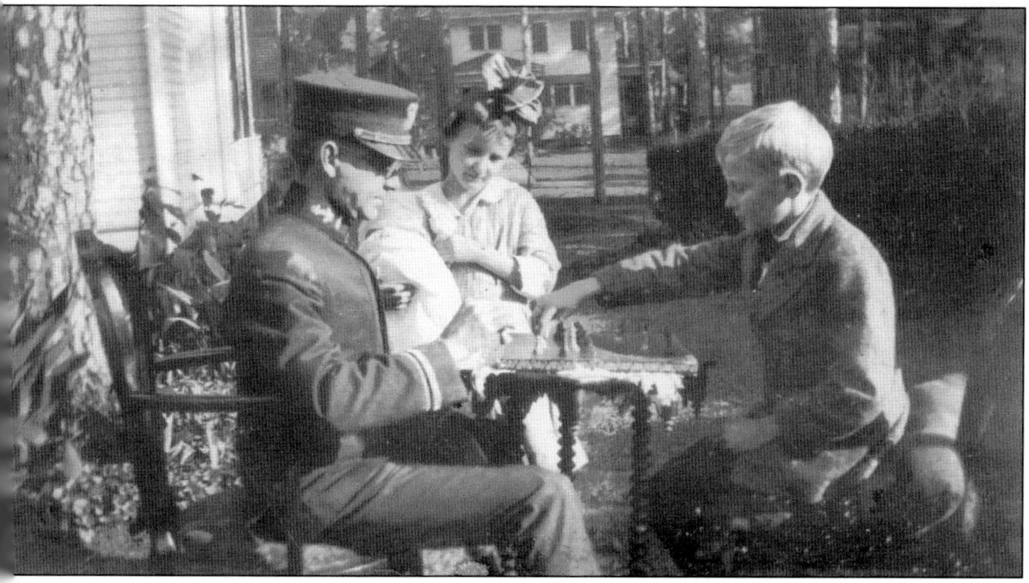

ı 1909, Dr. Paul S. Mertins Sr., dressed in his uniform, challenges his son, Paul Mertins Jr., to game of chess on the porch of the Mertins home at 1844 Galena Avenue. Jane Mertins looks ver her father's shoulder. (Courtesy Frances Durr.)

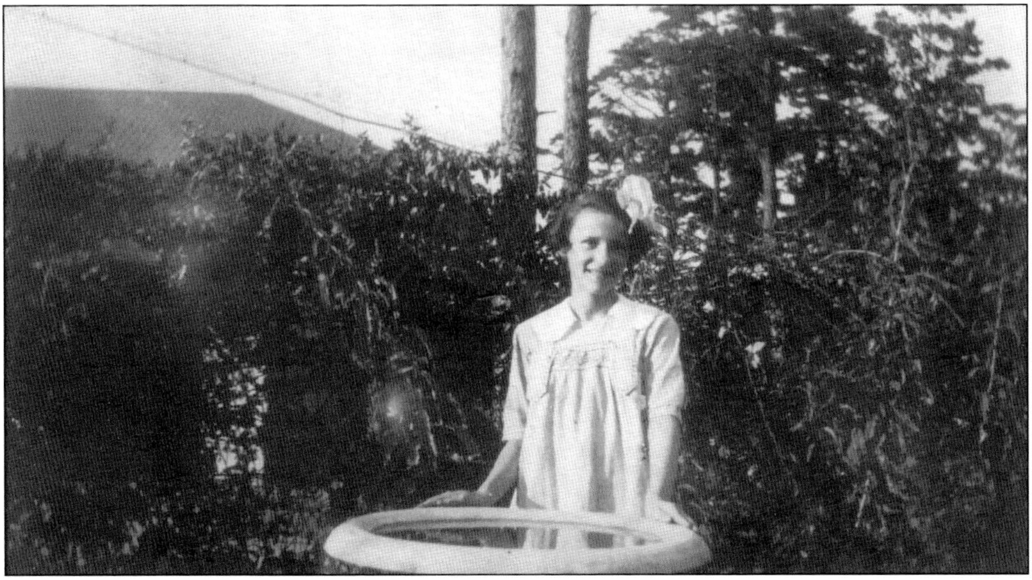

Jane Mertins stands beside the bird bath in the yard of the Mertins home at 1844 Galena Avenue. (Courtesy Frances Durr.)

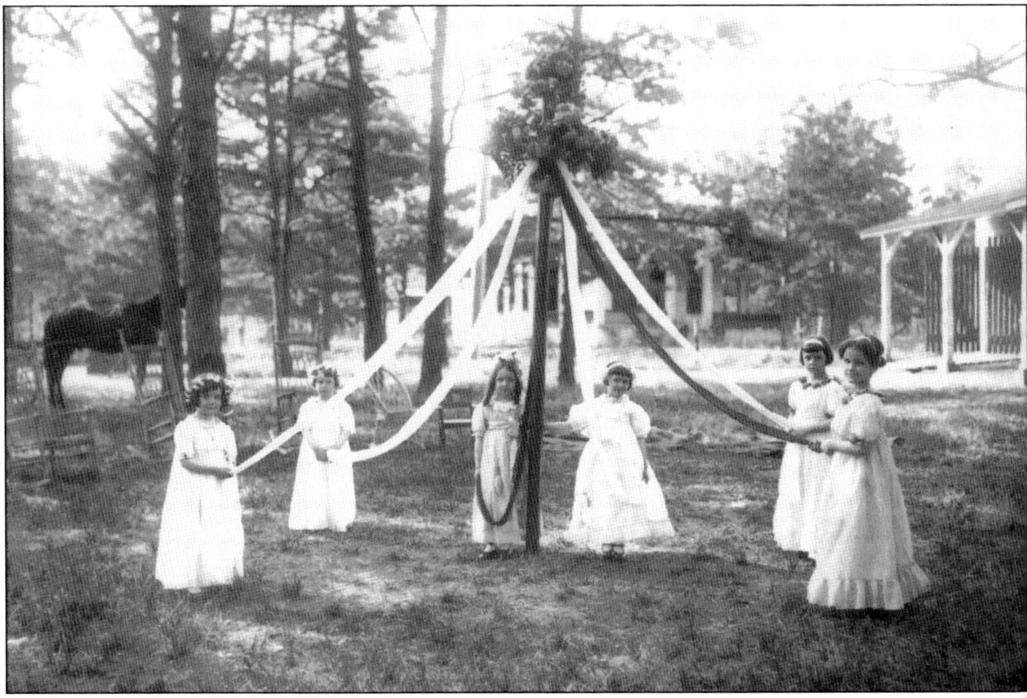

In 1910, from left to right, Ellen Duvall, Carolee Cobbs, Virginia Rothmore, Martha Cassel Caroline Davidson, and Theda Clark Peters participate in the popular spring tradition of th maypole dance. (Courtesy Ball family collection.)

Rev. Edward Ellerbe Cobbs and Edith Hurter Cobbs designed their home, the Pines, after a hunting lodge in England they saw on their honeymoon. Built between 1904 and 1906, the house stood where the First United Methodist Church now stands. Organizational meetings for the Church of the Ascension were held at the Cobbs' residence. (Courtesy Ball family collection.)

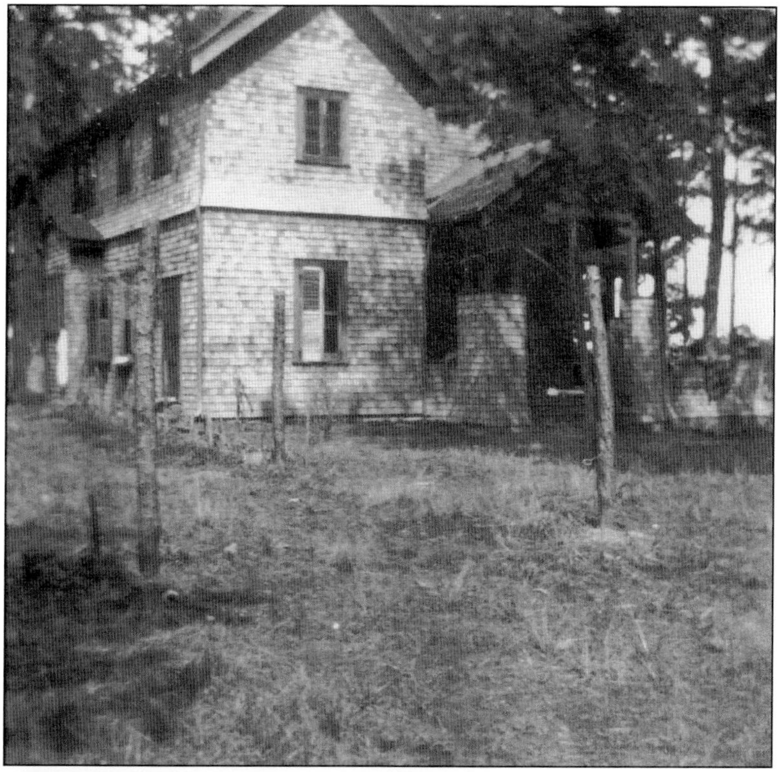

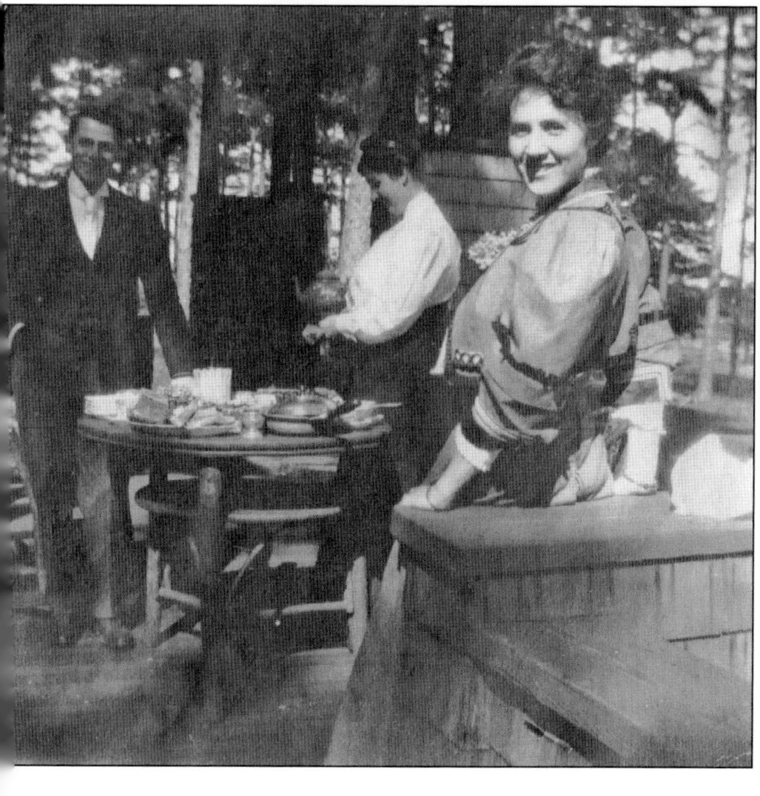

One of Cloverdale's first residents, Rev. Edward Ellerbe Cobbs was the youngest rector of St. John's Episcopal Church in Montgomery, where he served from 1902 to 1917. This 1907 family photograph is titled "tea at the Cobbs." From left to right preparing food are George Linder (noted as "Uncle George"), Edith Cobbs, and Kate Davidson (noted as "Aunt Kate"). (Courtesy Ball family collection.)

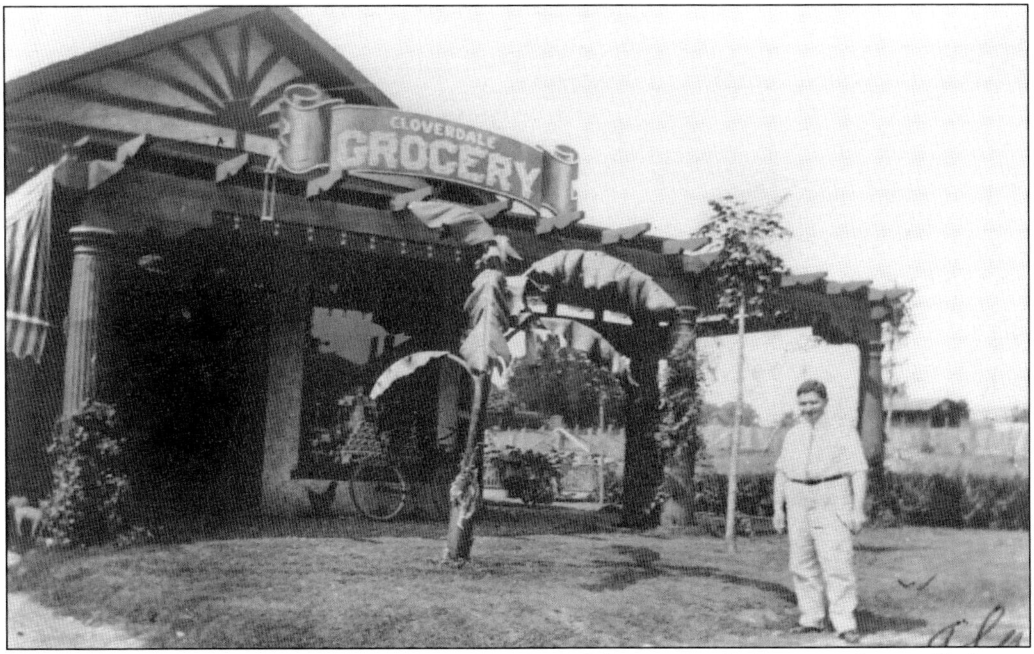

The Cloverdale Grocery was the first business in Cloverdale, opening before 1921. George Heilpern, the owner, stands in front of his business, which was located at the corner of Cloverdale Road and Decatur Street. (Courtesy MCHS.)

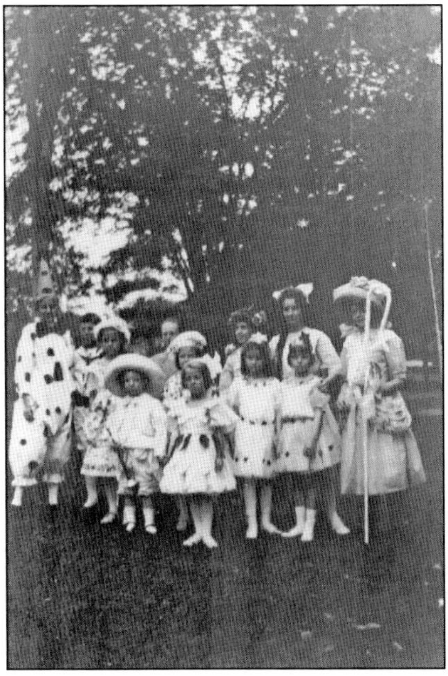

After a dance recital, the stellar cast posed for an informal photograph. Family history holds that two of the dancers are Caroline Lee Davidson and Theda Clark, but specific identification is uncertain. (Courtesy Ball family collection.)

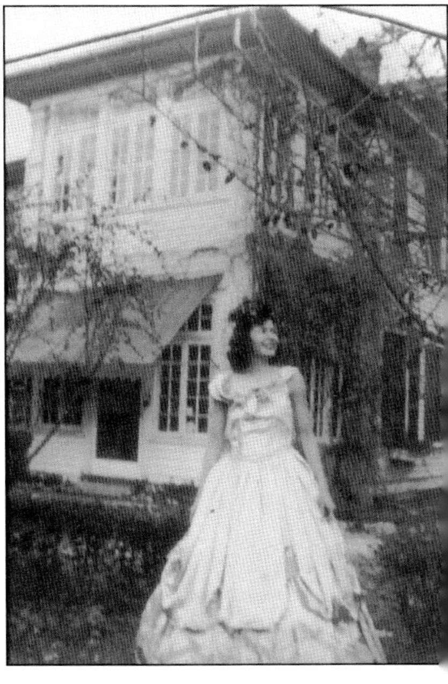

Jane Mertins poses in a lovely gown at the back of the Mertins family home. Note the second-story sleeping porch. (Courtesy Frances Durr.)

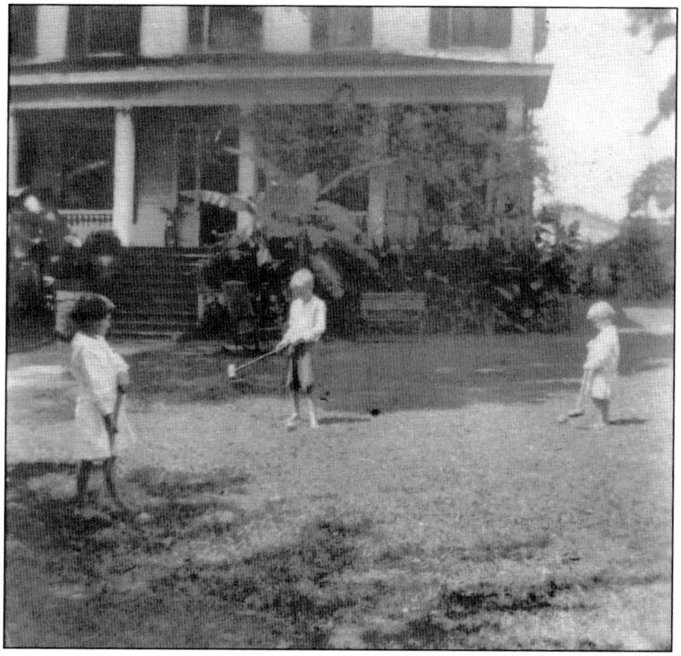

Children enjoy a game of croquet on the front lawn of the Mertins home. (Courtesy Frances Durr.)

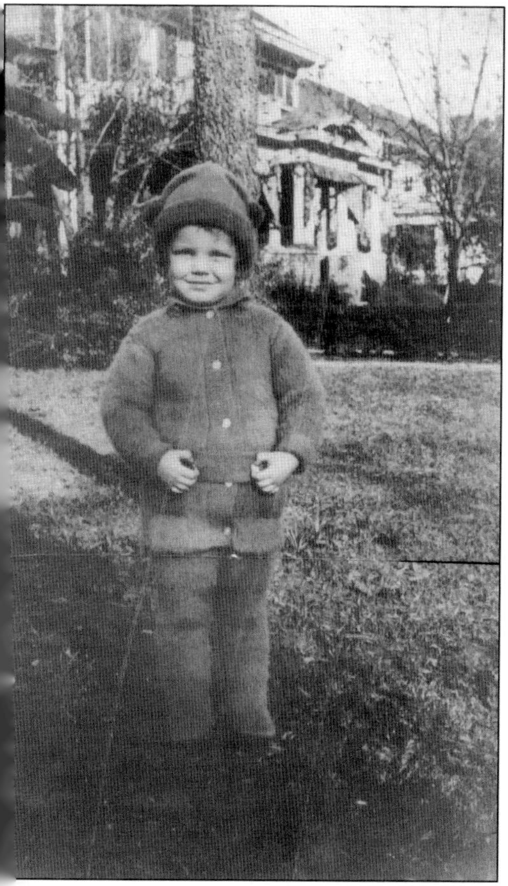

Charles Harris Jr. stands outside his home at 737 Felder Avenue in 1921. (Courtesy Montgomery Country Club.)

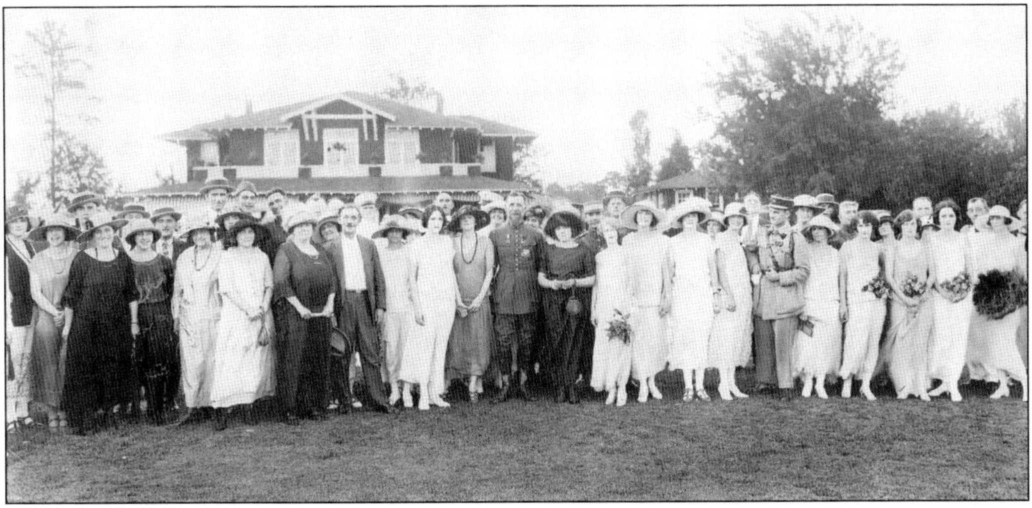

Gen. H. E. J. Gourand, French general and governor of Paris, was welcomed to Montgomery by Gov. William Brandon on Sunday, August 5, 1923, at the Montgomery Country Club. (Courtesy MCHS.)

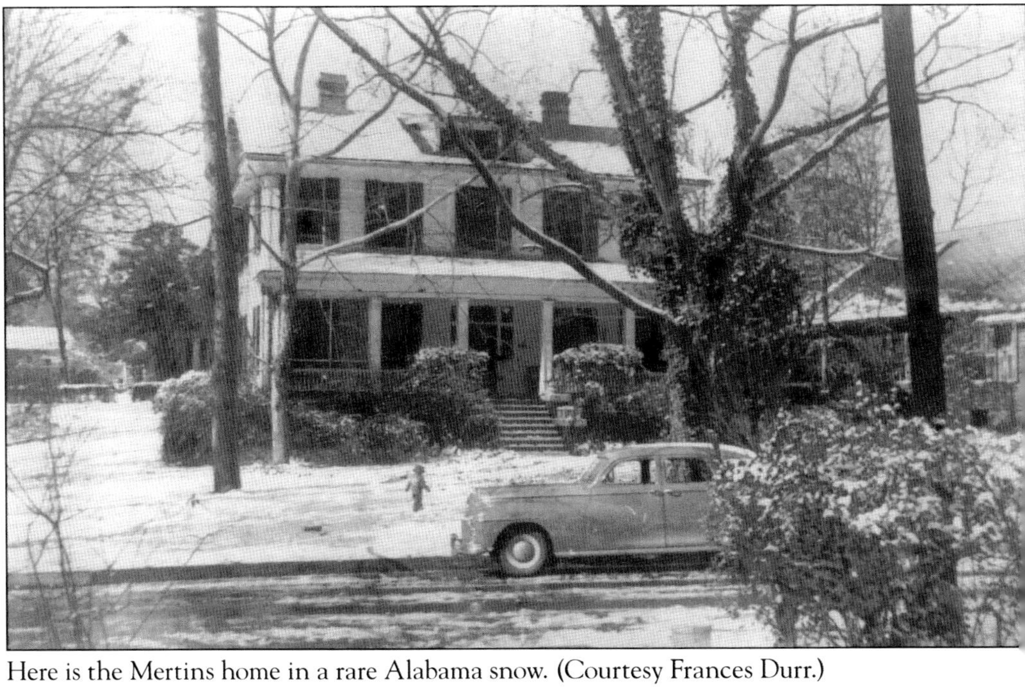

Here is the Mertins home in a rare Alabama snow. (Courtesy Frances Durr.)

On February 24, 1924, a *Montgomery Advertiser* article described children in Cloverdale enjoying skating on Galena Avenue. During the winter months, local officials roped off the street so the children could skate safely. (Courtesy Frances Durr.)

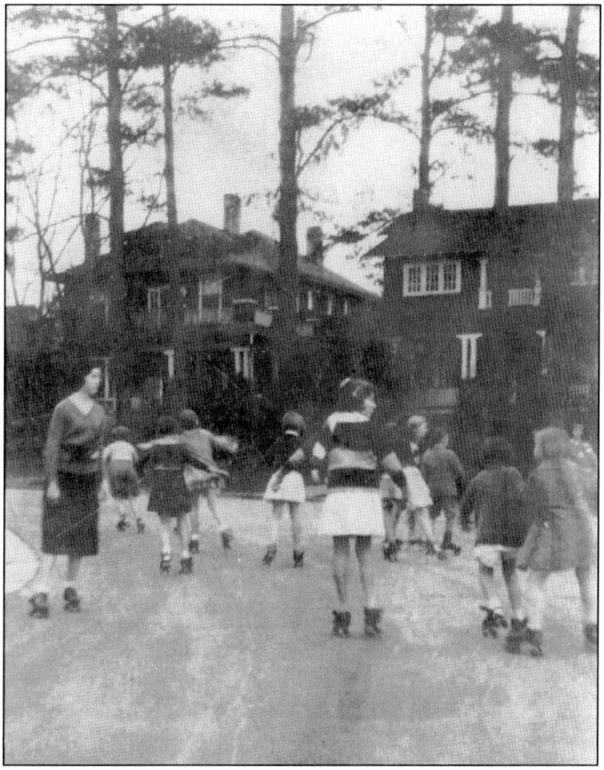

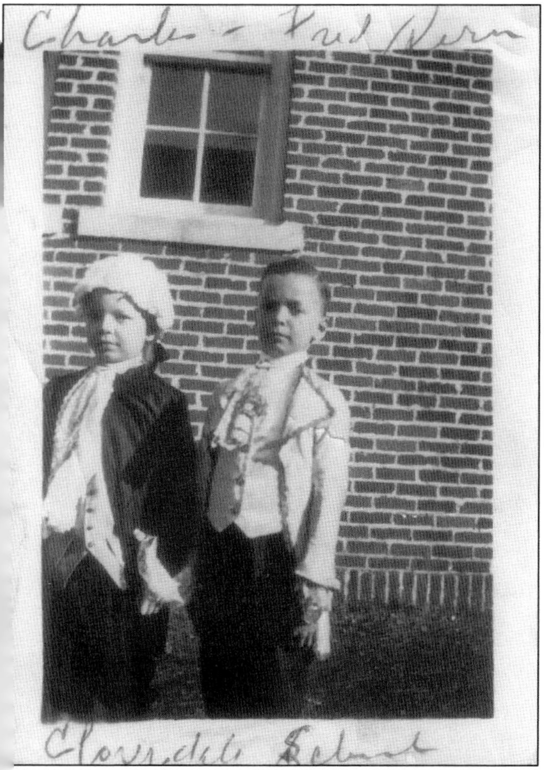

Charles Harris Jr. (left) and Fred Kern, dressed as founding fathers for their second grade's program on Colonial America, stand outside Cloverdale School in 1925. (Courtesy Montgomery Country Club.)

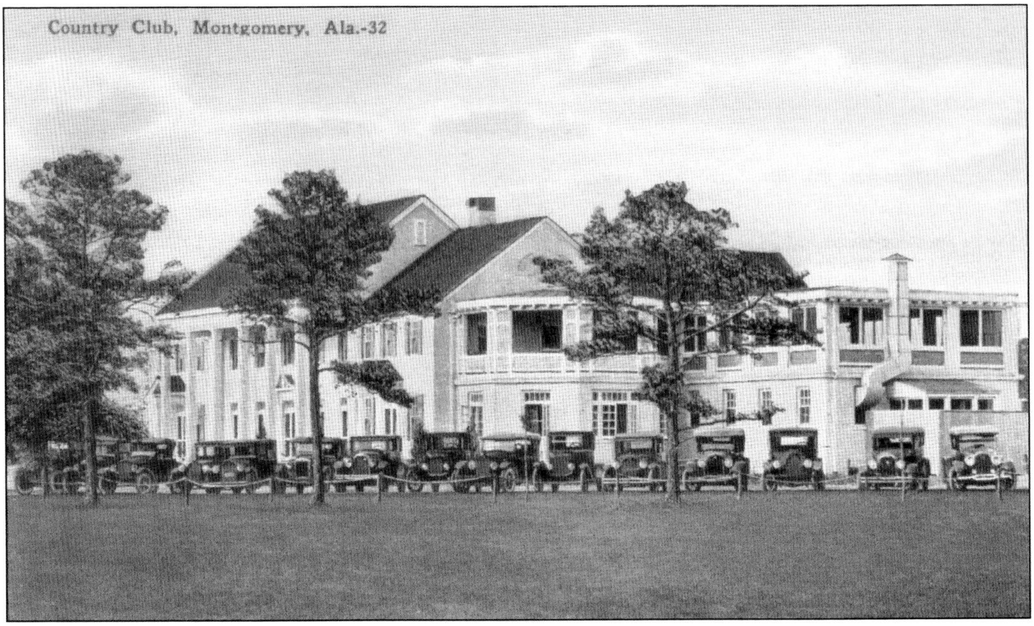

In 1926, the new Montgomery Country Club was built on Narrow Lane Road, which was not far from the first building. The design, however, changed drastically to accommodate the tastes of the Jazz Age. This building remained in use until 1989. (Courtesy Montgomery Country Club.)

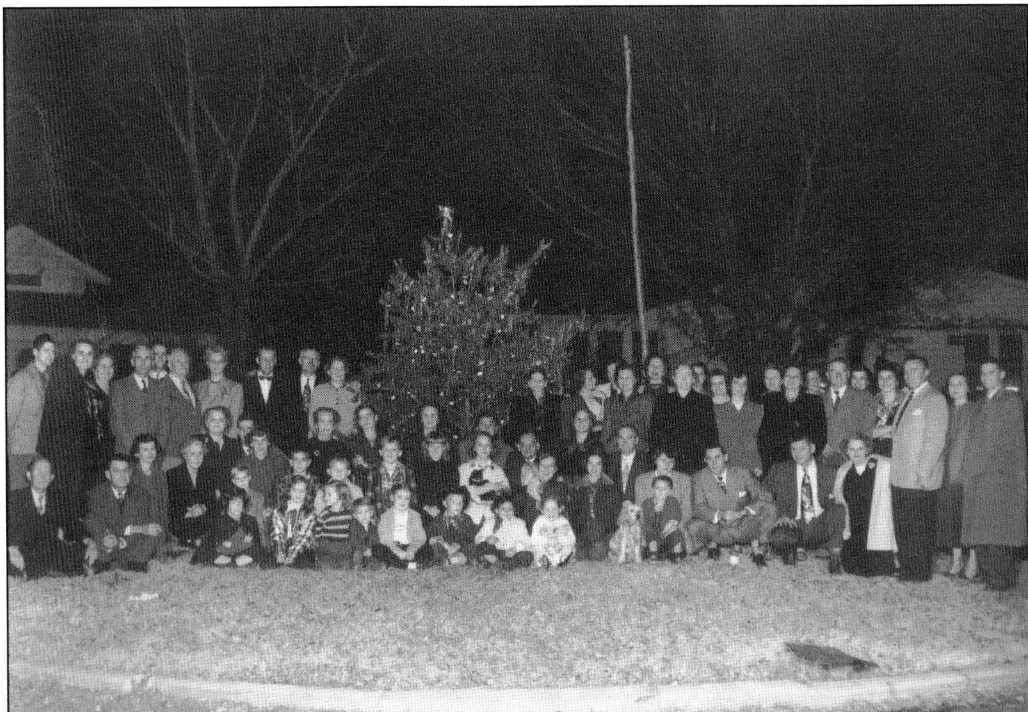

College Court, for a time, was one of several areas not originally considered part of the Cloverdale neighborhood. Here, in 1927, the annual College Court Christmas party and Christmas tree lighting shows families, cats, and dogs all enjoying the festivities. (Courtesy Barbara Moore.)

Mildred Green poses on the steps of Cloverdale High School on her graduation day in 1929. Note the unidentified student lurking behind post. (Courtesy Mastin family collection.)

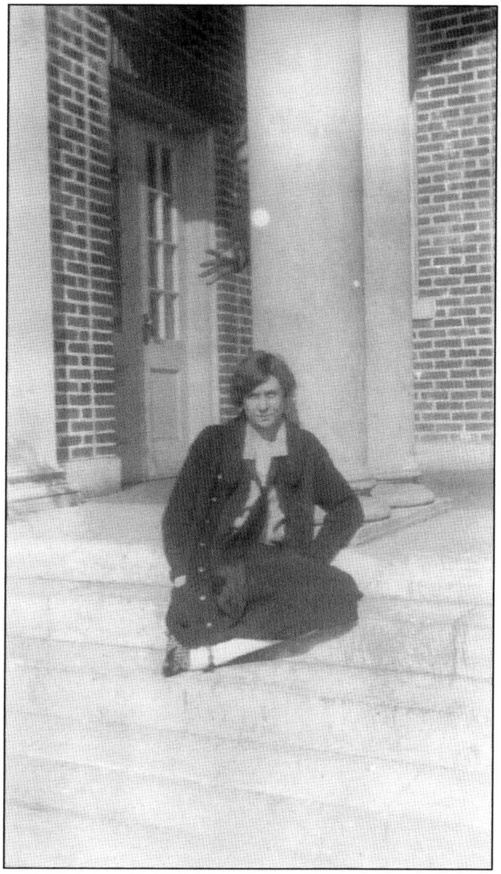

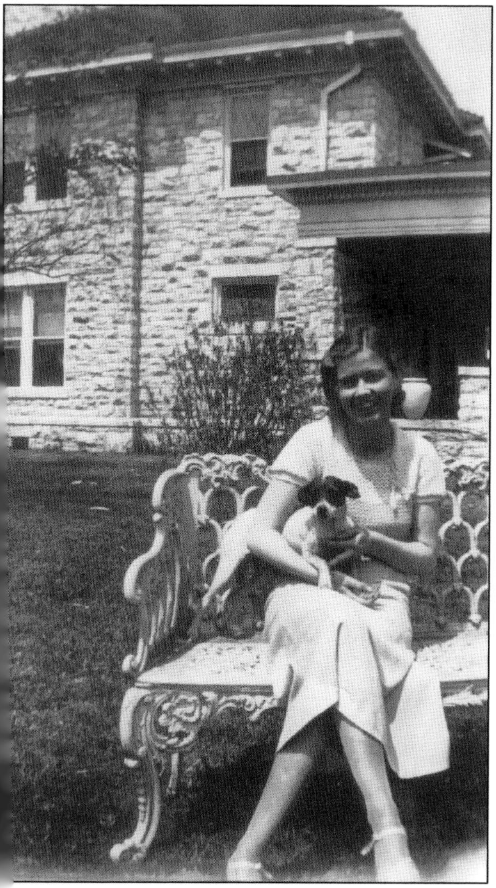

Mollie Shepard poses in the side yard of Stonecroft, the Crenshaw family home, on Narrow Lane Road around 1930. (Courtesy Barbara Moore.)

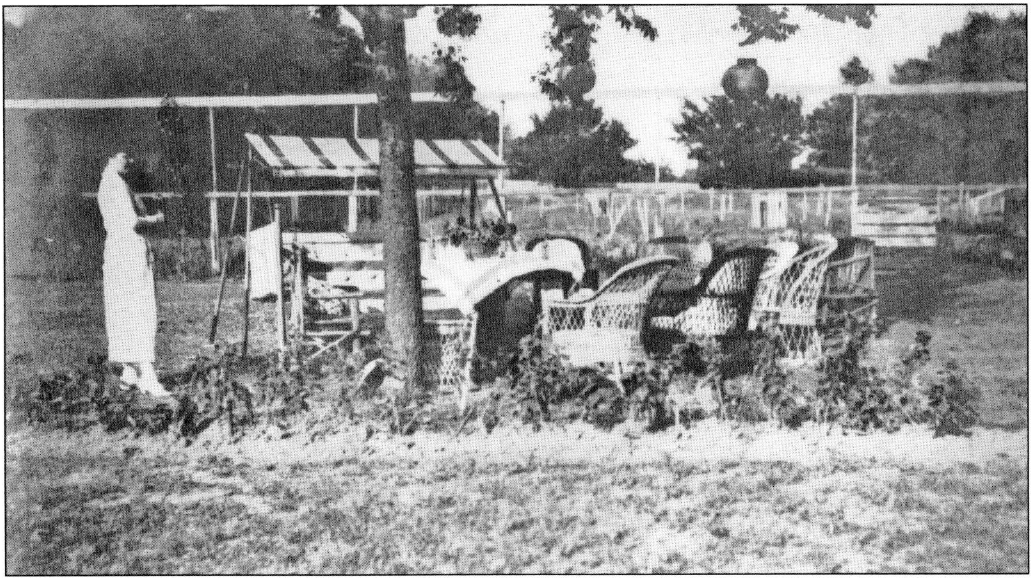

After Nick Marks died, Caroline Clark Davidson Marks married Dr. Brannon Hubbard, and they moved to 742 Felder Avenue. Here she prepares an outdoor party in Old Cloverdale on a sunny Alabama afternoon. (Courtesy Ball family collection.)

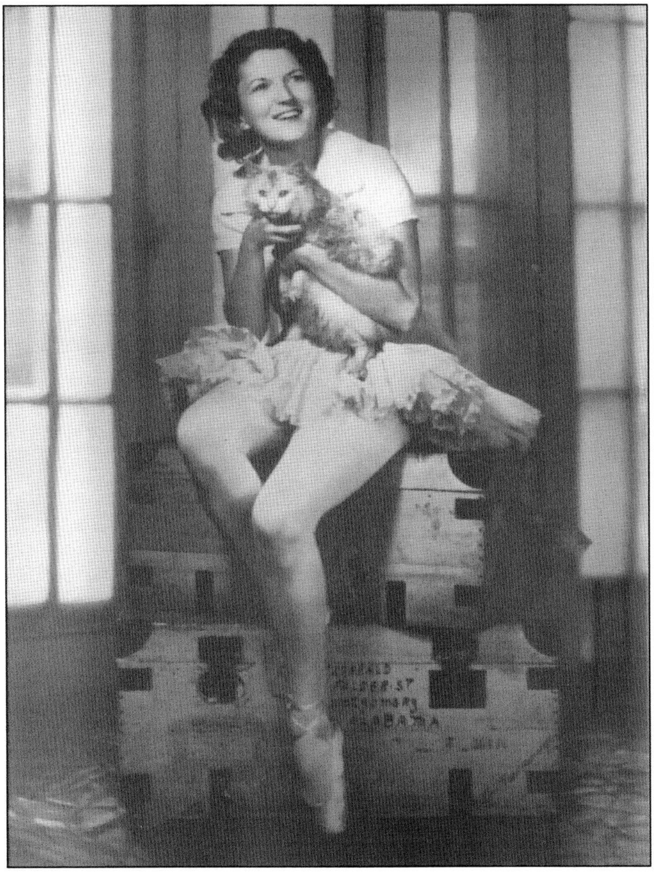

Zelda Fitzgerald posed for this photograph for the cover of her book *Save Me the Waltz* in the house at 919 Felder Avenue. (Courtesy *Romantic Egotists*.)

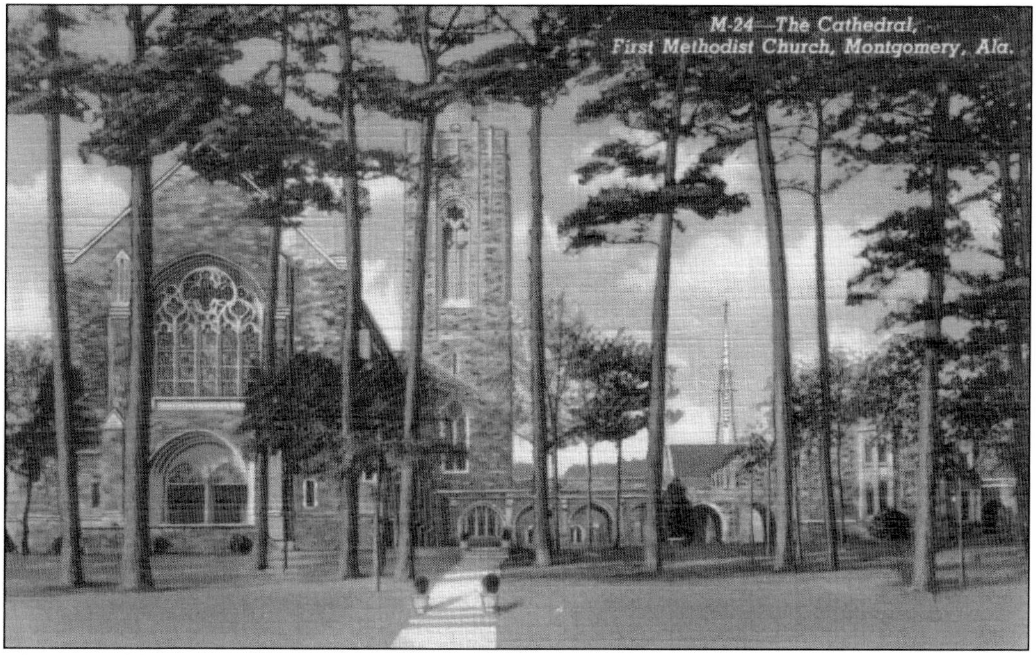

The ground-breaking for the First United Methodist Church and its education building was held on February 7, 1932. During final inspections on November 29, 1932, an explosion destroyed the majority of the new buildings. The sanctuary was not completed until July 1938. (Courtesy James Bozeman.)

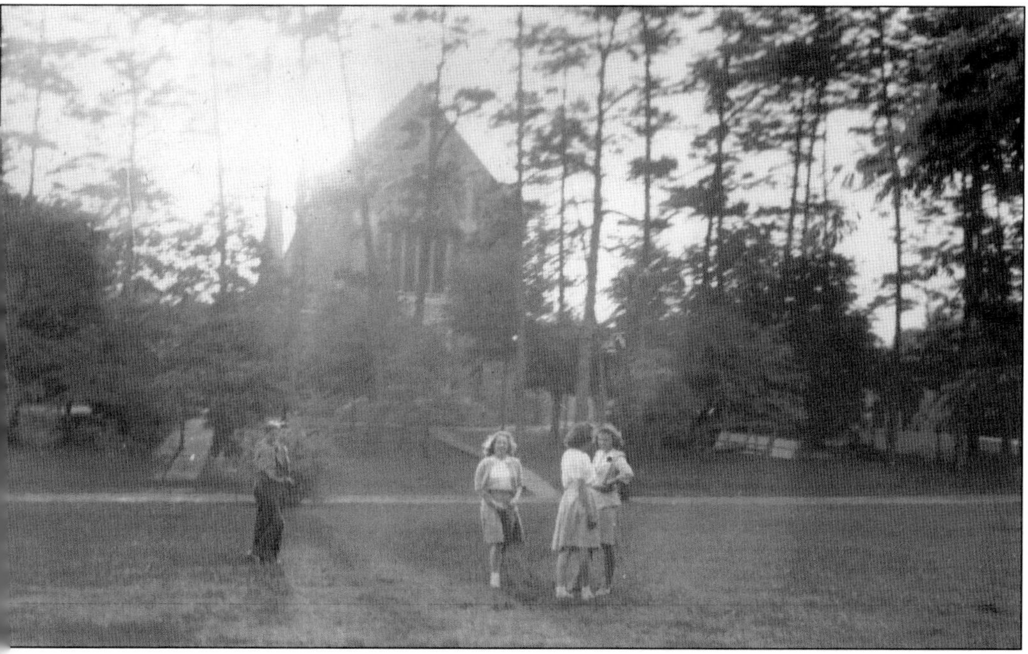

An unidentified group enjoys Cloverdale Park in front of the First United Methodist Church. (Courtesy Frazier family collection.)

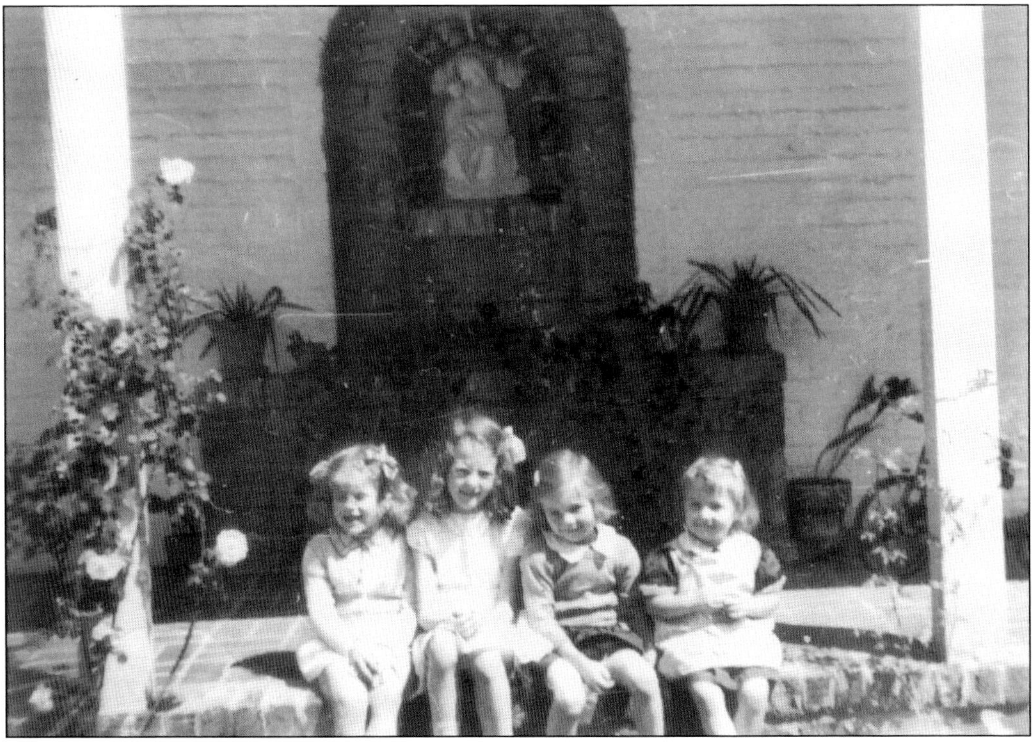

From left to right, Ellen Rogers, Helen Hatch, Fairlie Lane, and Elizabeth Lane sit in front of a Della Robia garden alcove at Hazel Hedge in the 1930s. Hazel Hedge, a well-loved collection of cottages owned and rented by Jean Read, stood at the end of College Avenue. (Courtesy Sallie Millsap and Fairlie Haynes.)

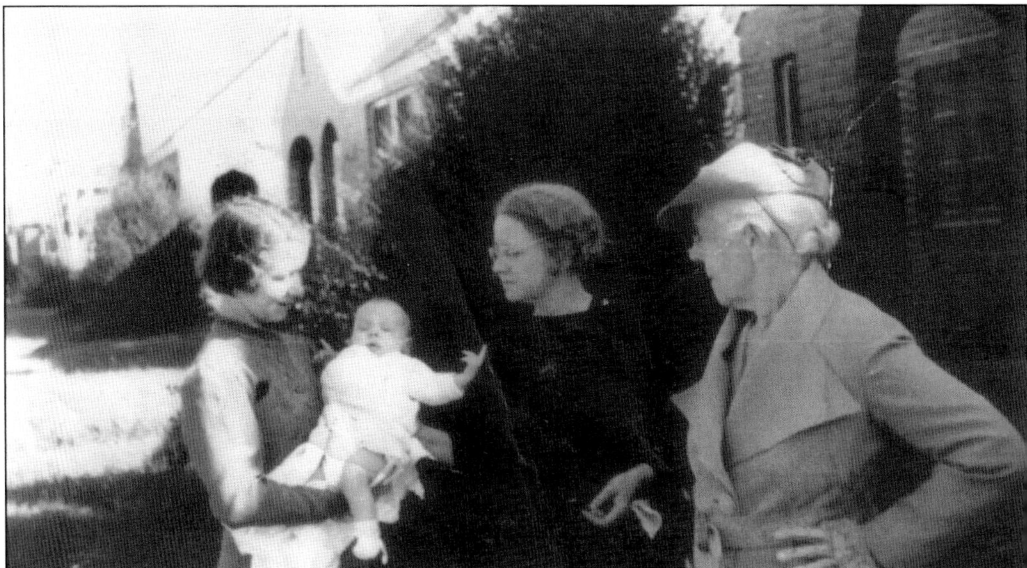

Four generations of women stand close to the Crenshaw family home, Stonecroft, on Narrow Lane Road in the summer of 1937. They are, from left to right, Mollie Cottle holding Barbara (Babs) Cottle, Babs Shepard, and Mollie Crenshaw. (Courtesy Barbara Moore.)

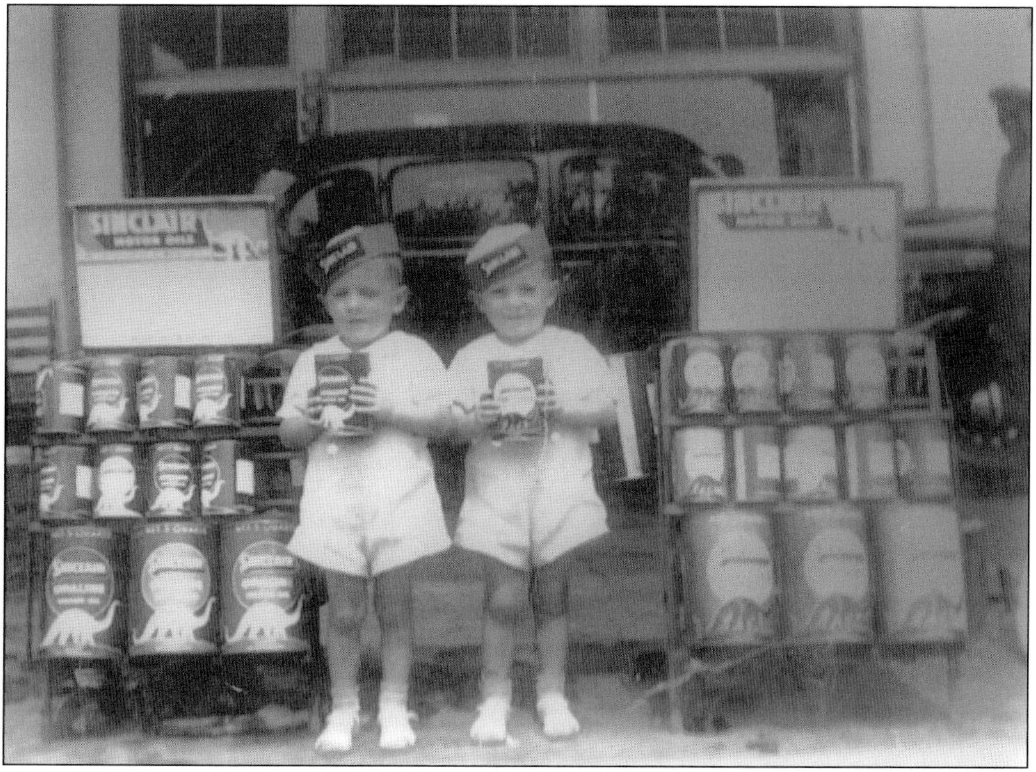

The Williamson twins pose for an advertisement for Sinclair Motor Oil in front of Sinclair's filling station. (Courtesy Sinclair's Restaurant.)

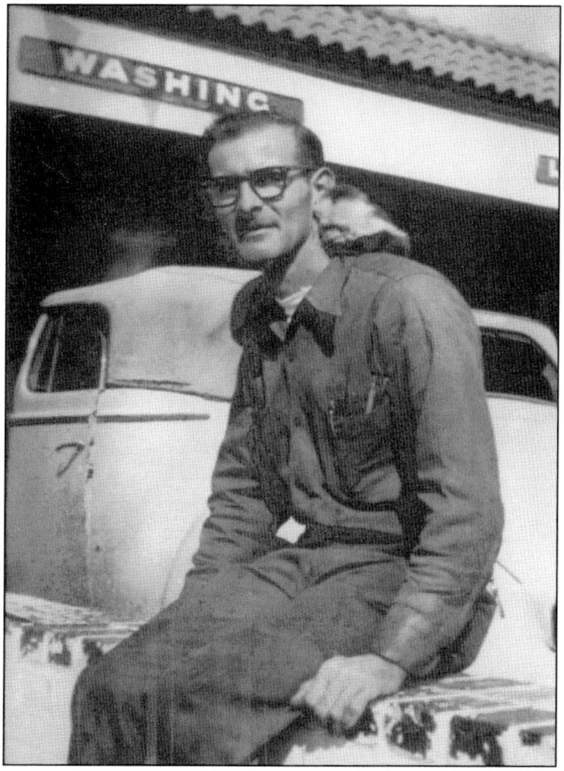

eff, the service attendant at Sinclair's illing station at the corner of Fairview nd Boultier Avenues, is shown ere with his pet monkey, Pedro. Courtesy Sinclair's Restaurant.)

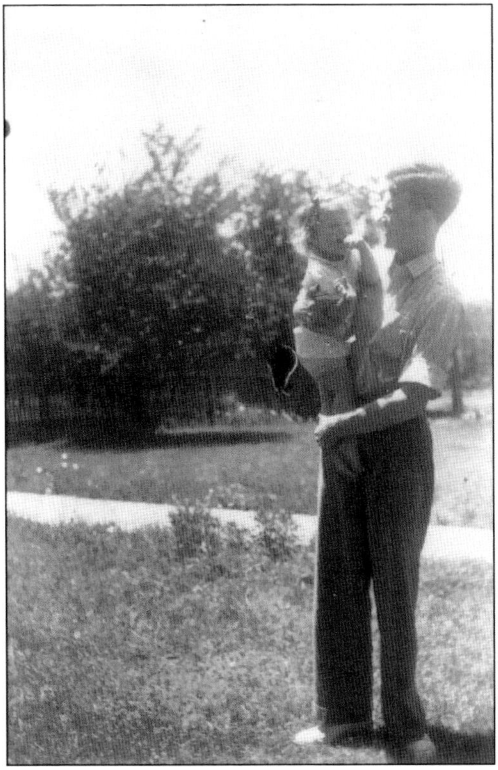

Herbert Morton stands on the lawn and holds his baby daughter, Gerry, in 1938. (Courtesy Barbara Moore.)

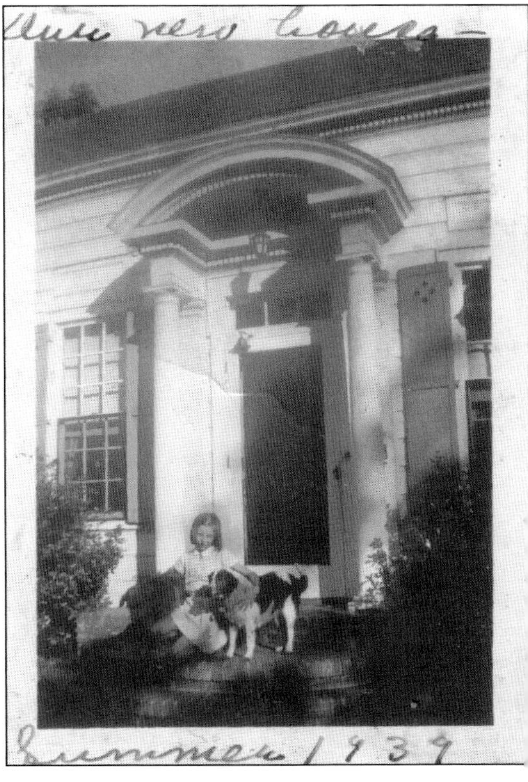

The Wood family moved to their new home at 910 Park Avenue in the summer 1939. Sallie Wood sits on the front steps with Spot. (Courtesy Sallie Millsap.)

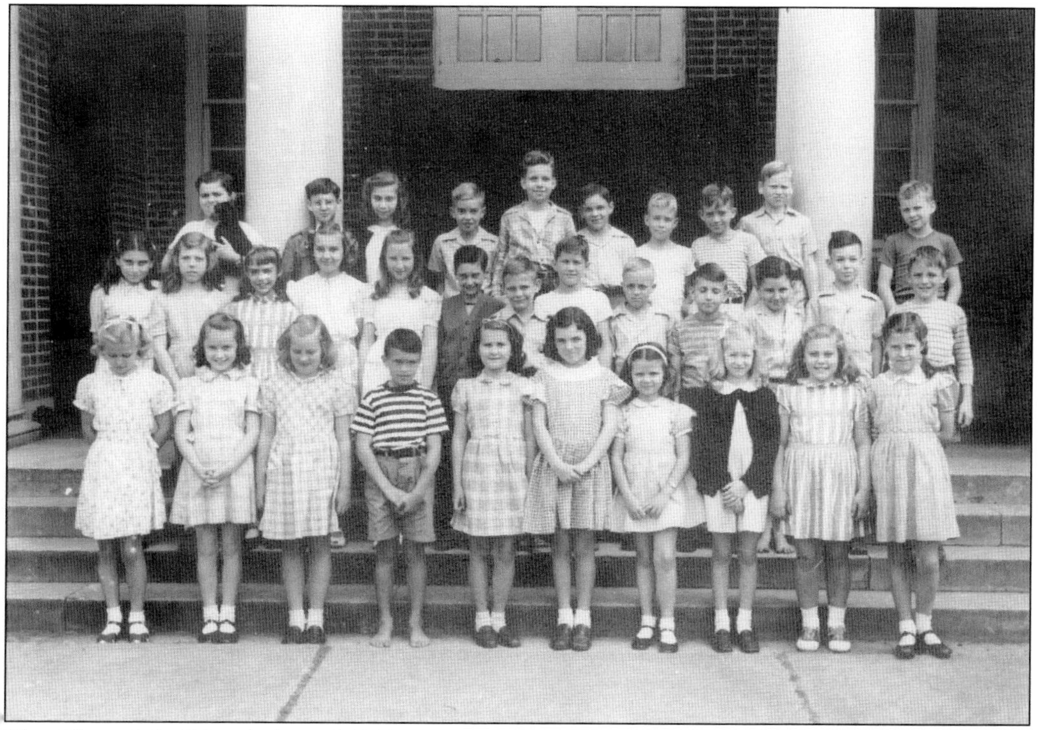

The Cloverdale School class of 1940 poses for its group photograph in front of Cloverdale School on Fairview Avenue. (Courtesy MCHS.)

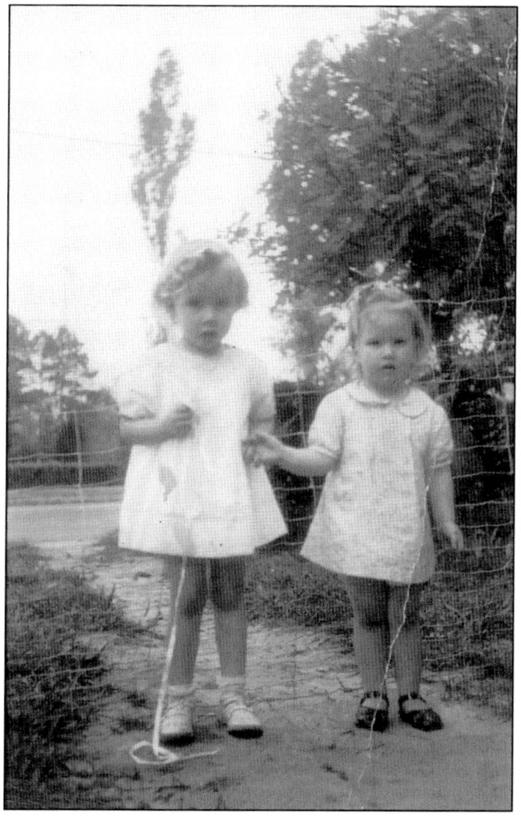

ɪest friends and neighbors Barbara (Babs) ;ottle (left) and Gerry Morton stop playing ɔng enough for this picture to be taken ı 1940. (Courtesy Barbara Moore.)

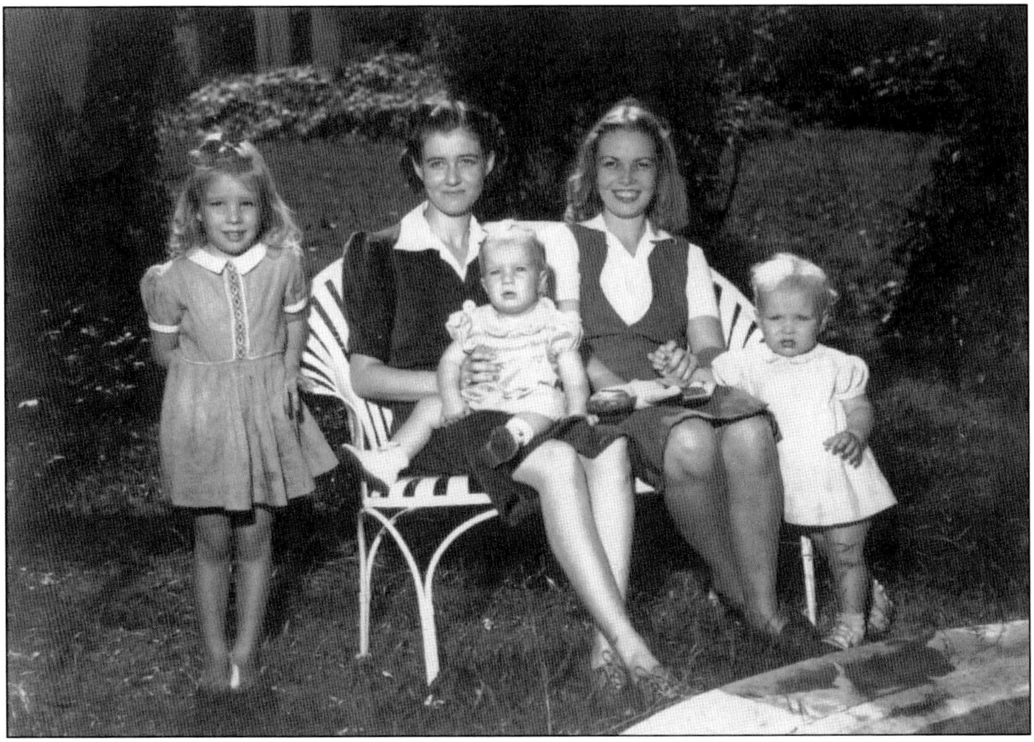

Posing in the side yard of the Crenshaw family home, Stonecroft, on Narrow Lane Road in 1942 are, from left to right, Barbara (Babs) Cottle, Mollie Shepard Cottle holding Betty Cottle, Anne Shepard Lawn, and Priscilla Lawn. (Courtesy Barbara Moore.)

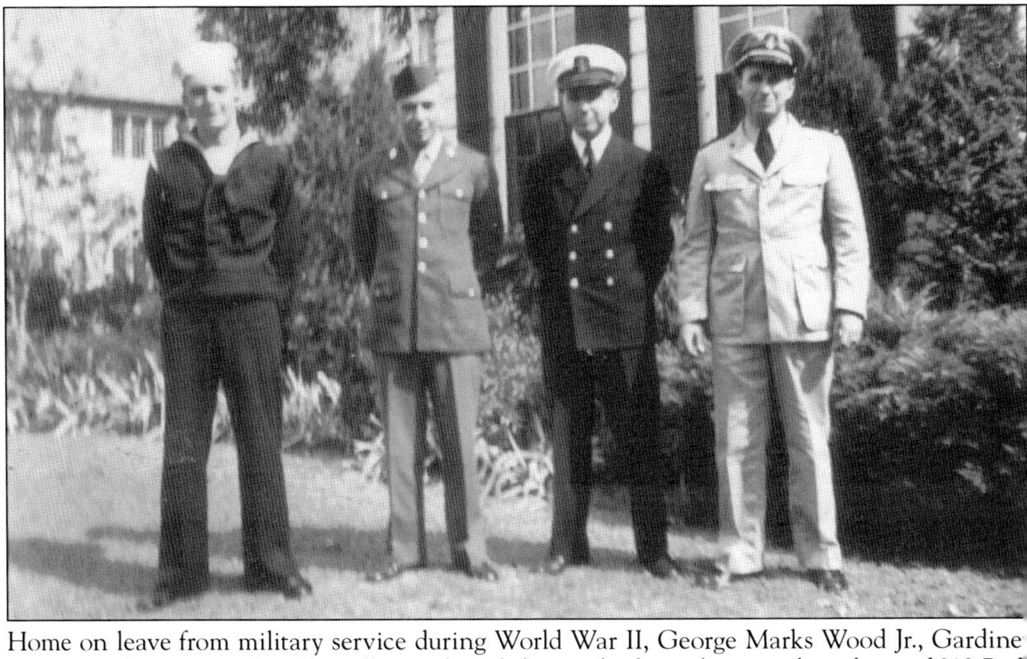

Home on leave from military service during World War II, George Marks Wood Jr., Gardine Parker, Dick Rives, and Wiley Hill pose from left to right for a photograph in front of 910 Par Avenue. Note First Methodist Church in background. (Courtesy Sallie Millsap.)

Frank Broadway Jr. stands with his bicycle in front of Cloverdale School in 1945. (Courtesy Frank Broadway Jr.)

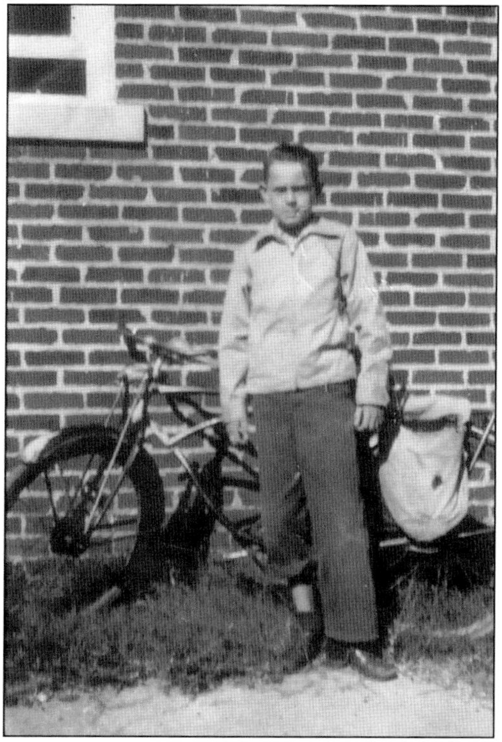

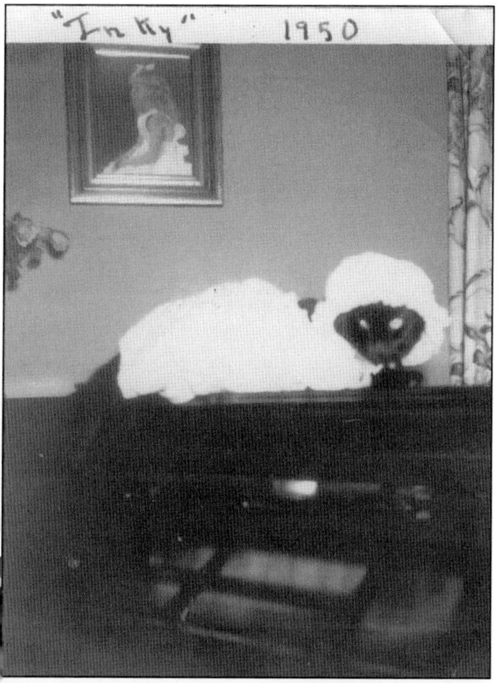

Families in Cloverdale enjoyed their pets. This photograph shows Betty Cottle's cat, Inky, dressed in baby clothes and happily resting in his favorite place on top of the piano. (Courtesy Barbara Moore.)

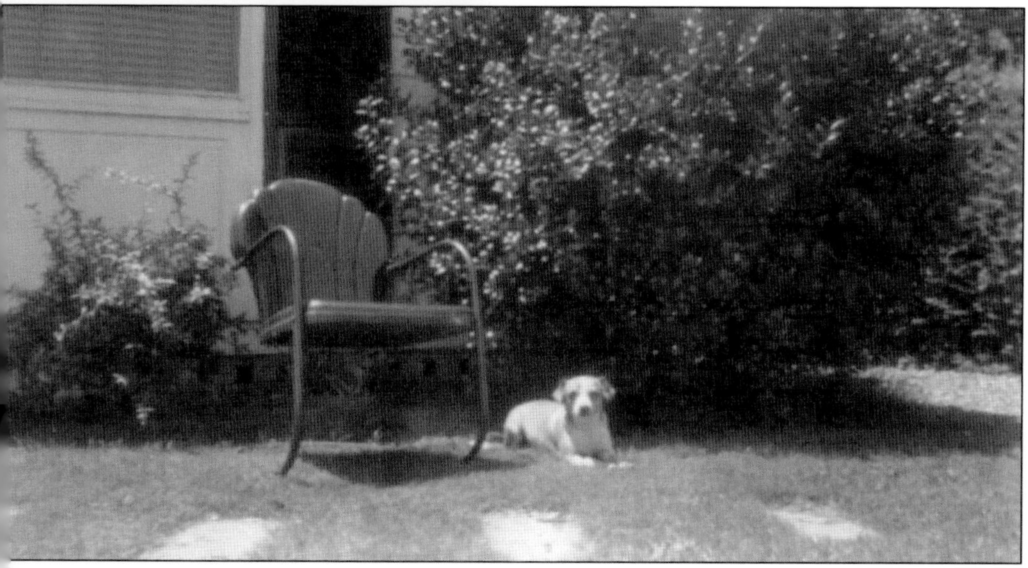

'he Broadway family dog waits for company beside a lawn chair at 1248 Westmoreland Avenue ı 1949. (Courtesy Frank Broadway Jr.)

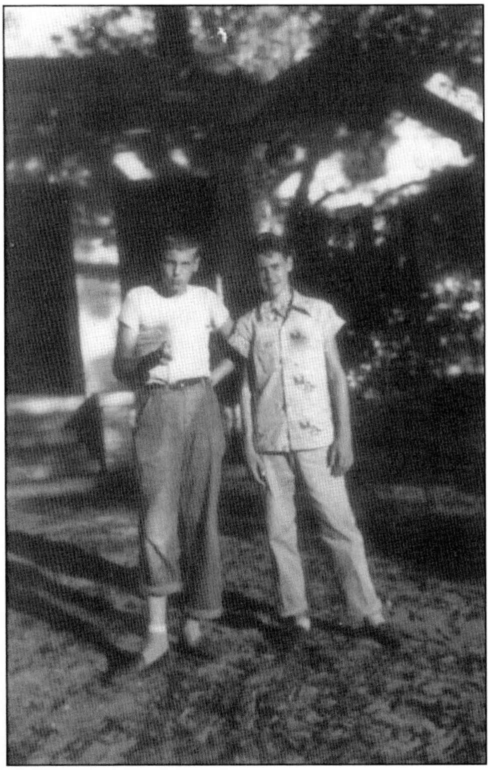

Bill Buettman (left) and Frank Broadway Jr. stand under the huge willow oak on Cloverdale Road in 1949. The willow oak is reputed to be the second largest in the county. (Courtesy Frank Broadway Jr.)

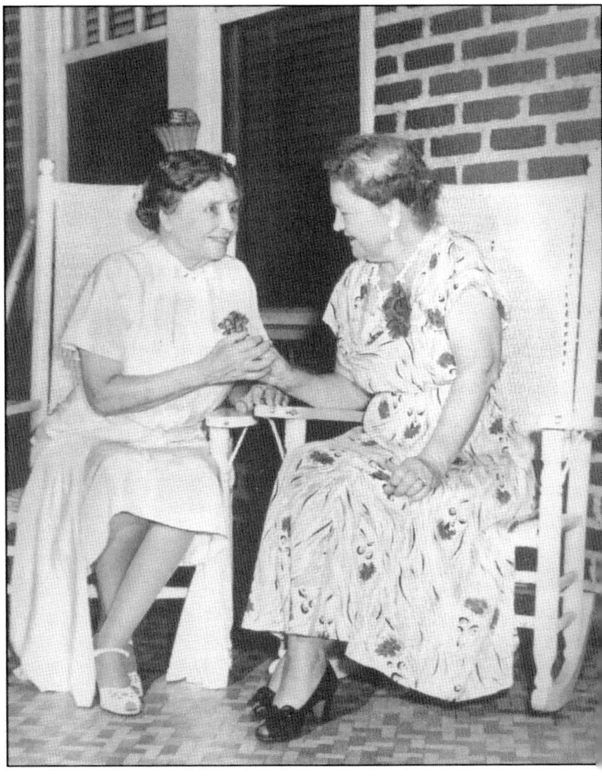

Helen Keller (left) and her sister, Mildred Keller Tyson, sit on the front porch of 831 Felder Avenue in 1955. Helen, a frequent visitor, enjoyed the company of her nieces, Mildred's three daughters—Patty, Mildred, and Katherine. (Courtesy Leslie McPhillips.)

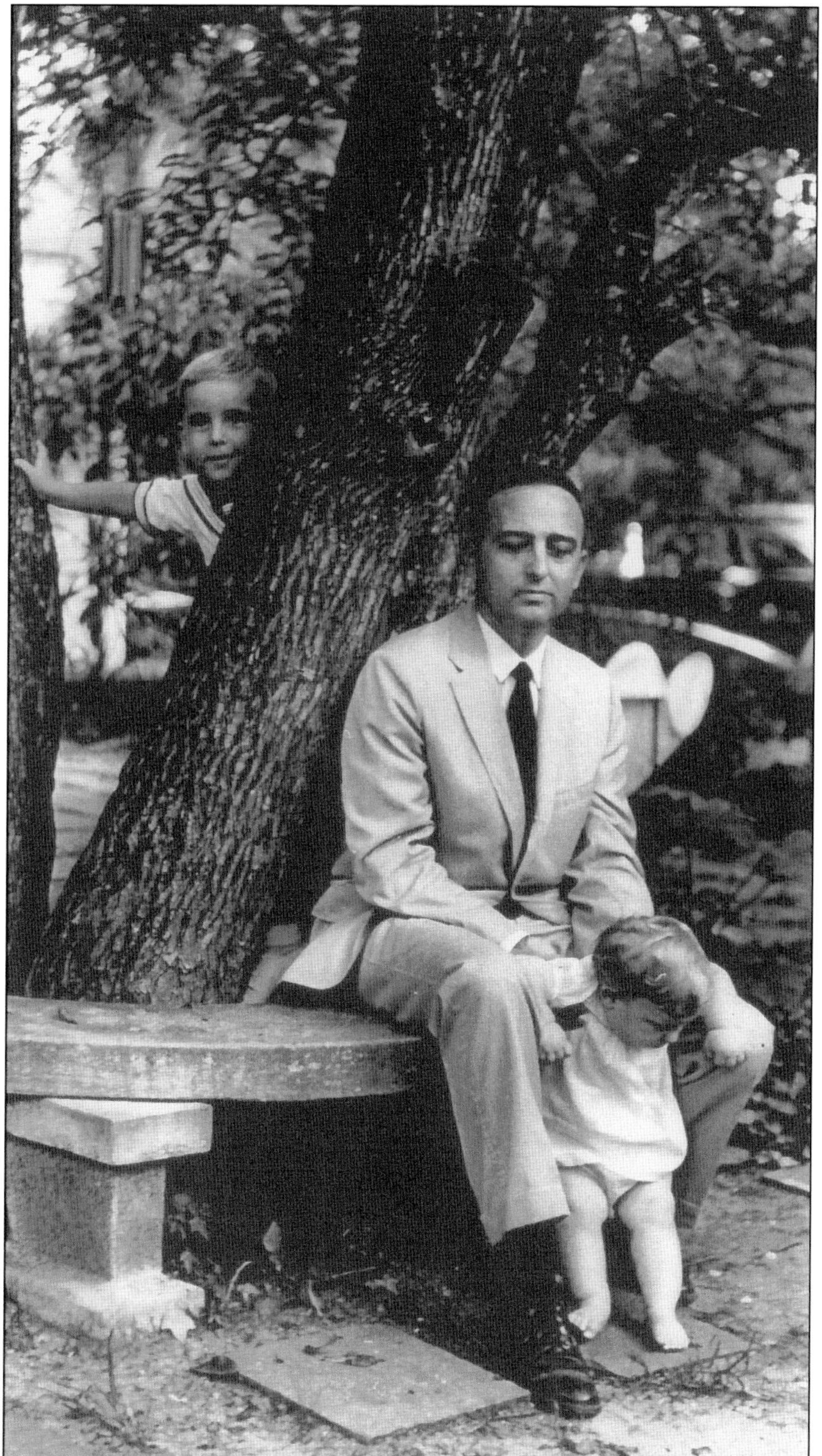

Gene Millsap sits on the bench in the 1960s under the mock orange tree at Hazel Hedge with his small sons, Temple (left) and Mark. (Courtesy Sallie Millsap.)

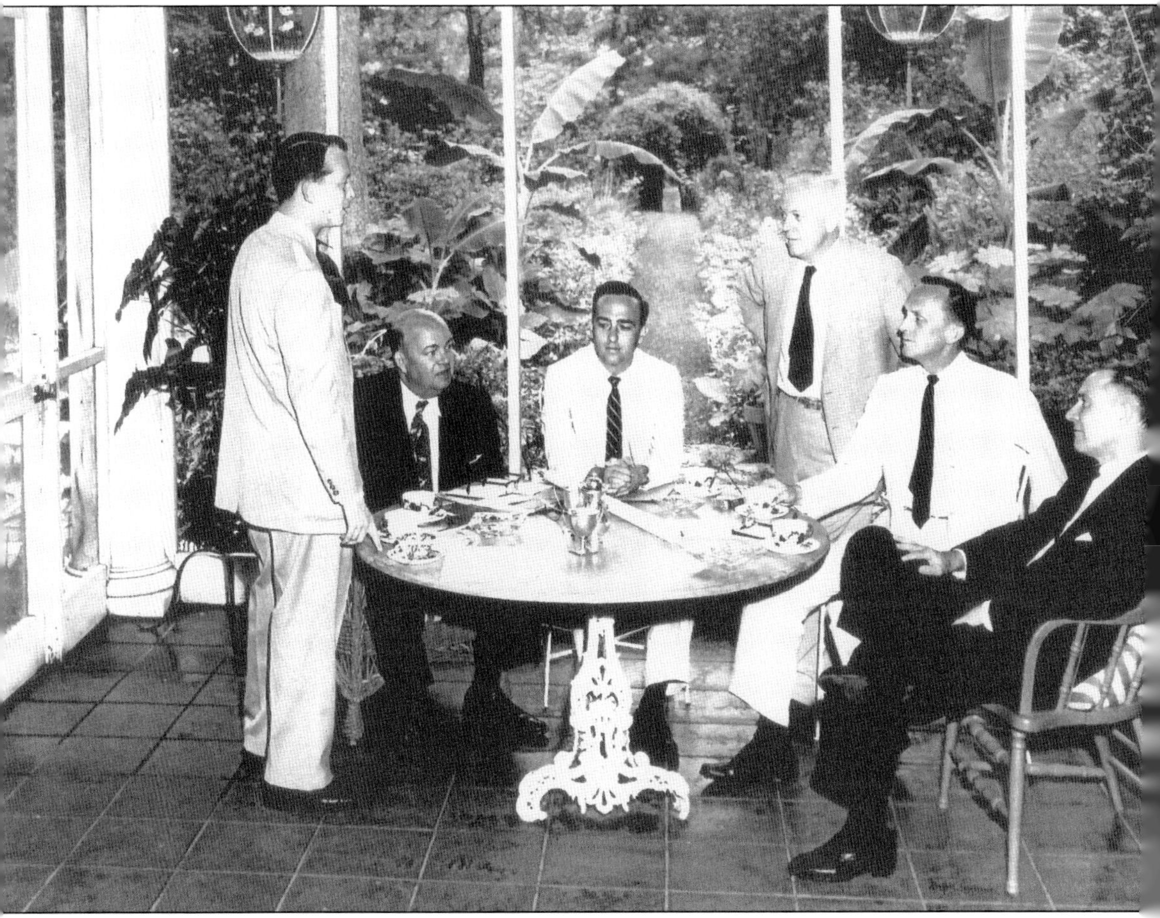

The architectural firm of Sherlock, Smith, and Adams enjoyed board meetings at Miss Jean's screen porch at Hazel Hedge around the 1960s. From left to right are John Shaffer, Dick Adams, Gene Millsap, Moreland Smith, Charles Kelley, and Colquitt Lane. (Courtesy Sallie Millsap.)

Eight

Capitol Heights

Capitol Heights was named for both its proximity to downtown and the fact that its location is 150 feet higher than the main part of the capital city. In this postcard, Col. J. S. Pinkard's home, Rockhaven, the Van Pelt home, and trolley tracks are visible on Madison Avenue. Col. J. S. Pinkard, one of Capitol Heights' developers and prominent residents, donated land for the elementary school and served as mayor. (Courtesy James Bozeman.)

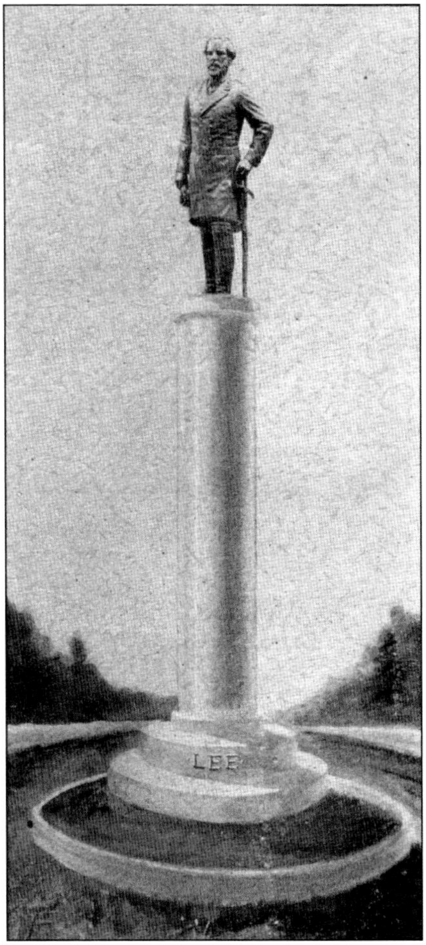

The statue of Robert E. Lee marked the new residential area, Lee Place, on North Madison Terrace (formerly Vickers Street). This photograph is from the program of the unveiling ceremony held on June 12, 1908. The Lee statue now stands in front of Robert E. Lee High School. (Courtesy Landmarks Foundation of Montgomery.)

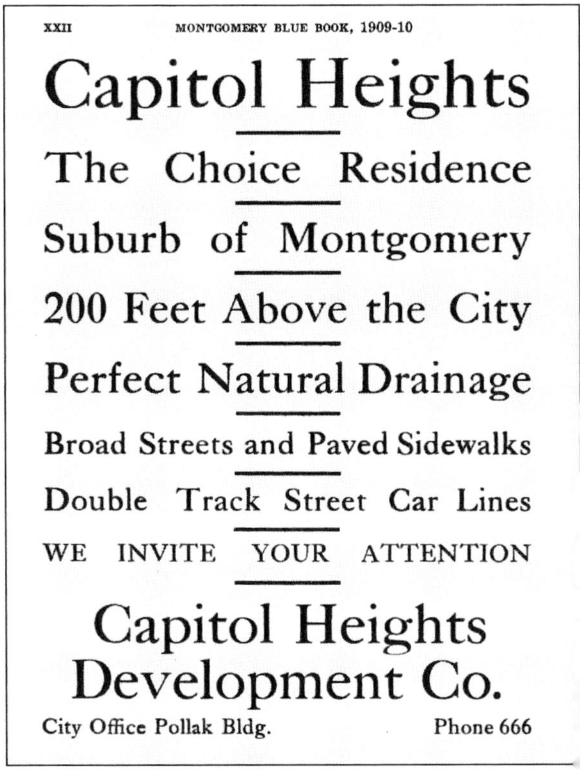

Capitol Heights' advertisements promoted its higher elevation from downtown Montgomery. Residential areas near downtown endured constant threats from mosquitoes and yellow fever due to their close proximity to the Alabama River. Anyone reading the advertisement's references to the "height" in Capitol Heights understood that its location offered clean air and cool breezes. (Courtesy Landmarks Foundation of Montgomery.)

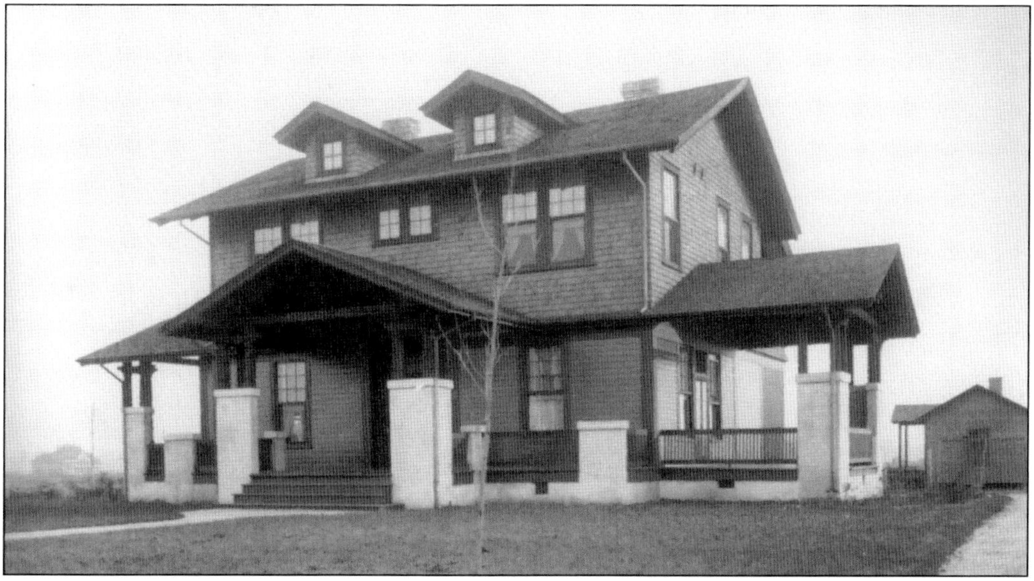

The William H. Ragland House on Madison Avenue was included in the 1907 gravure photographs taken of outstanding homes in Montgomery. (Courtesy Art Work Collection.)

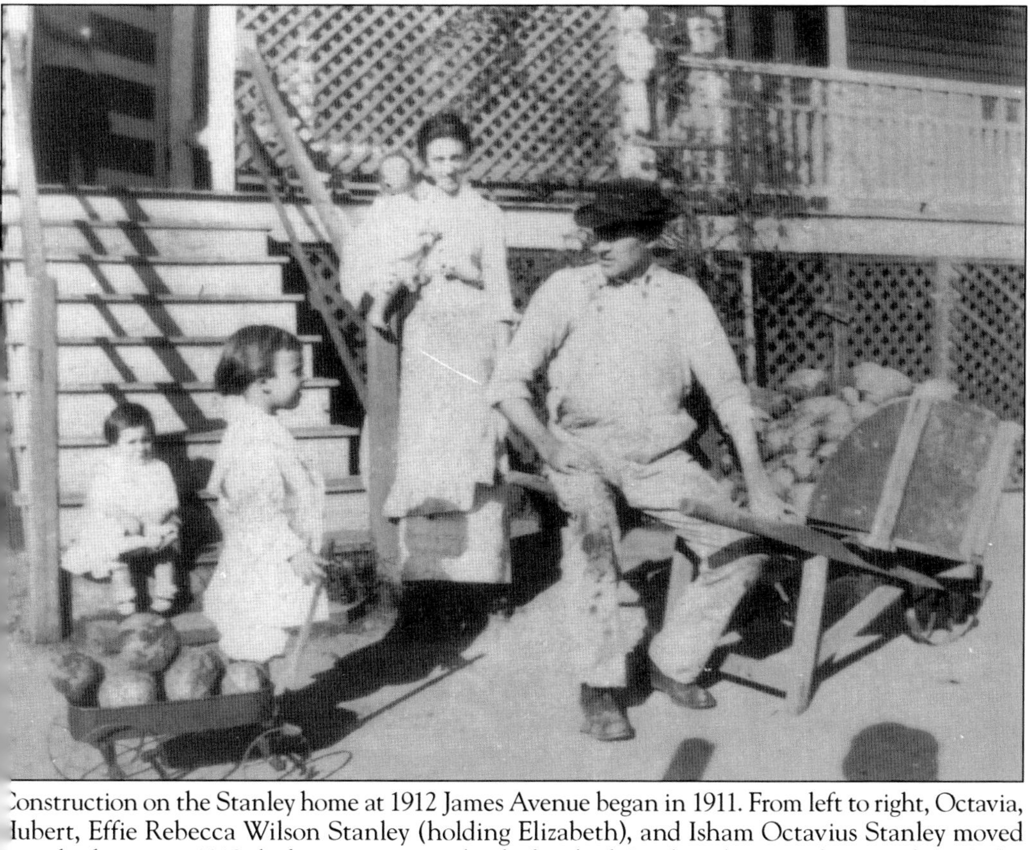

;onstruction on the Stanley home at 1912 James Avenue began in 1911. From left to right, Octavia, lubert, Effie Rebecca Wilson Stanley (holding Elizabeth), and Isham Octavius Stanley moved ıto the house in 1912, before it was completely finished. In this photograph around 1915, the ımily harvests sweet potatoes at the back of their house. (Courtesy Stanley family collection.)

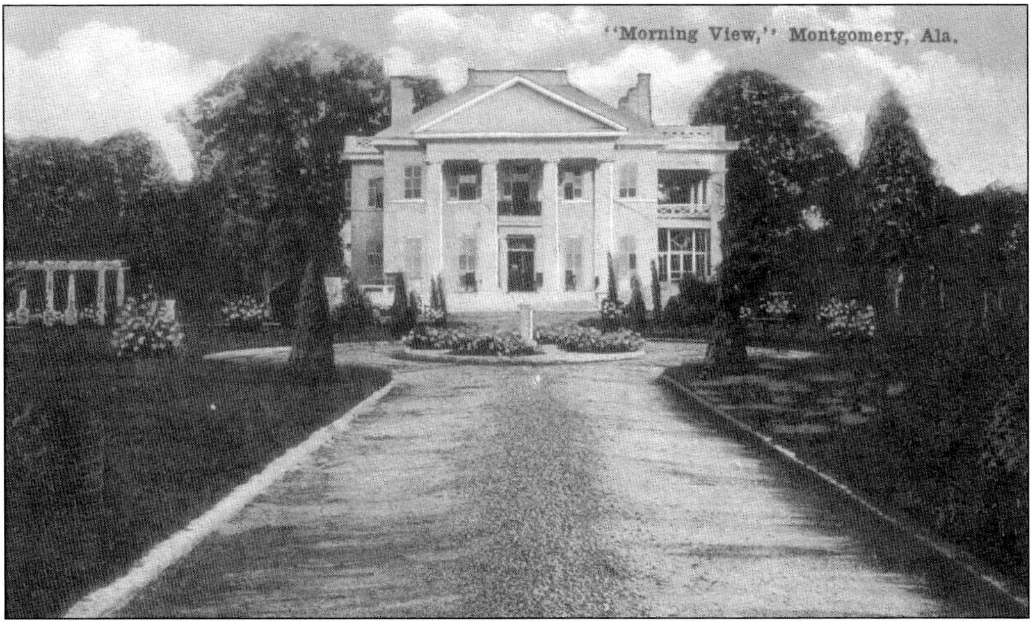

Morning View, the home of Gen. Mitchell B. Houghton, stood at the far boundary of Capitol Heights where Ann Street and Madison Avenue now intersect. The home was built in 1915 over the basement of an antebellum structure and was surrounded by over 100 acres of fruit trees and gardens. (Courtesy MCHS.)

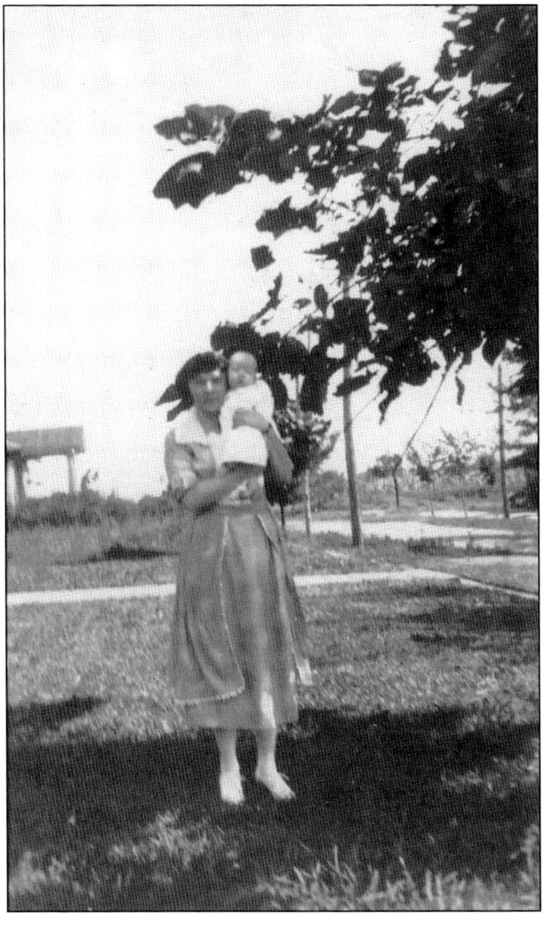

Danylou Belser holds George Quiggin Jr. in the side yard of the Belser House at 103 North Lewis Street around 1915. Architect Richard Whaley designed and built the home for himself in 1908. The Belser family bought the home and lived there until 1993. (Courtesy Fred Williams, Bobby Golden, and Wendy Slaton.)

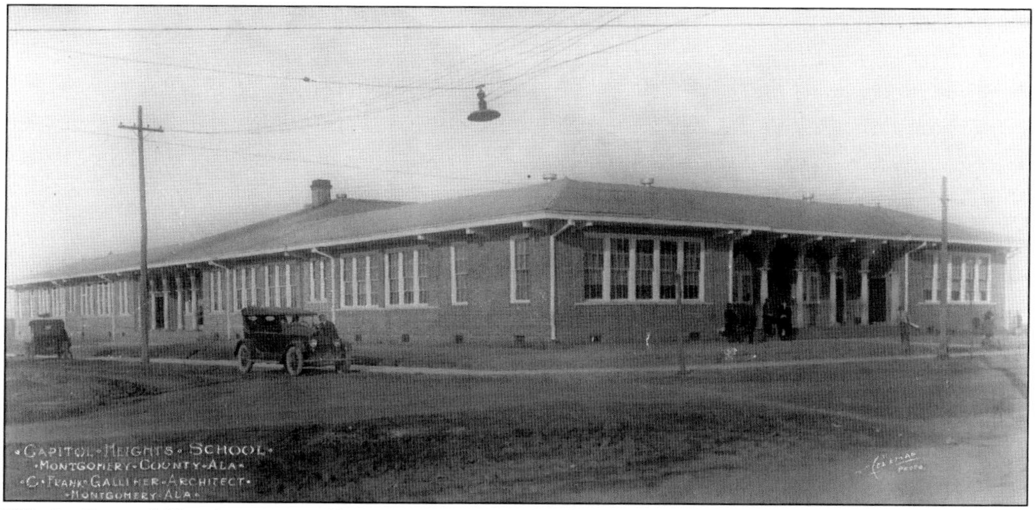

While Capitol Heights was still a new town, city leaders donated land for an elementary school. The community partnered with the Montgomery County Board of Education and built Capitol Heights Elementary School. Designed by architect C. Frank Galliher, the school opened in the fall of 1917. Capitol Heights Elementary School attracted national attention as the first unit of consolidation of Montgomery County Schools. (Courtesy Landmarks Foundation.)

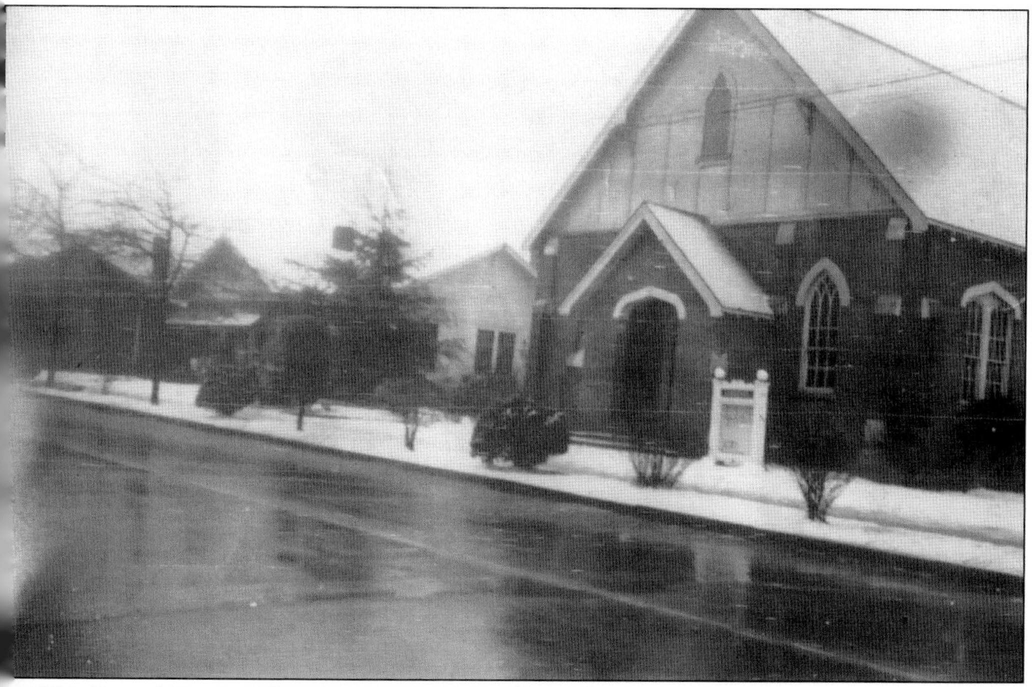

ı 1924, Capitol Heights United Methodist Church was the first church built in the Capitol Heights eighborhood. The original building stood facing Winona Avenue at the corner of Florida and Vinona Avenues. (Courtesy Capitol Heights United Methodist Church.)

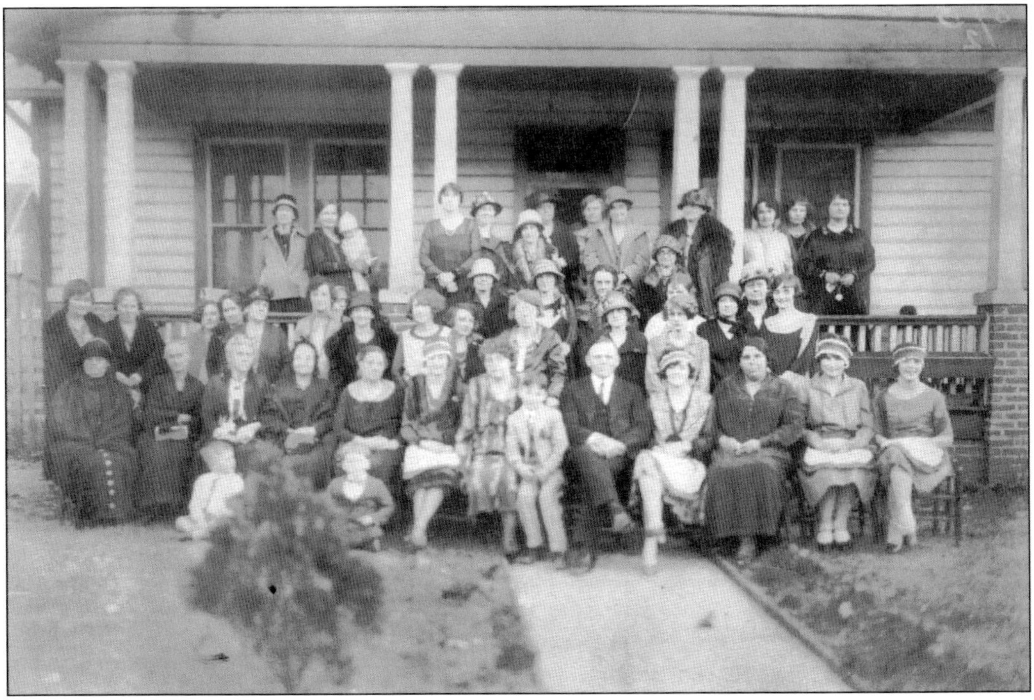

Capitol Heights United Methodist Church members gather in front of the parsonage on Winona Avenue. (Courtesy Capitol Heights United Methodist Church.)

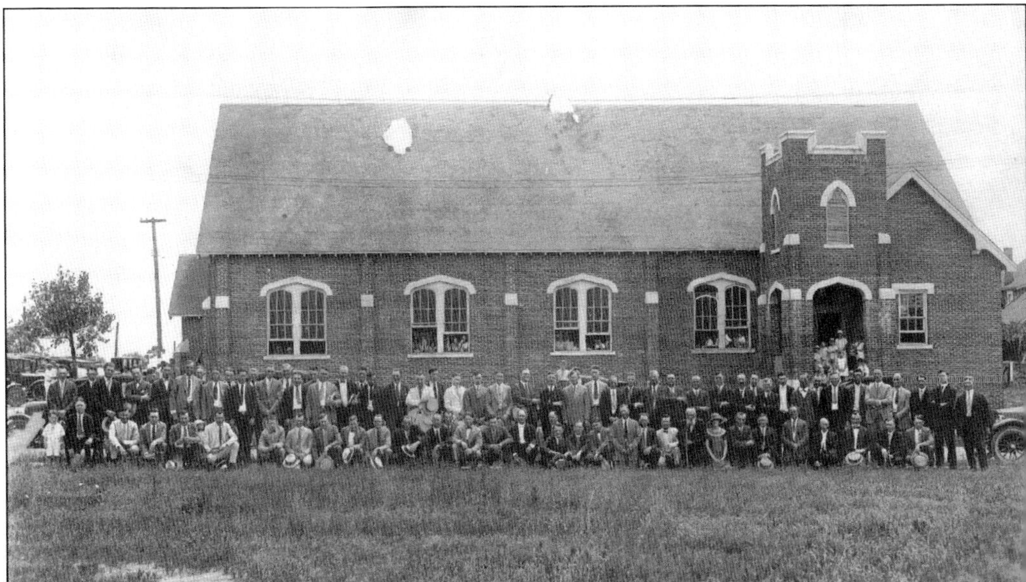

Capitol Heights United Methodist Church members pose on the Florida Street side of the church around 1923. (Courtesy Capitol Heights United Methodist Church.)

In this photograph, Ruby Lee Hattemer pretends to be a cowgirl. Perhaps posing for this photograph with a pony made an impression upon her, because when she grew up and married James. P, Richardson, they went to Arizona to homestead. After retirement in 1922, they returned to the home on 1701 Madison Avenue. (Courtesy Richardson family collection.)

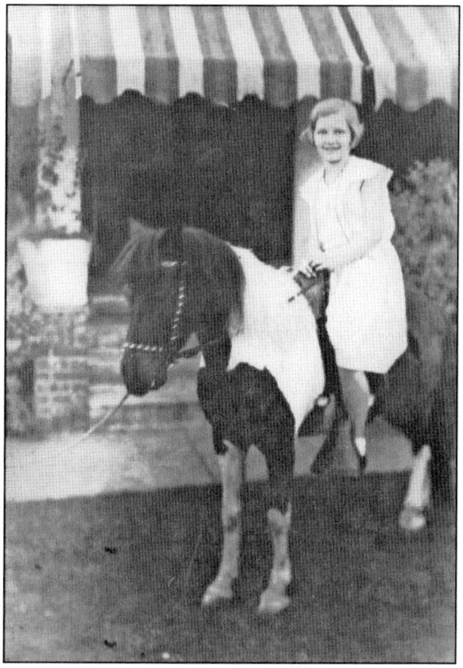

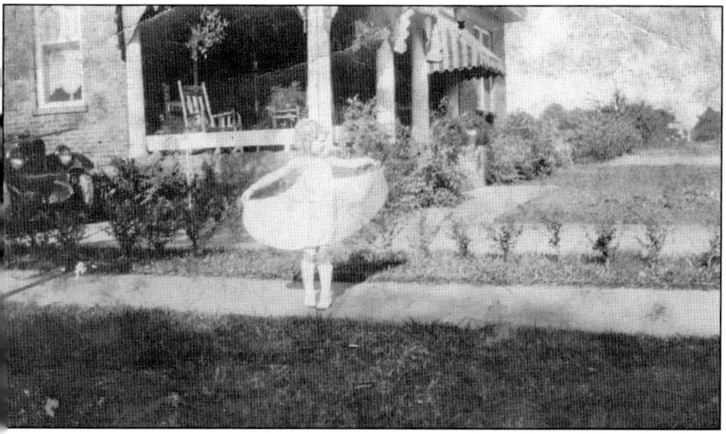

Ruby Lee Hattemer's parents bought their home in 1922. Ruby grew up in the Capitol Heights neighborhood and attended Capitol Heights Elementary School and Capitol Heights Junior High School. Here, however, Ruby is simply happy being a little girl in front of her home at 1701 Madison Avenue. (Courtesy Richardson family collection.)

The Children's Home was founded n 1918 by the Montgomery ederation of Women's Clubs n association with several city gencies. Property on Upper Vetumpka Road was purchased o allow "country life [to] ontribute to the improvement nd development of the little nes." (Courtesy Landmarks oundation of Montgomery.)

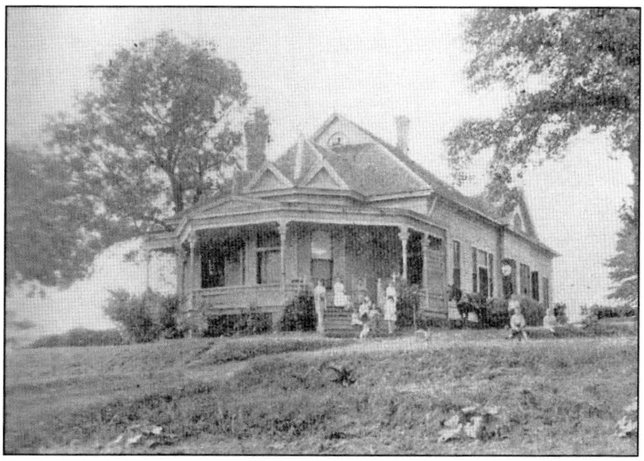

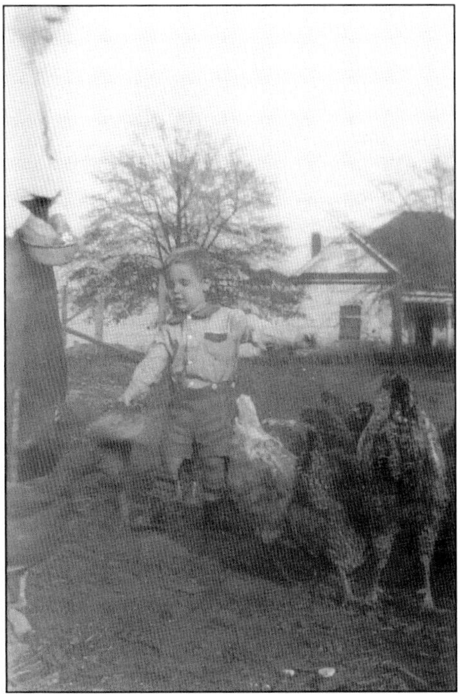

Marvin Hunter Pearson stands in front of his home on Lassester Street on June 10, 1920. Lassester Street was named for Frank S. Lassester, a prominent contractor who built many home in Capitol Heights. (Courtesy Pearson family collection.)

In February 1927, Marvin Pearson and his son, Bill, visit the chickens on Lassester Street, which is now called North Capitol Parkway. (Courtesy Pearson family collection.)

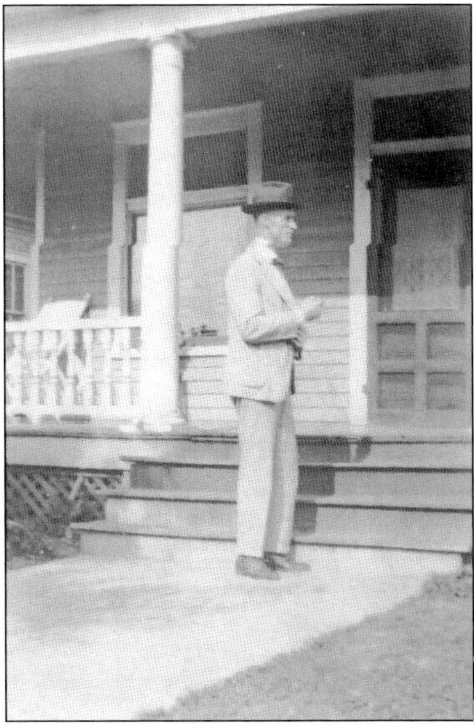

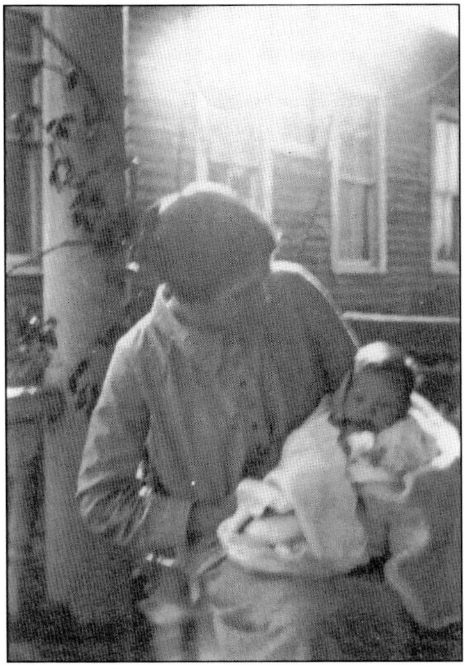

Lena Collins Pearson stands on her porch of her home on Lassester Street with her baby, William Marvin Pearson, in January 1925. The house is lost to the neighborhood, but the houses on either side of it are still homes of Capitol Heights residents. (Courtesy Pearson family collection.)

Capitol Heights Baptist Church organized in 1934 and met in Capitol Heights Elementary School. Land was purchased from H. S. Houghton (of Morning View). The cornerstone was laid in 1937. (Courtesy Capitol Heights Baptist Church.)

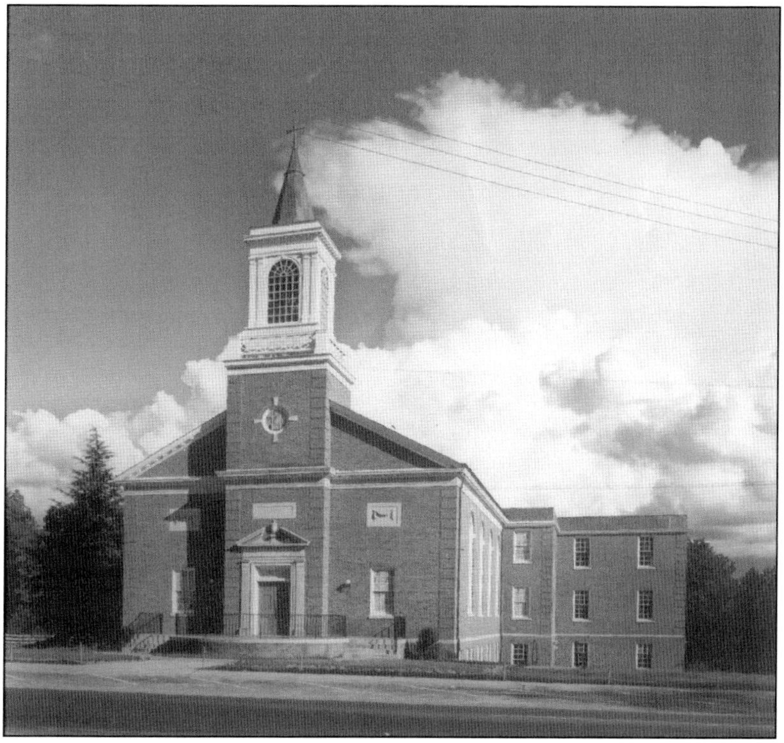

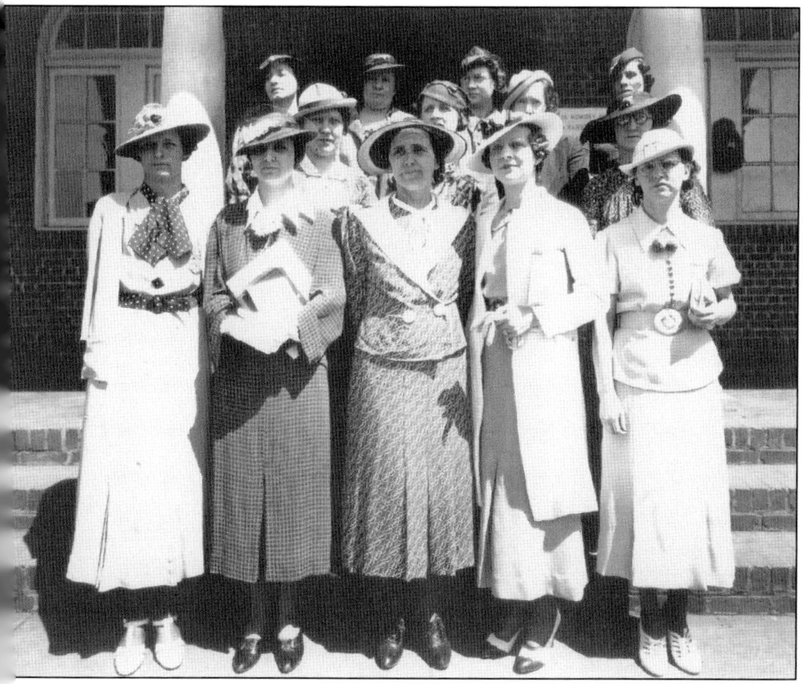

In 1935, the Phebean Class, Mrs. T. H. Temple's Sunday school class, posed for a photograph in front of the Capitol Heights Elementary School where they met. (Courtesy Capitol Heights Baptist Church.)

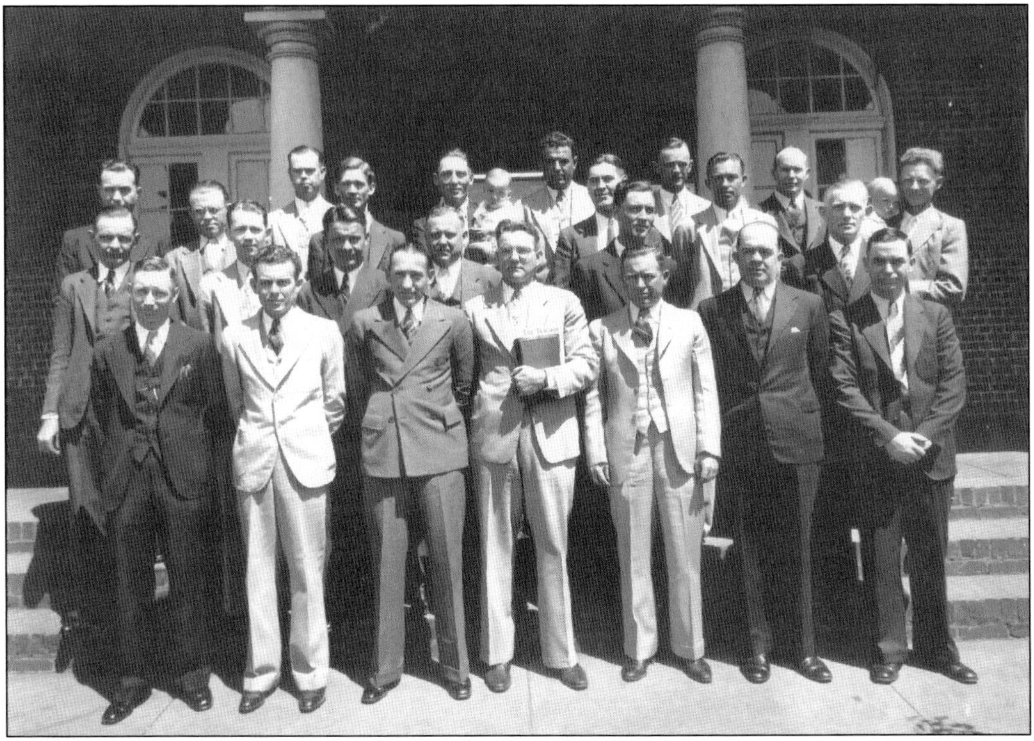

In 1935, the Good Fellows Bible Class, taught by Harry J. Weeks, posed for a photograph in front of the Capitol Heights Elementary School where they met. (Courtesy Capitol Heights Baptist Church.)

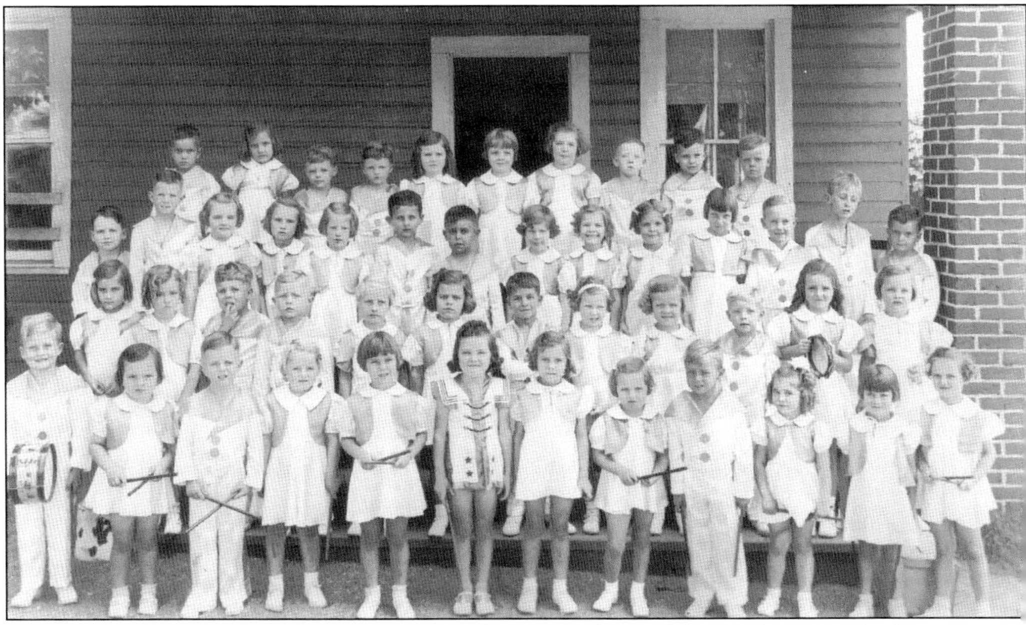

The Yancey Park Kindergarten Rhythm Band poses in front of the kindergarten building around 1938. The building still stands at the corner of North Madison Terrace and Upper Wetumpka Road. Yancey Park is now the site of the Children's Center of Montgomery. (Courtesy Ruth Ott.)

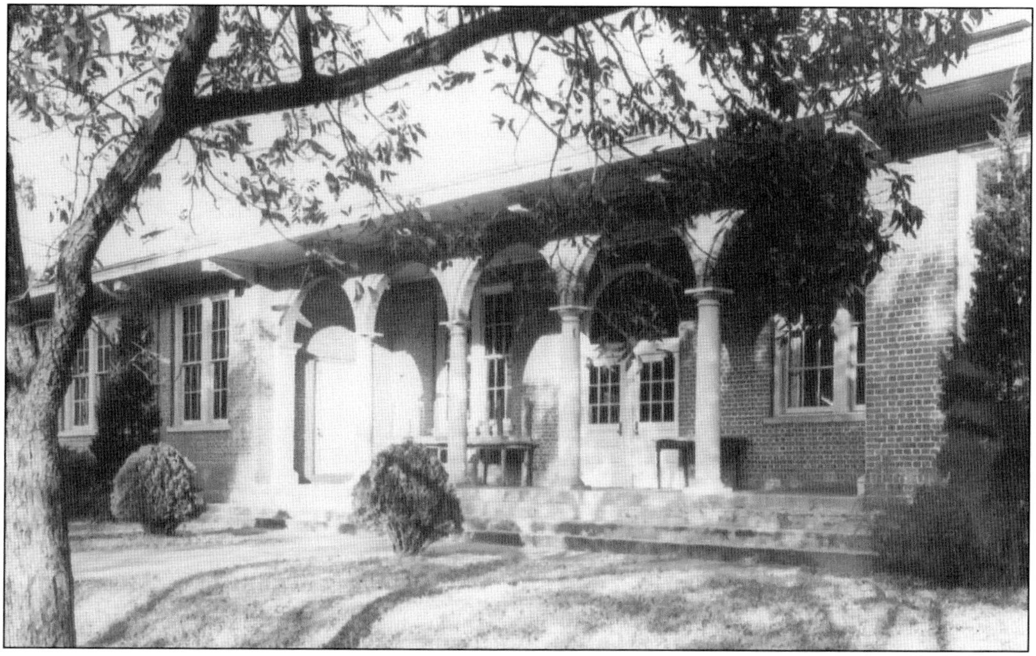

Capitol Heights Elementary School was well loved and well used by the community. This 1930s photograph was taken by the Capitol Heights Baptist Church to document its use of the facility on Sundays for the three years prior to the church being completed. (Courtesy Capitol Heights Baptist Church.)

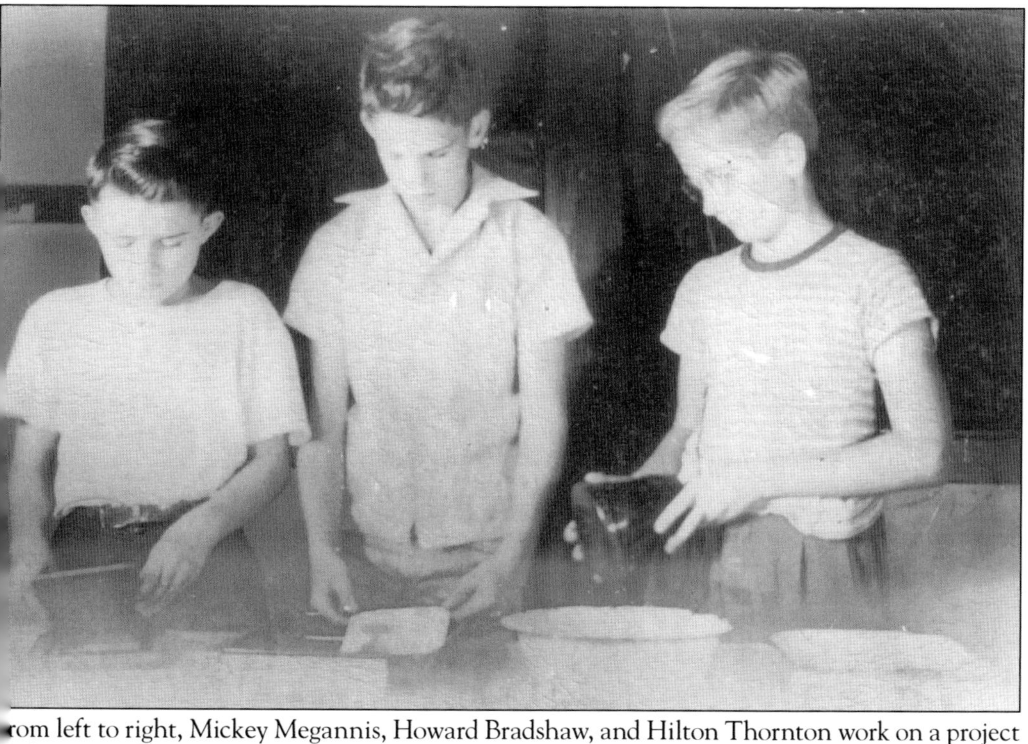

rom left to right, Mickey Megannis, Howard Bradshaw, and Hilton Thornton work on a project the Capitol Heights Elementary School in the 1930s. (Courtesy Howard Bradshaw.)

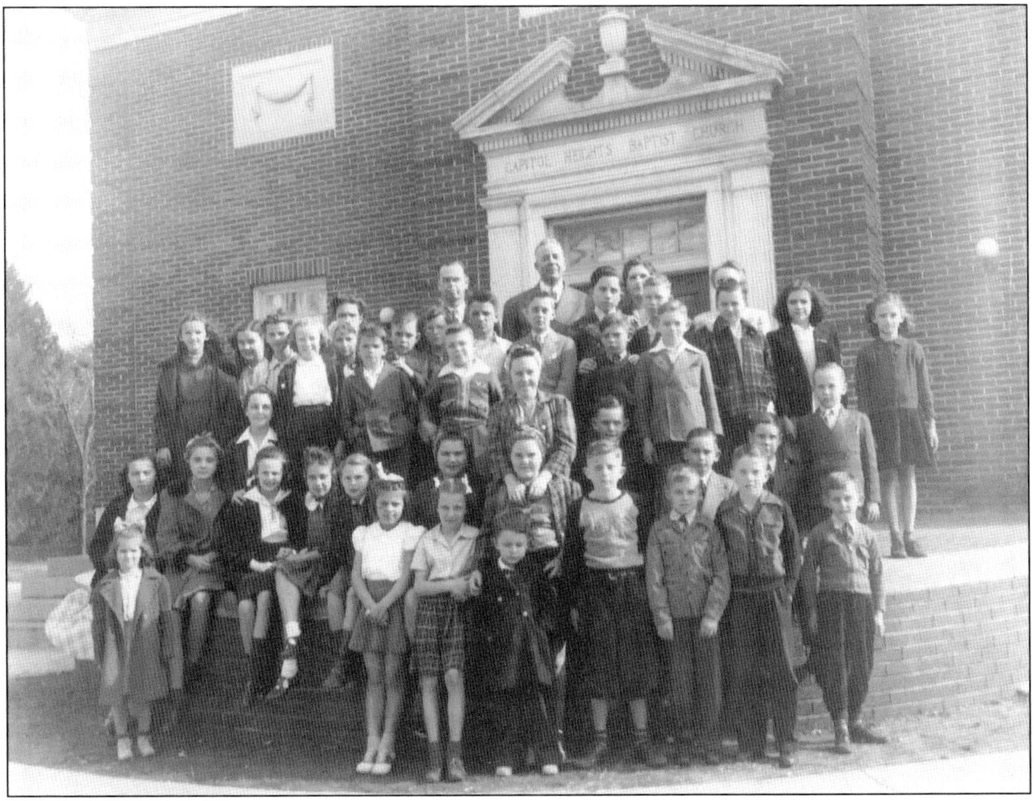

The children's Sunday school class poses in front of the Capitol Heights Baptist Church's new building around 1937. (Courtesy Capitol Heights Baptist Church.)

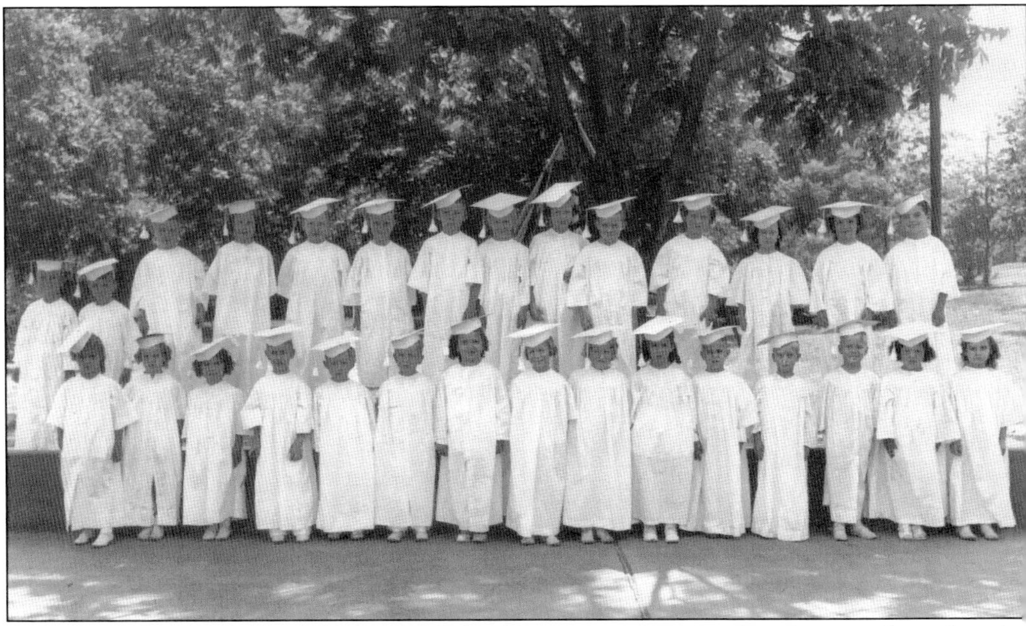

The 1940 graduating class of Yancey Park kindergarten gathers for this photograph at the edg of the basketball court behind the pavilion at Yancey Park. (Courtesy Ruth Ott.)

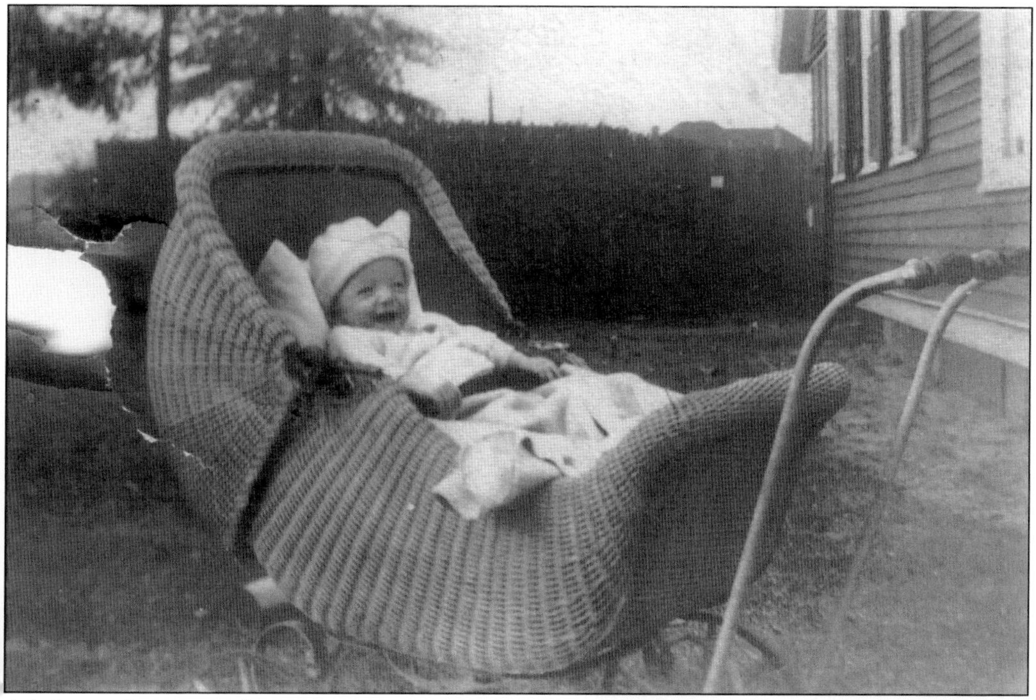

A baby smiles in a wicker carriage in the side yard of 401 St. Charles Avenue. (Courtesy Claire Bost Steindorf.)

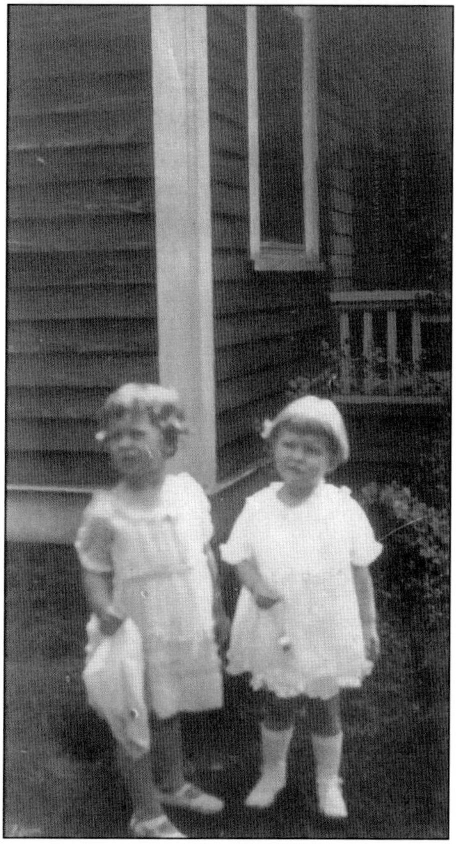

Martha Terry Bost (left) and Ann McMorris stand in the side yard of 401 St. Charles Avenue. (Courtesy Claire Bost Steindorf.)

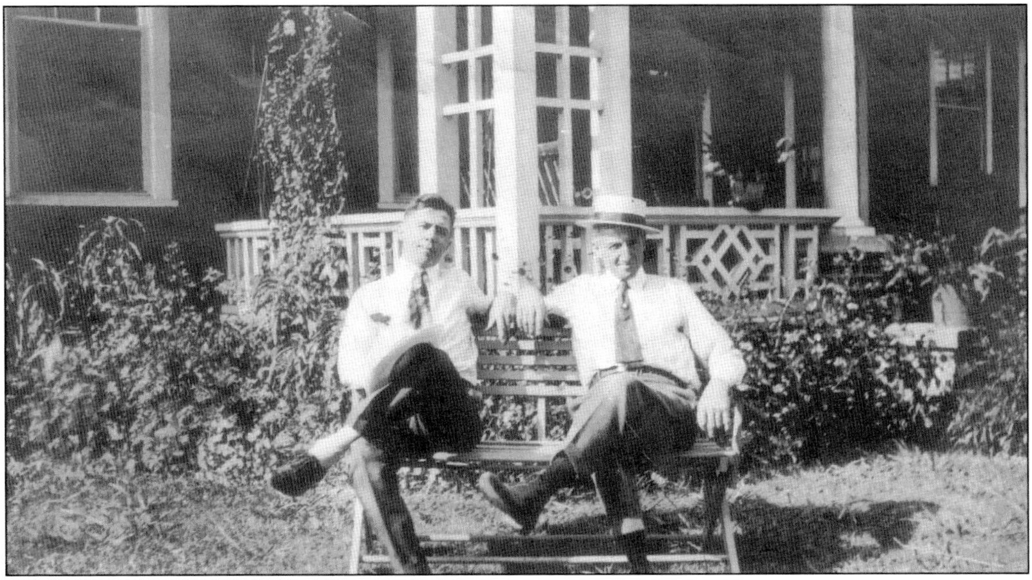

William Edward Bost (left) and his brother, Roy, rest on a bench in the yard of 401 St. Charles Avenue. (Courtesy Claire Bost Steindorf.)

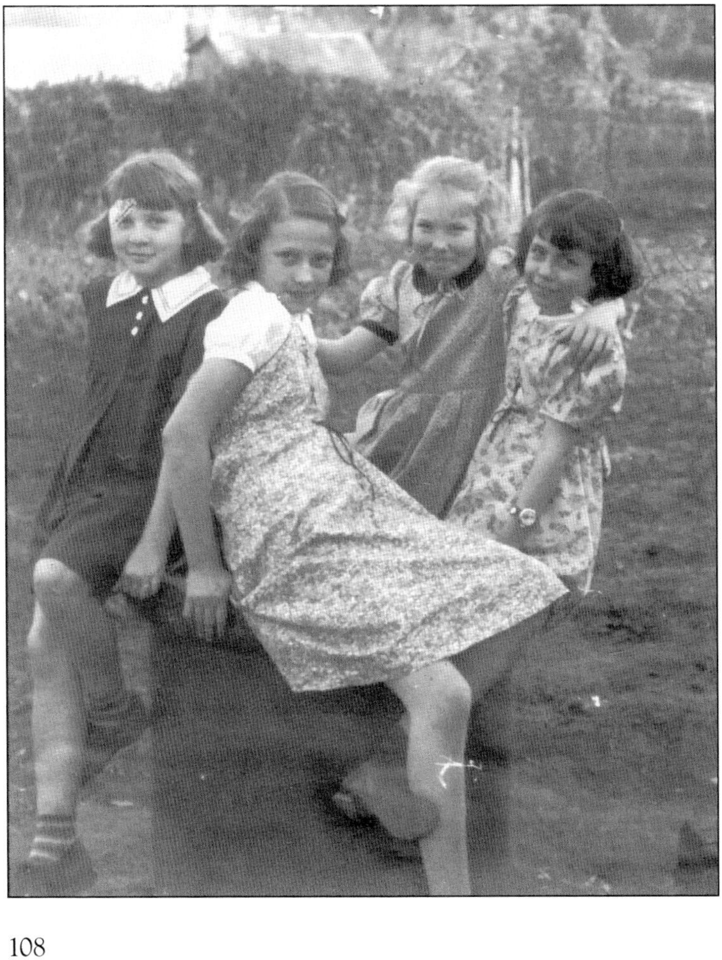

Neighborhood girlfriends from left to right, are unidentified, Mary Virginia Key, Tula Mae Williams, and Dot Bost. (Courtesy Claire Bost Steindorf.)

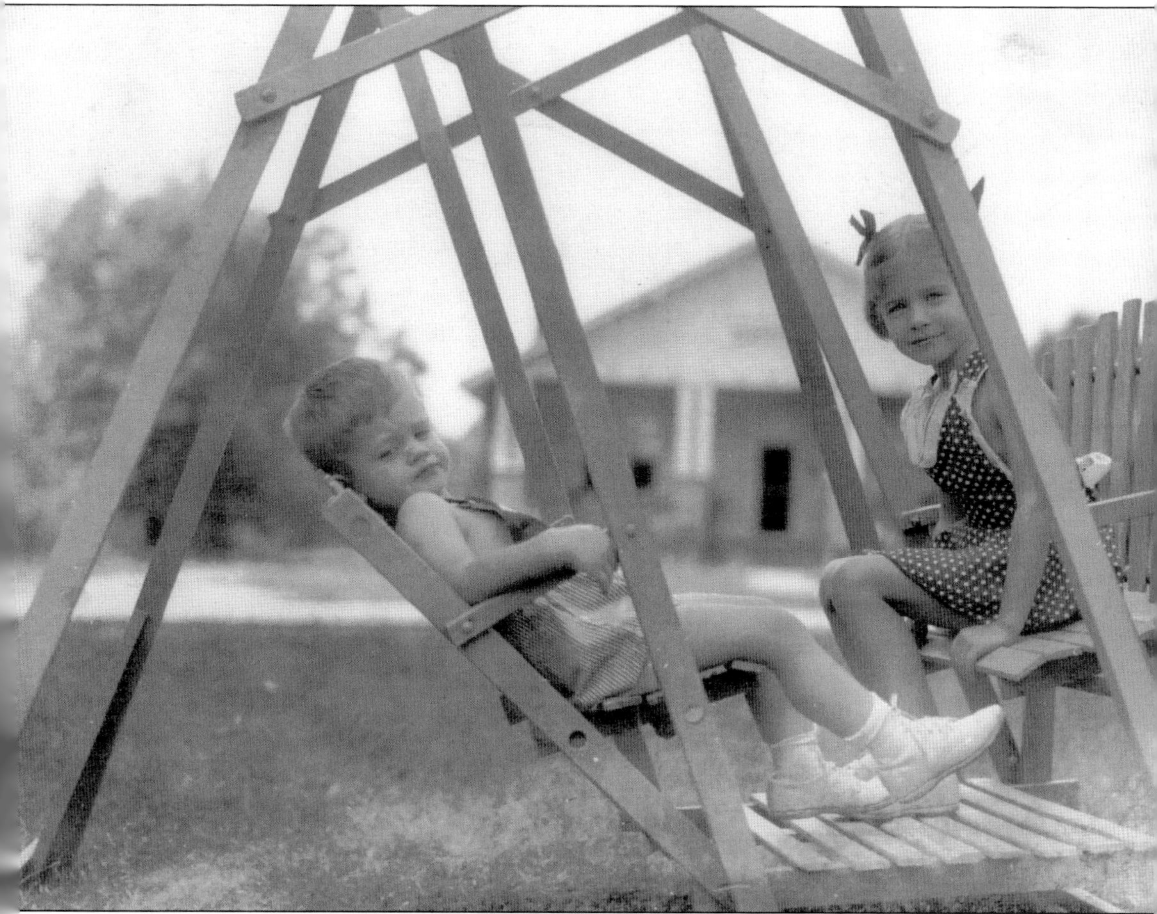

Neighborhood children enjoy the swing in the front yard of 401 St. Charles Avenue. (Courtesy Claire Bost Steindorf.)

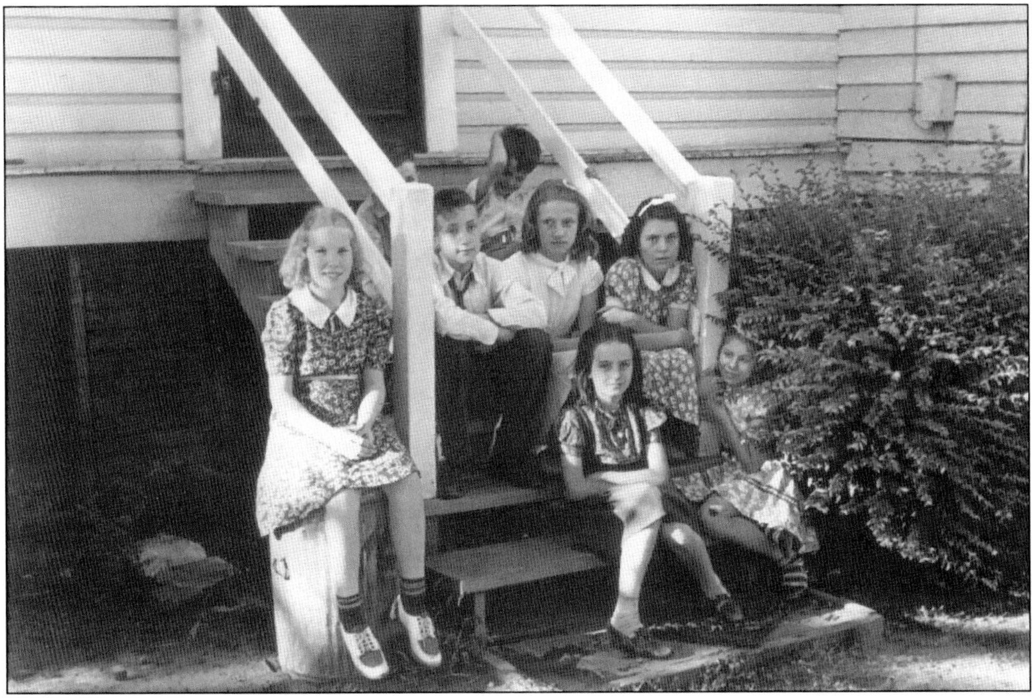

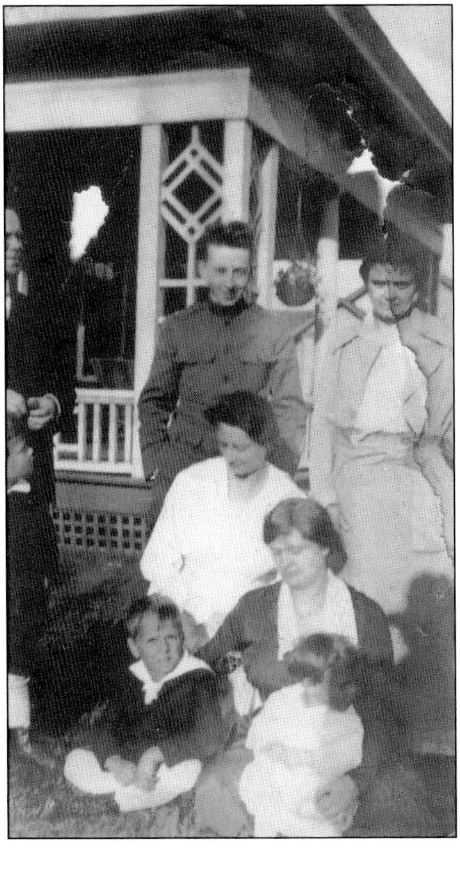

Sitting on the back steps are, from left to right, Tula Mae Williams; (top step) two unidentified; (third step) David Hughes, Mary Virginia Key, and Connie Norman; (bottom step) Joan Hughes and Dorothy Virginia Bost. (Courtesy Claire Bost Steindorf.)

Folks gather for a group photograph in the side yard of 401 St. Charles Avenue. (Courtesy Claire Bost Steindorf.)

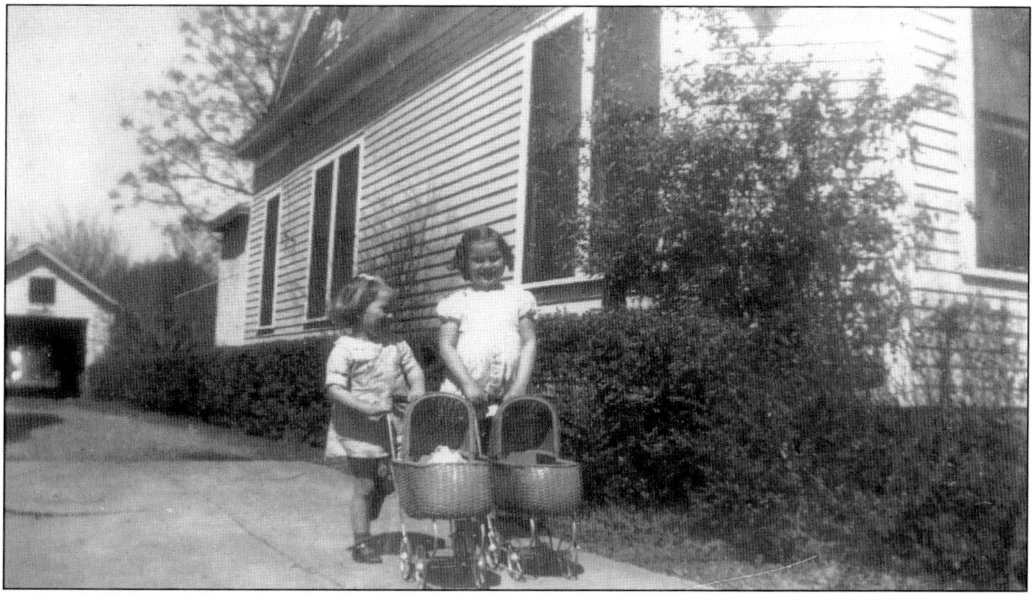

Lena Ruth, age four, and her sister, Valeria Mitchell, age six, play in the yard of their home at 1923 Winona Avenue (then 407) around 1941. (Courtesy Ruth Ott.)

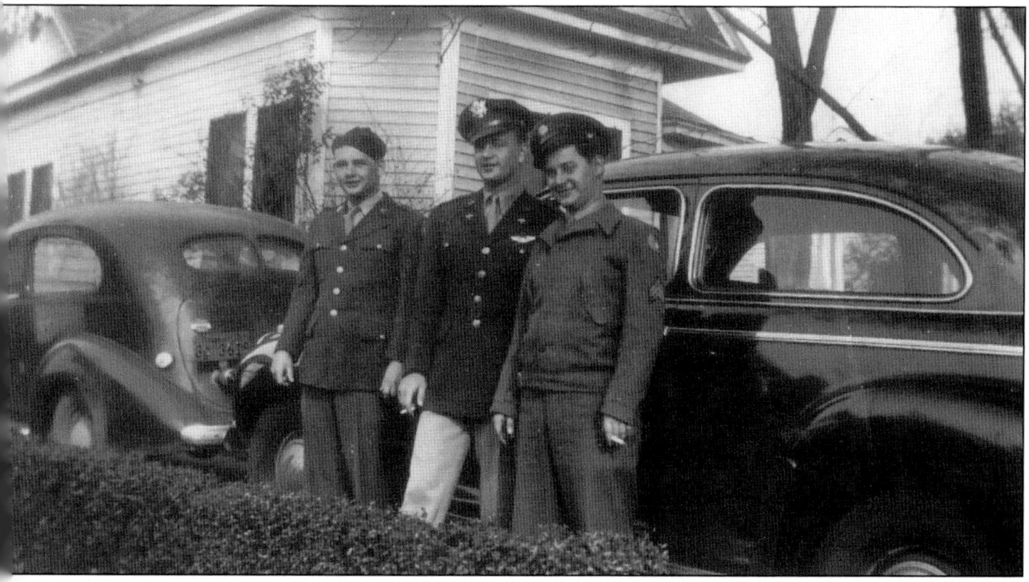

rom left to right, Sewell and Robert Mitchell and Gaines Jeffcoat, on military leave, visit the litchells' parents' home in Capitol Heights in 1942. (Courtesy Ruth Ott.)

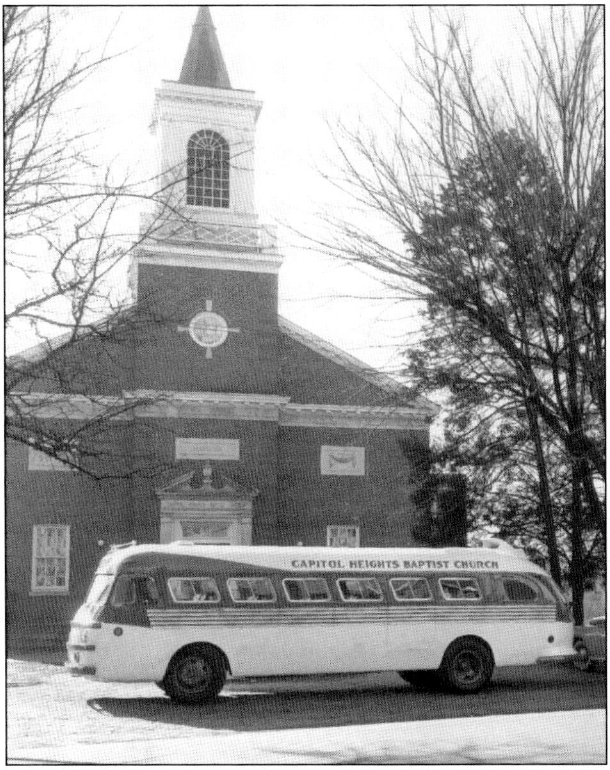

By the 1940s, automobiles and buses had replaced the trolleys, as pictured at left. The Capitol Heights Baptist Church had a sleek bus for transporting members. (Courtesy Capitol Heights Baptist Church.)

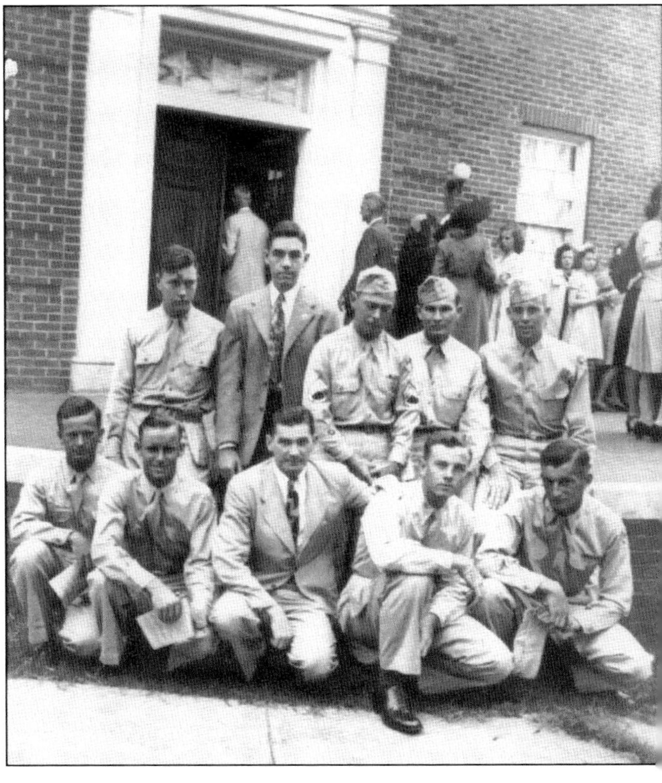

Pictured on the right during World War II, Capitol Heights Baptist Church created a Sunday school class for soldiers stationed in Montgomery. Taken on September 24, 1944, this photograph shows, from left to right (kneeling), David Bryant (Alabama), Louis Dobson (Florida), C. H. Ward (teacher), Glynn Hill (Tennessee), and Joe Hoover (Kentucky); (standing) Marvin Burley (South Carolina), Jack Blue (Alabama), Paul Hamrick (North Carolina), Bill Lankford (South Carolina), and Maury Perry (Mississippi). (Courtesy Capitol Heights Baptist Church.)

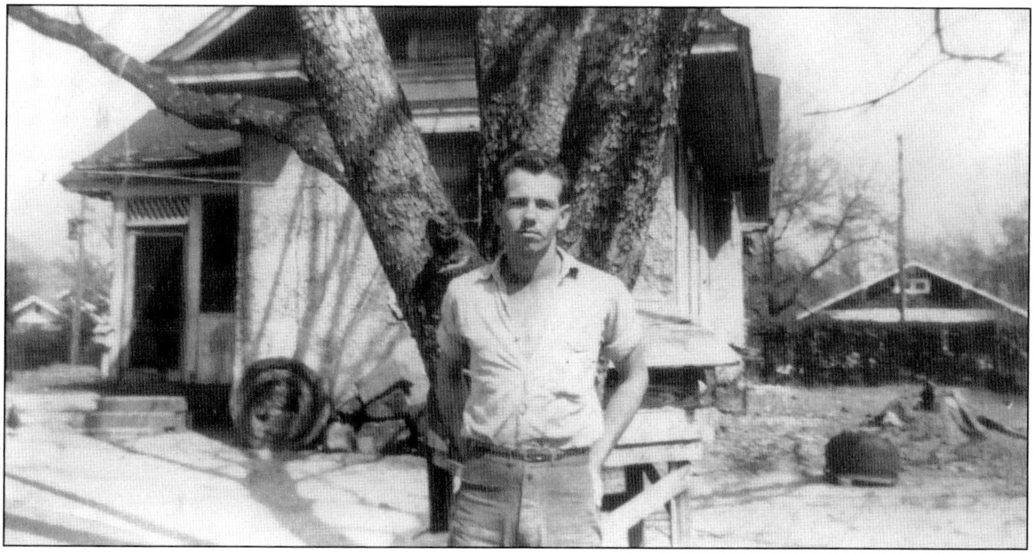

Robert Osborne, home on leave from military service in 1946, stands behind 109 North Lewis Street. (Courtesy Cotie Mae Osborne.)

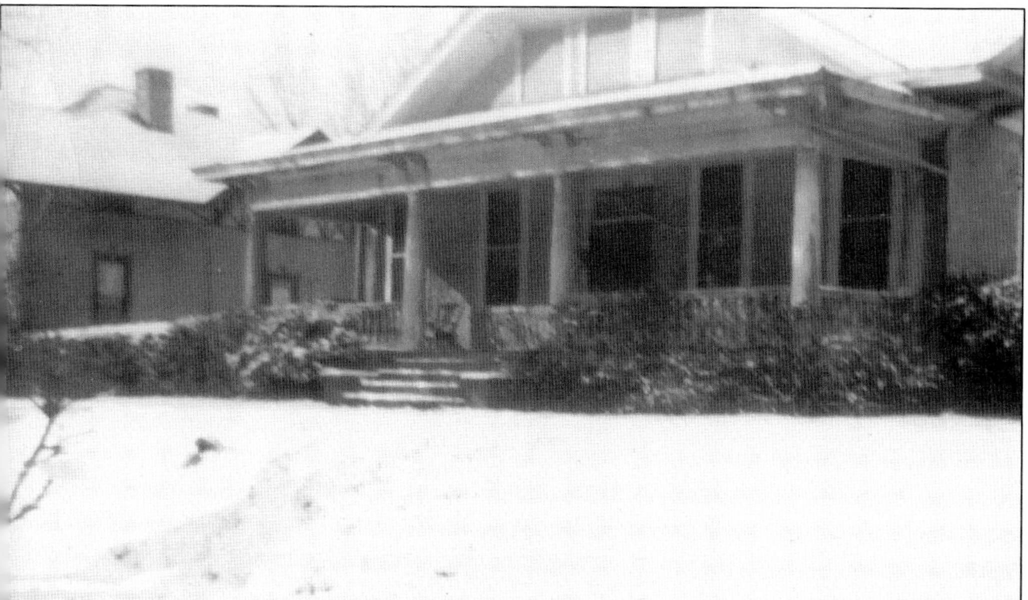

'his photograph shows 109 North Lewis Street in a rare snow in 1946. During World War II, the ouse was made into apartments and housed military families. (Courtesy Cotie Mae Osborne.)

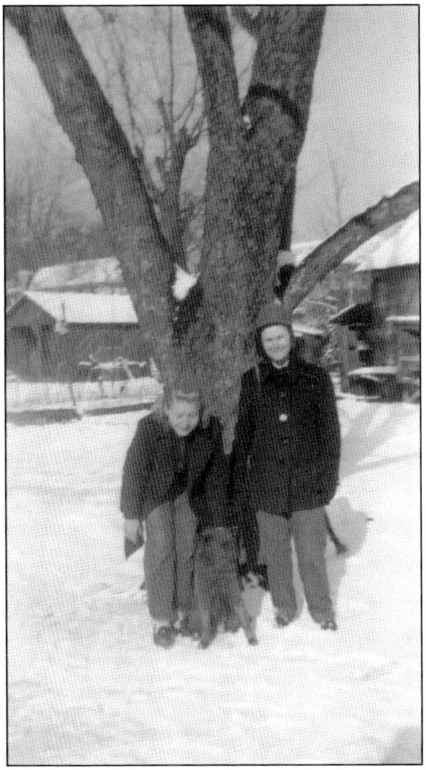

Melanie Blake (left) and Cotie Mae Osborne stands in the snow in 1946. The house in the background is 117 North Lewis Street. (Courtesy Cotie Mae Osborne.)

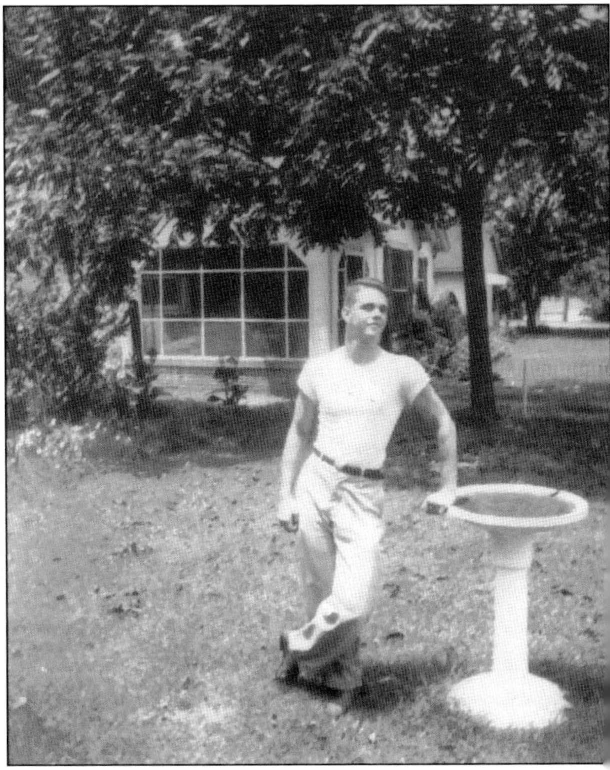

Howard Bradshaw strikes a pose in his parents' yard at 1914 McKinley Avenue in November 1951. (Courtesy Howard Bradshaw.)

Blooming azaleas surround the porch and Bradshaw neighbor William Reynolds at 1914 McKinley Avenue in June 1954. (Courtesy Howard Bradshaw.)

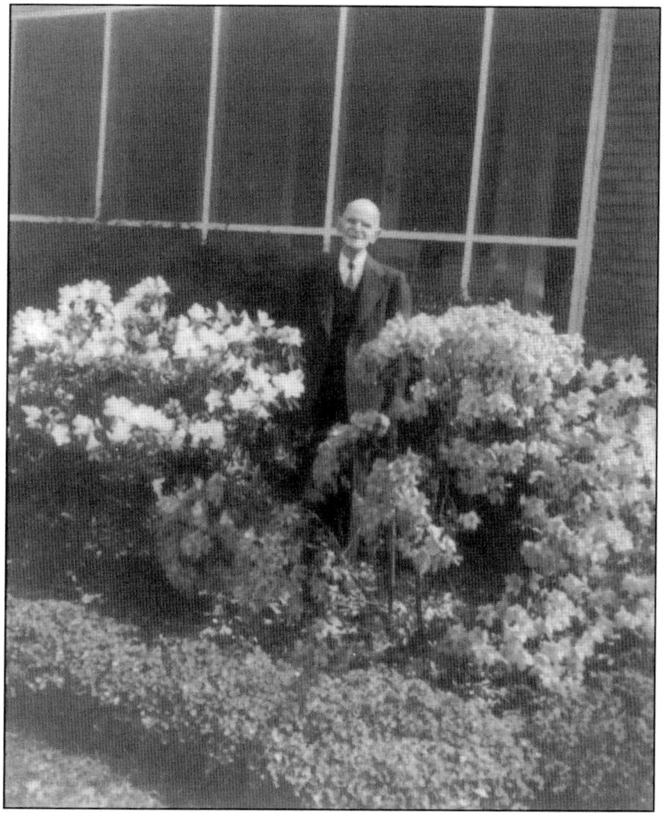

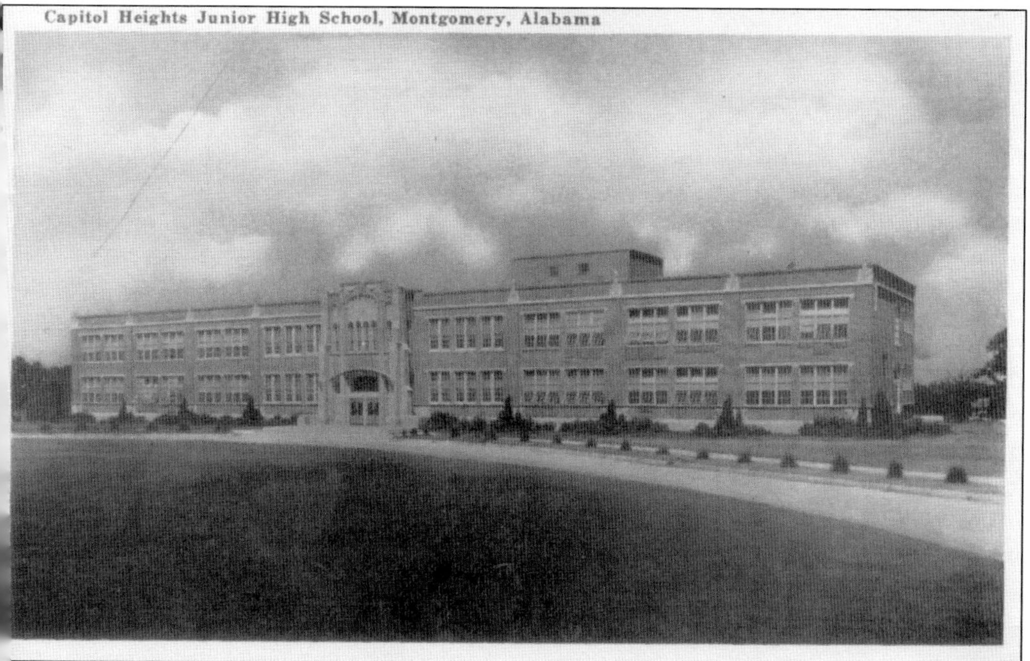

'his photograph shows Capitol Heights Junior High School on Federal Drive. (Courtesy ımes Bozeman.)

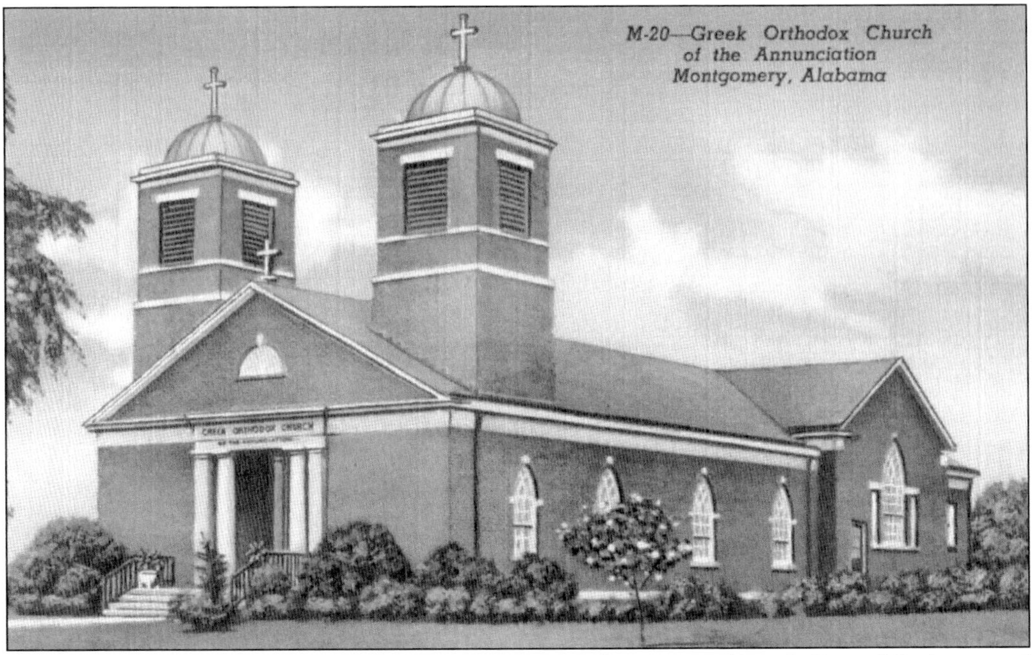

The Greek Orthodox Church of the Annunciation, on the corner of South Capitol Parkway and Mount Meigs Road, received its charter in 1945, but construction was delayed because of a lack of building supplies during World War II. The church held its first service, the Divine Liturgy of Christmas Day, on Christmas Day in 1947. (Courtesy MCHS.)

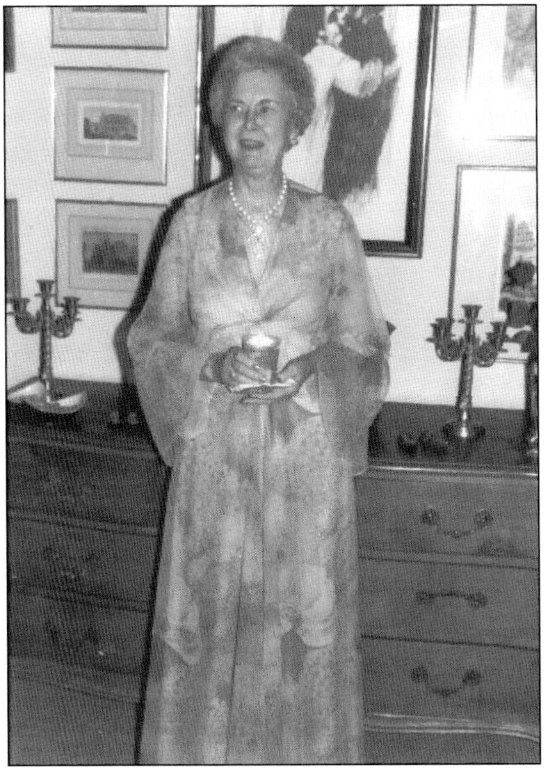

"Miss Dorothy" Belser stands in her dining room at 103 North Lewis Street around the late 1940s. She inherited the Belser house from her husband's aunts, the Belser sisters. (Courtesy Meta Harris.)

Nine

CLOVERDALE IDLEWILD

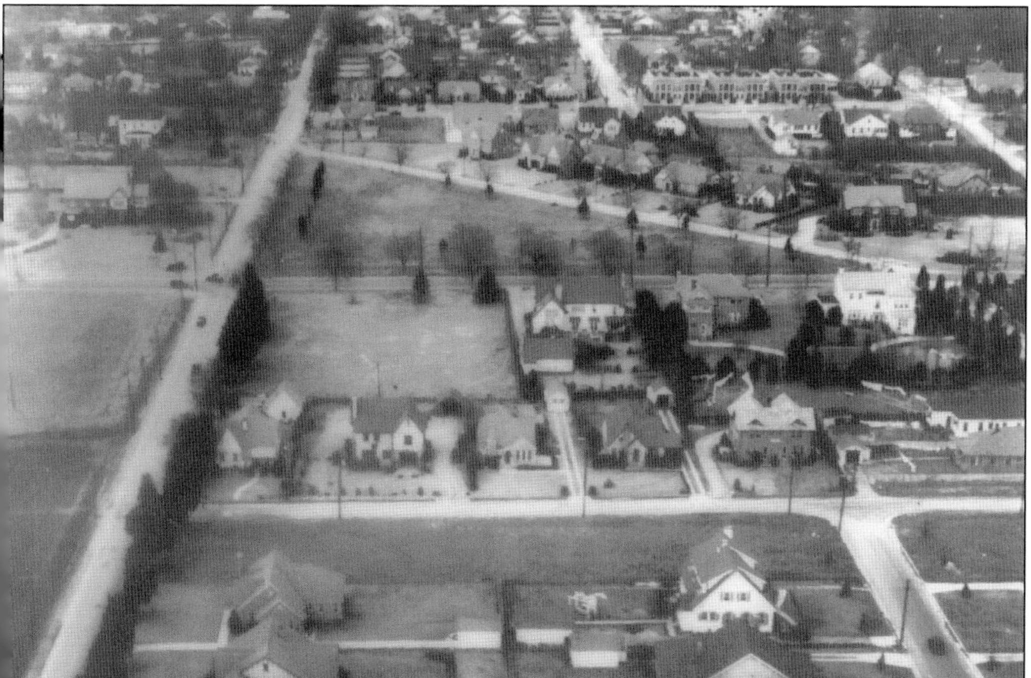

'his aerial view looking north shows the residential neighborhoods that continued to develop. 'he intersection of Norman Bridge Road and Fairview Avenue is visible along, with empty lots nd newly built homes. (Courtesy Fred Drehr Collection.)

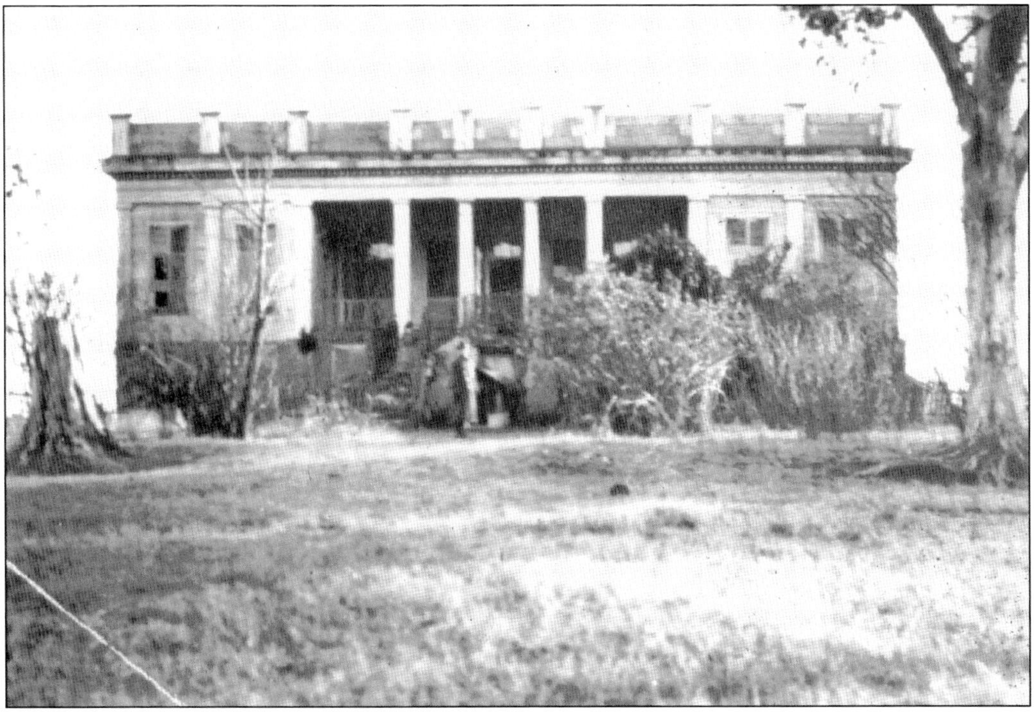

Peter B. Mastin arrived in Montgomery County about 1836. He bought extensive land and by 1851 had moved his family into his house, named Fairview. The Mastin family raised three generations in the home, and so it became known in later years as the "Old Mastin Homeplace." Fairview Avenue is named for the house and Mastin Lane for the Mastin family. (Courtesy Mastin family collection.)

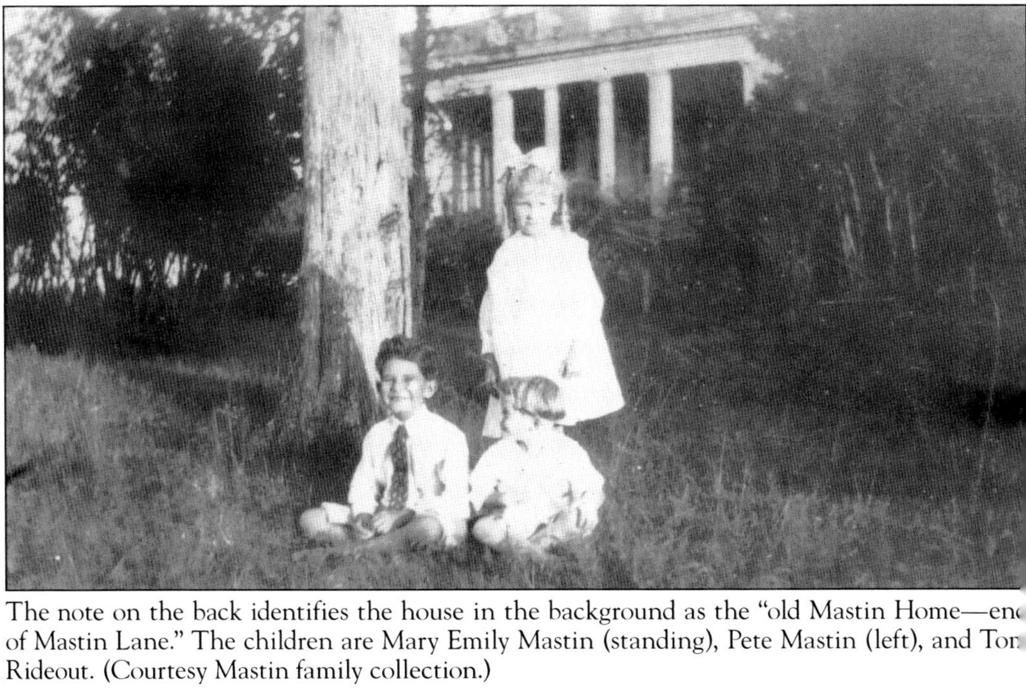

The note on the back identifies the house in the background as the "old Mastin Home—end of Mastin Lane." The children are Mary Emily Mastin (standing), Pete Mastin (left), and Tom Rideout. (Courtesy Mastin family collection.)

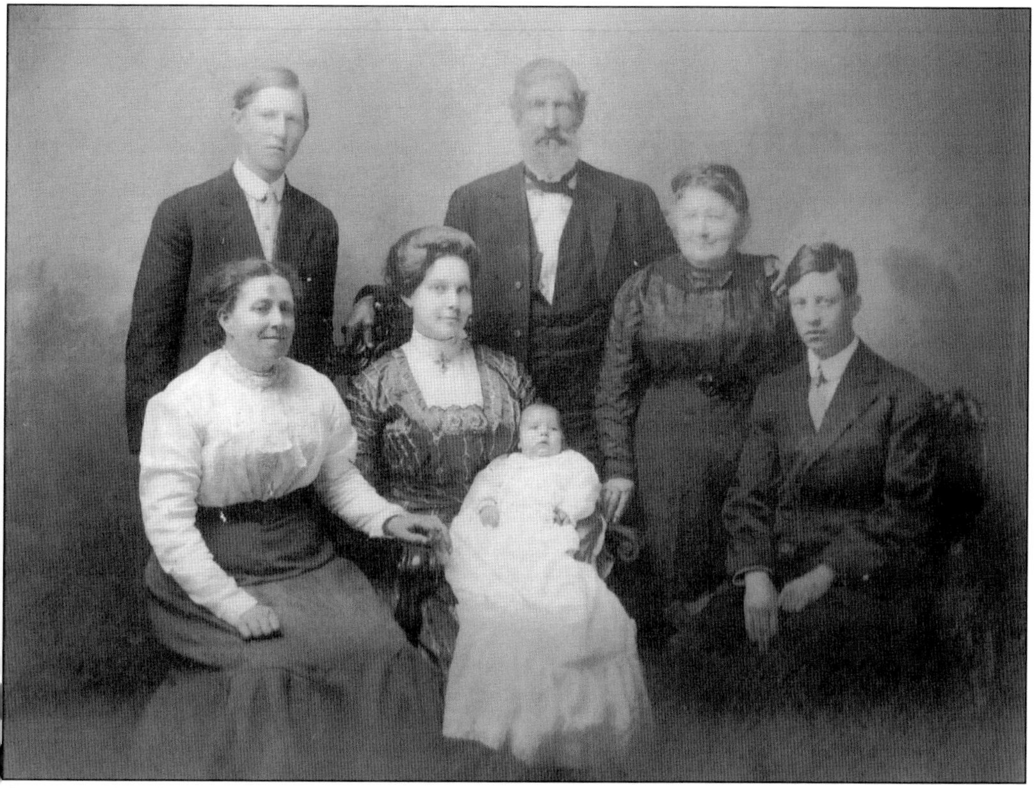

A Mastin family portrait shows, from left to right, (first row) Mattie Mastin Jones and Mary Jones Rideout (holding Thomas Rideout); (second row) Robert A. Jones, Capt. Peter Blackwell Mastin, Mary Elizabeth Harris Mastin, and Peter B. Mastin. (Courtesy Mastin family collection.)

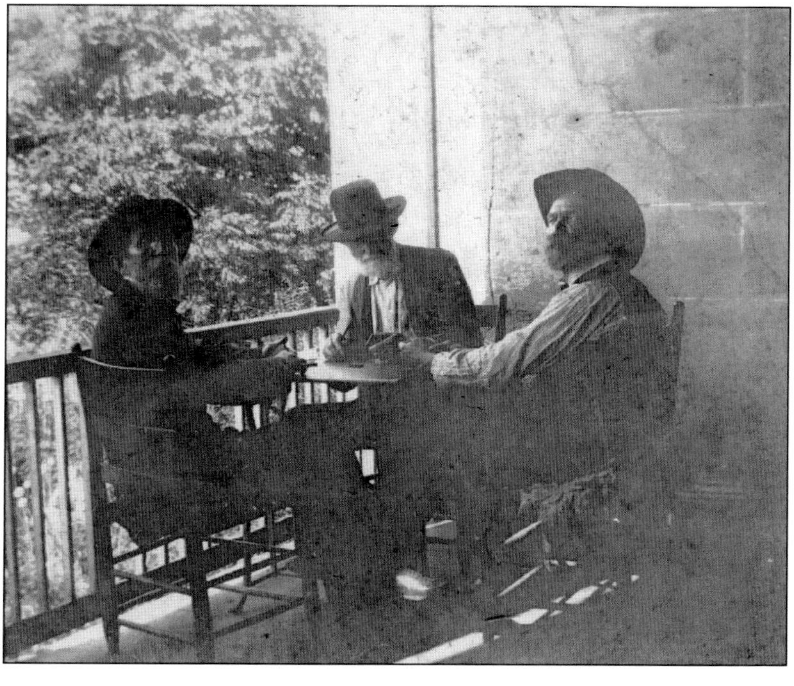

Sitting on the front porch of Fairview playing cards are, from left to right, George Clisby, Don Loper, and Capt. Peter Mastin in the 1900s. (Courtesy Mastin family collection.)

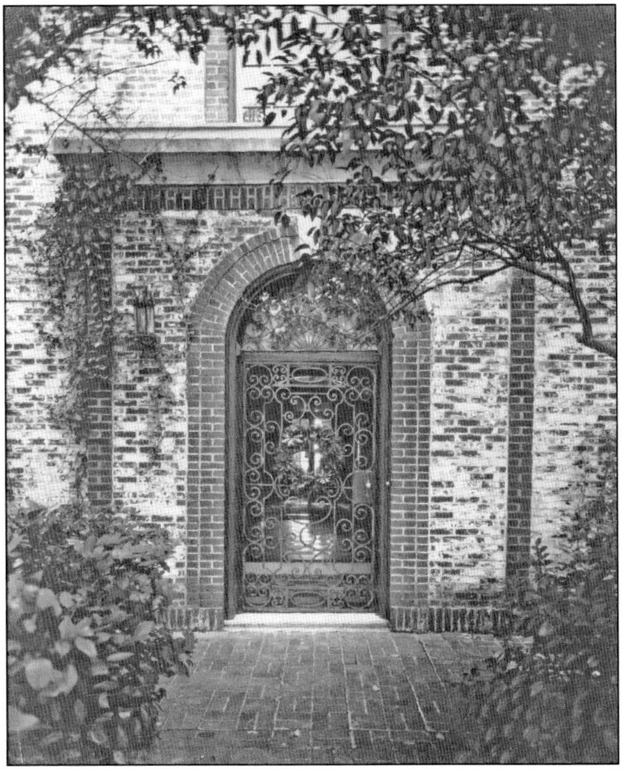

Caroline and Dr. Brannon Hubbard built a new home designed by well-known architect Frank Lockwood on the site of the Mastin homeplace, Fairview, in 1924. That home, known as Lane's End, was demolished in the early 1970s due to foundation problems. (Courtesy Ball family collection.)

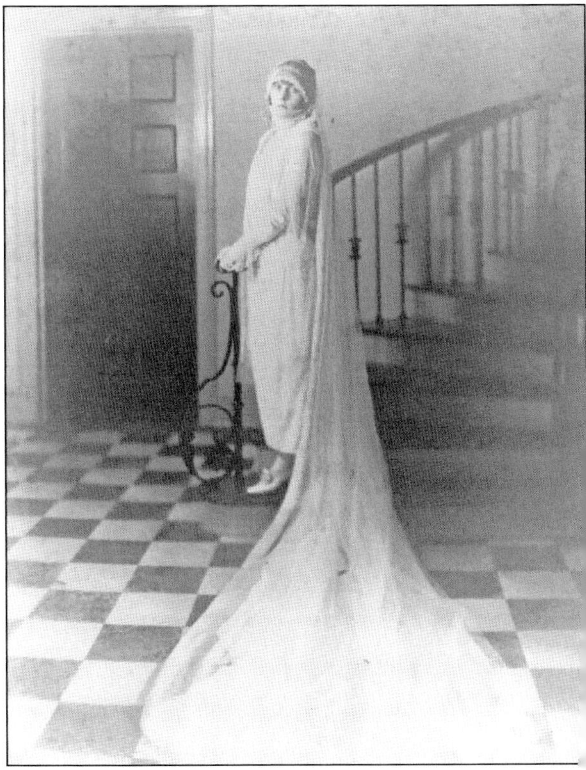

Caroline Lee Davidson married Frank Ball Jr. in 1924 at St. John's Episcopal Church. Caroline was the daughter of Caroline Davidson Hubbard. This wedding portrait is in the entrance foyer of Lane's End prior to the wedding. (Courtesy Ball family collection.)

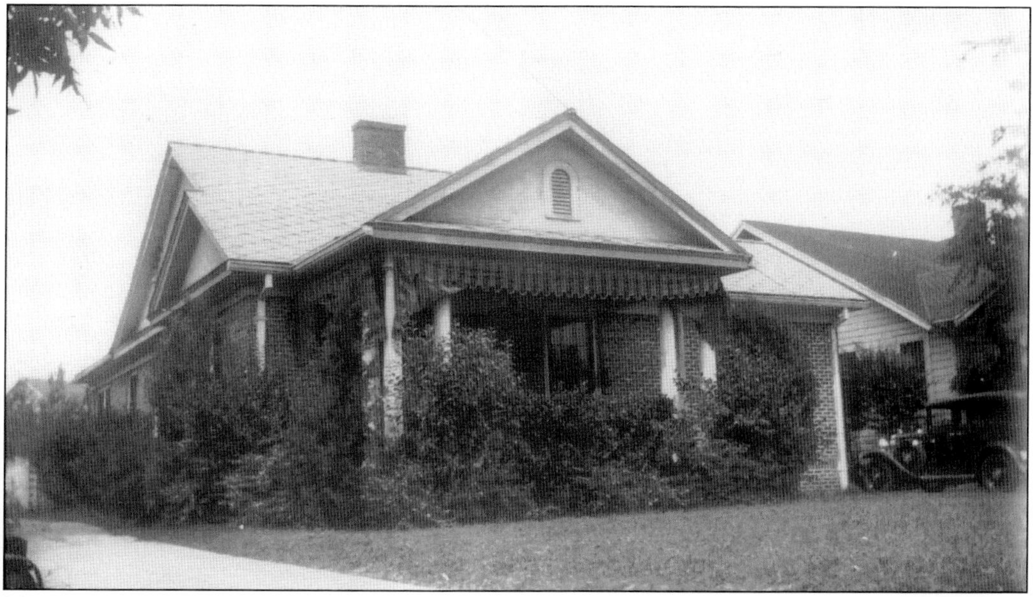

Marvin Hunter Pearson and Lena Collins Pearson built their home at 17 Woodley Road House in the late 1920s. (Courtesy Pearson family collection.)

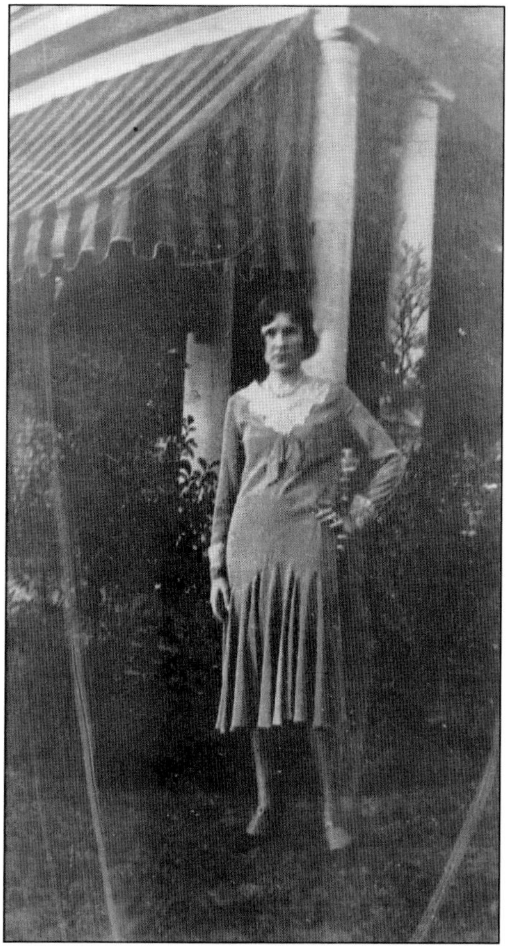

'ell Pearson Williford poses in front ' 17 Woodley Road around 1926. Courtesy Pearson family collection.)

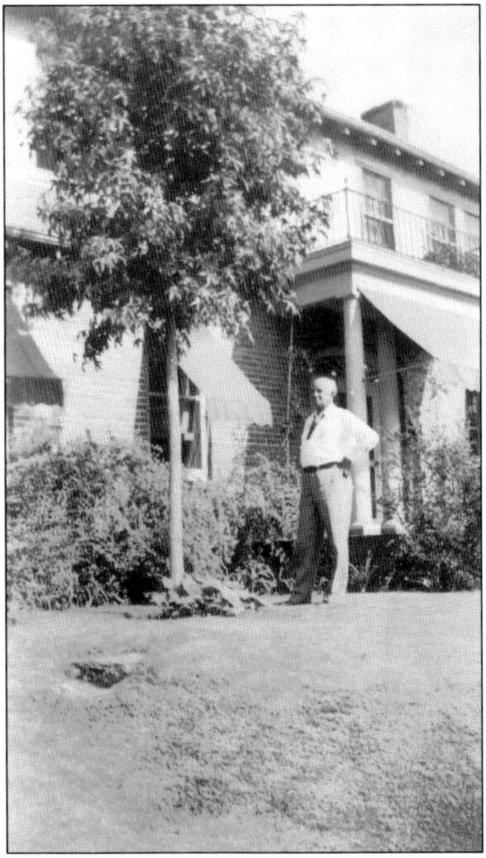

Col. Hartley Allen Moon stands in front of the home he built in 1928 at 105 Lexington Road. Colonel Moon was the adjutant general of Alabama from 1919 to 1927. (Courtesy Young family collection.)

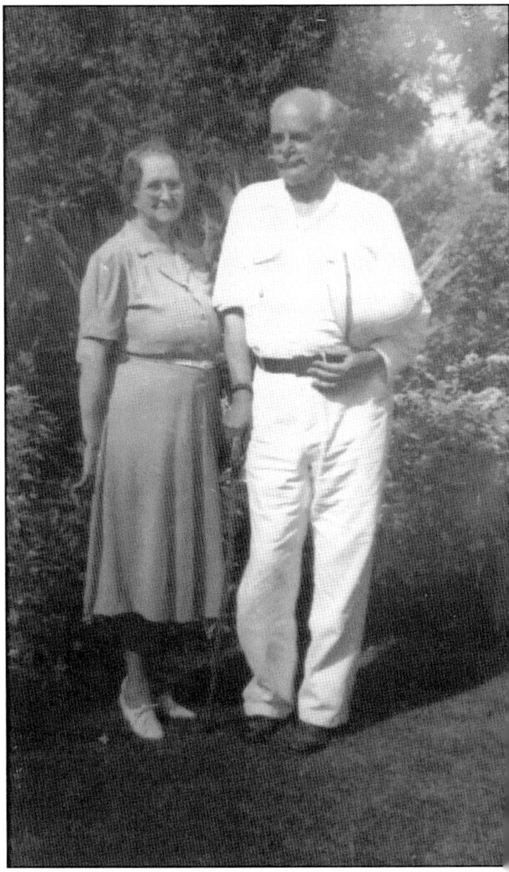

Colonel Moon and his wife, Mary Middleton Moon, stand in the garden at their home at 105 Lexington Road in 1928. (Courtesy Young family collection.)

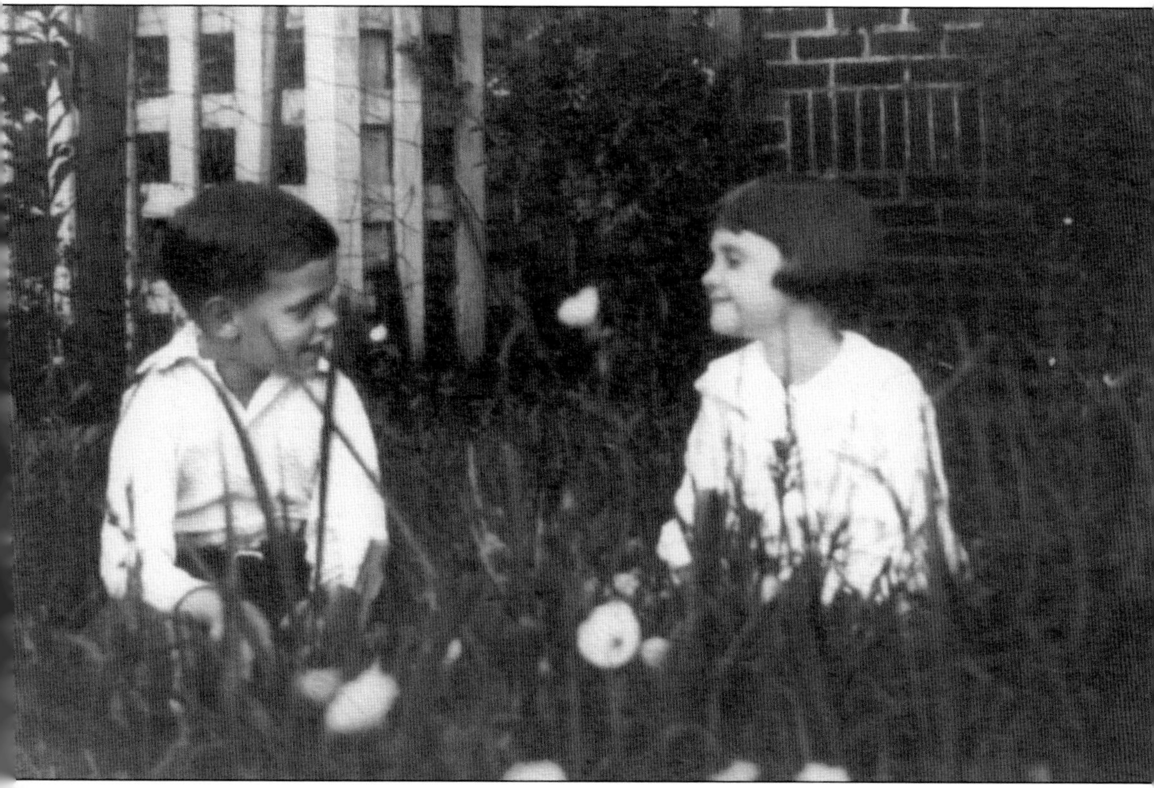

William (Bill) Marvin Pearson and neighbor Betty Buck Tatum play in the backyard of 17 Woodley Road around 1930. (Courtesy Pearson family collection.)

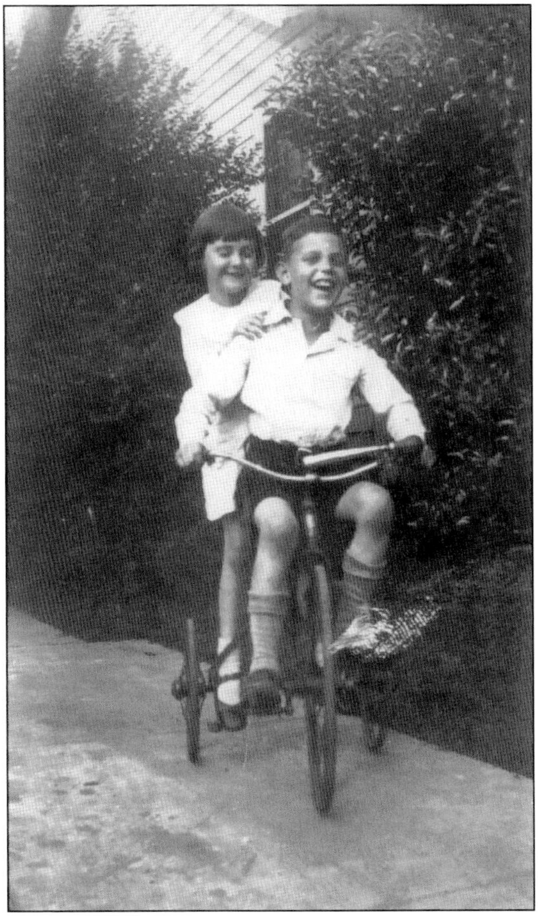

William (Bill) Marvin Pearson and neighbor Betty Buck Tatum take off on Bill's bike around 1930. (Courtesy Pearson family collection.)

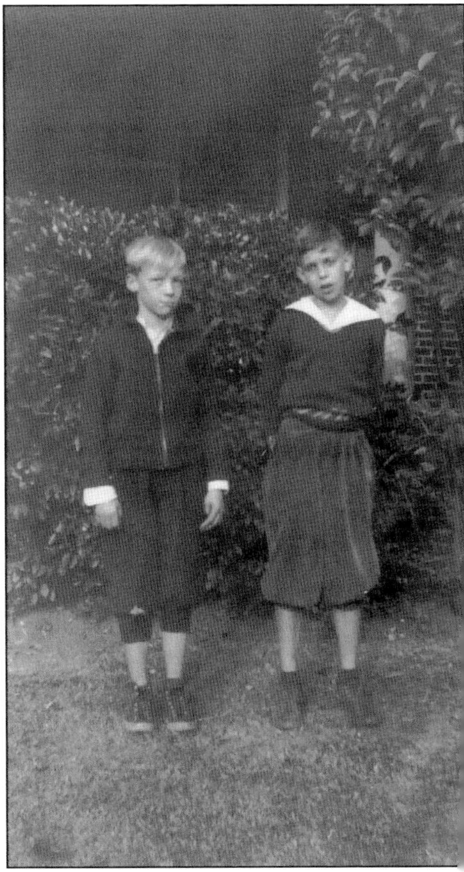

John Matthews (left) and William (Bill) Pearson pose in front of 17 Woodley Road. (Courtesy Pearson family collection.)

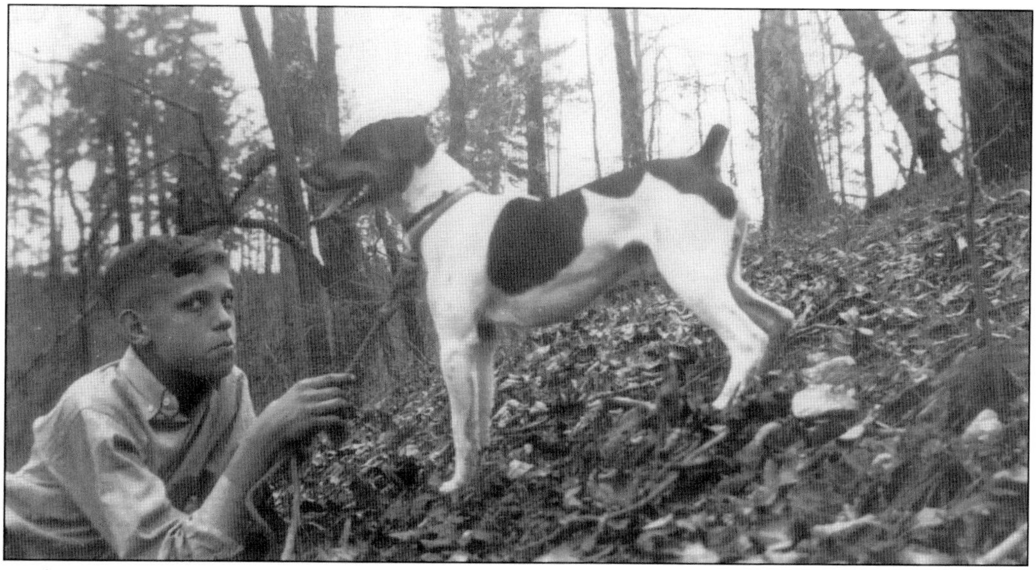

In the 1930s, the area around the Pearson house was wooded. In this photograph, Bill and his dog, Blinks, pose with a stick. (Courtesy Pearson family collection.)

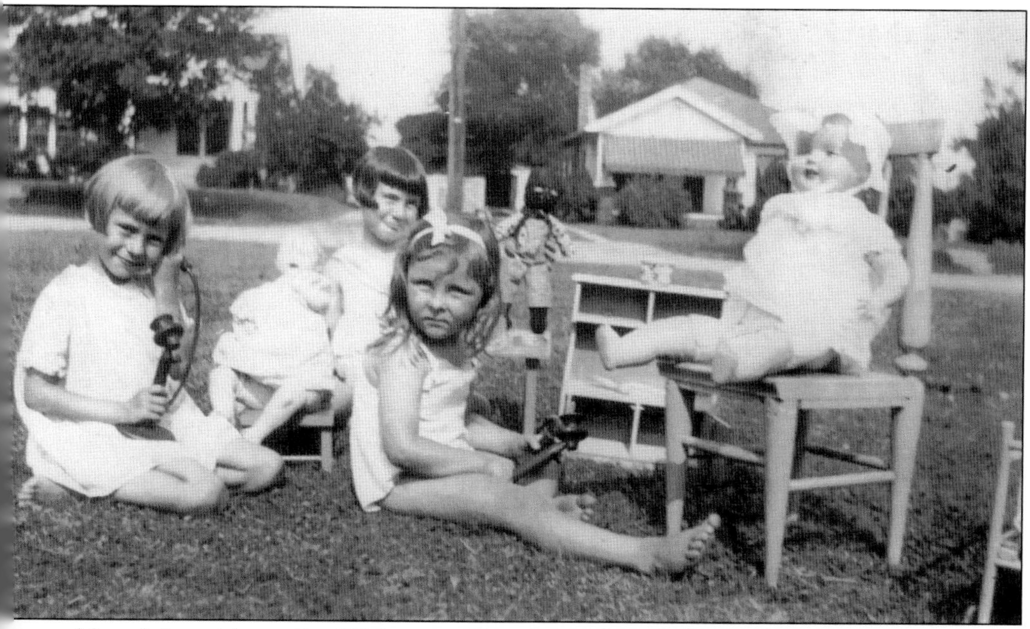

ıctured from left to right are Pen Williamson, Betty McMahan, Sallie Watkins Wood, and Big Dolly ıjoying a tea party on the front lawn of 218 LeBron Avenue in 1933. (Courtesy Sallie Millsap.)

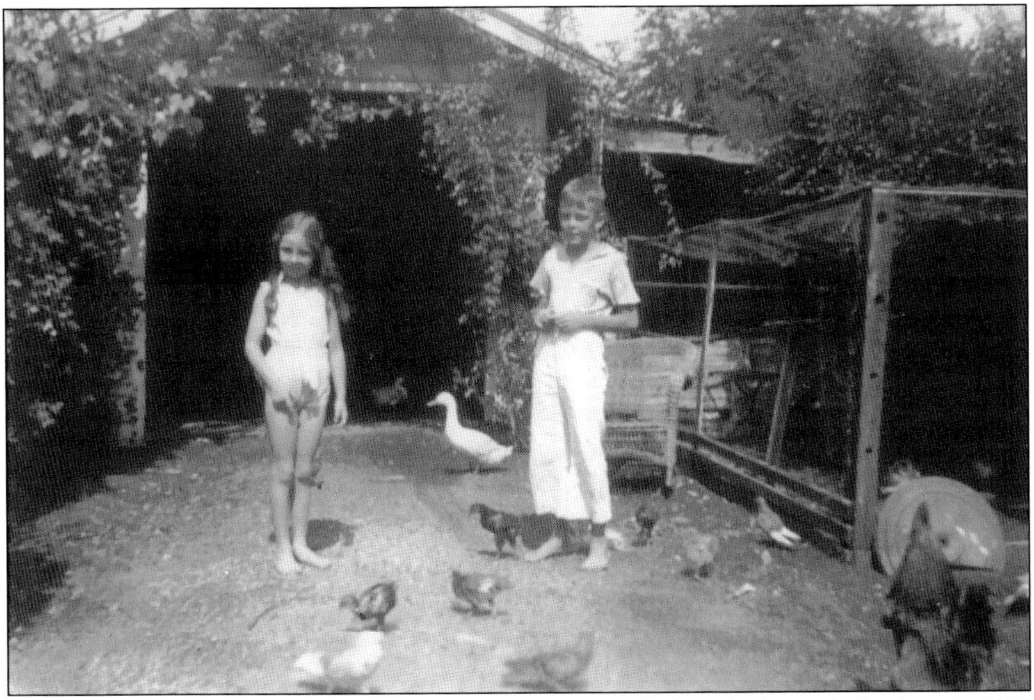

Sallie Watkins Wood and George Marks Wood Jr. play with their ducks in the backyard of 218 LeBron Avenue in 1936. The caption of the photograph in the family album reads, "Before breakfast." (Courtesy Sallie Millsap.)

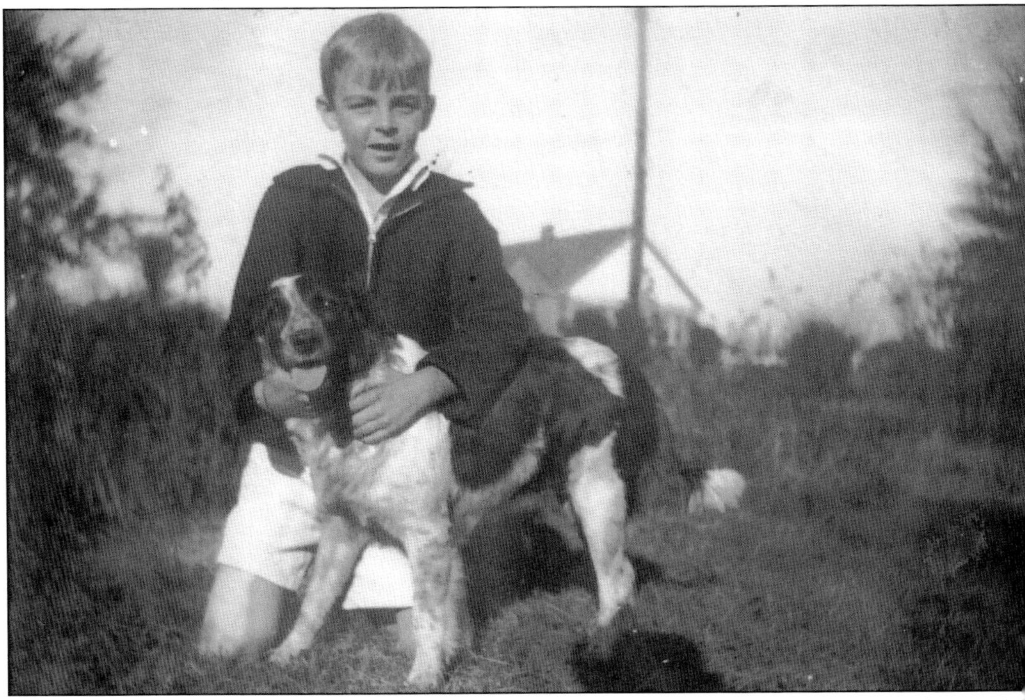

George Marks Wood and his dog, Spot, smile for the camera on Cloverdale Road in 1934. (Courtesy Sallie Millsap.)

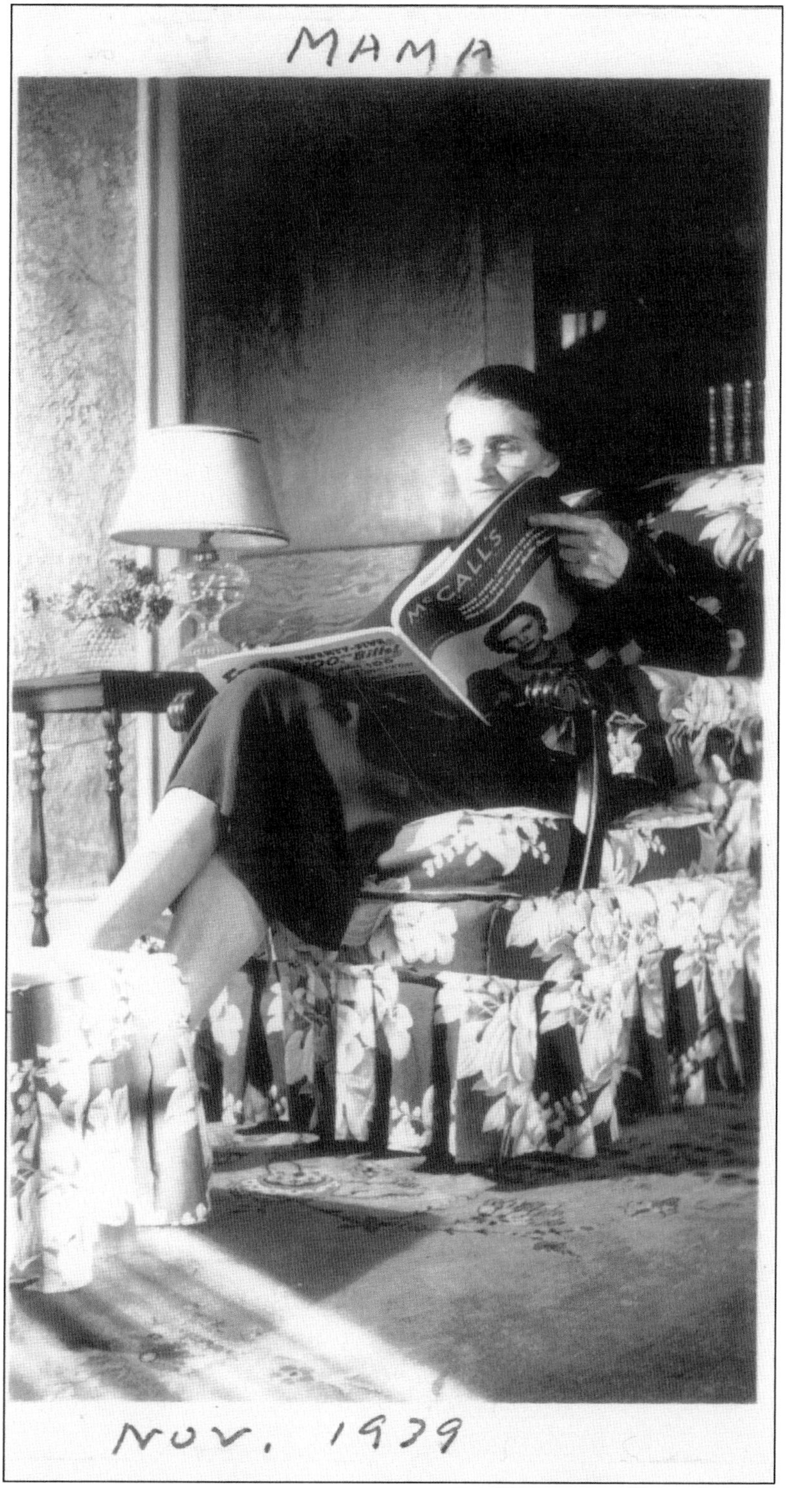

ena Collins Pearson takes some time to read her *McCalls* at her home at 17 Woodley Road on ovember 26, 1939. (Courtesy Pearson family collection.)

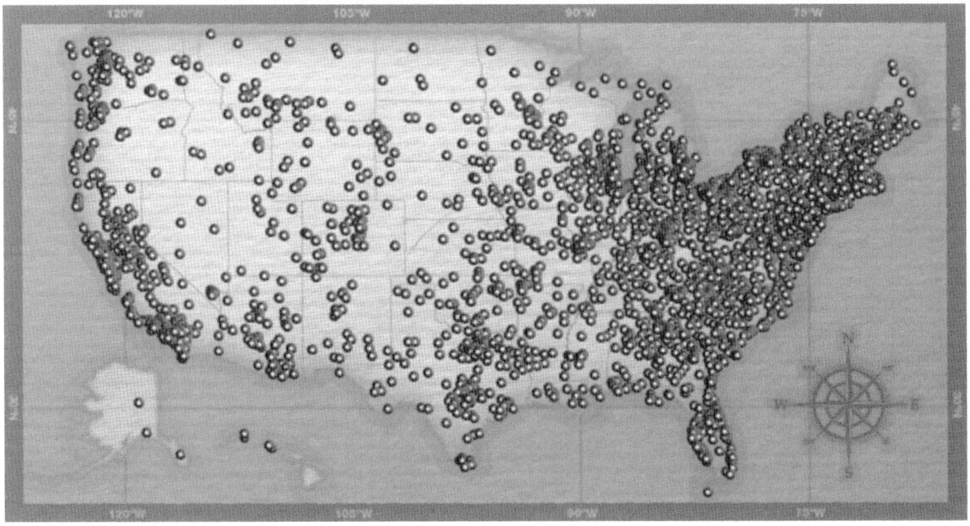

Consistent with our mission to preserve history on a local level, this book was printed in South Carolina on American-made paper and manufactured entirely in the United States. Products carrying the accredited Forest Stewardship Council (FSC) label are printed on 100 percent FSC-certified paper.

MADE IN THE USA